More Praise for *Thinking Like Your Editor*

"What a smart and useful book *Thinking Like Your Editor* is. No other book in print addresses the art and craft of writing serious nonfiction books—the kinds of books that change minds, enrich our intellectual lives, win major awards—with anything like the clarity of expression and depth of practical knowledge to be found herein. And unlike most books of advice, it is a positive pleasure to read. May it find a wide audience among writers—and editors too, for that matter. I'll certainly be recommending it to both camps."
—Gerald Howard, editorial director, Broadway Books

"At last—a sensitive, thorough, and creative guide to writing nonfiction proposals and manuscripts. In forty-five years in publishing, I have never read better advice then this book offers. Bravo."
—Hugh Van Dusen, vice president and executive editor, HarperCollins Publishers

"Rabiner and Fortunato take you through the corporate Oz of the publishing world, behind the smoke and mirrors, yet leave you with your creative heart intact."
—Dale Maharidge, Stanford School of Journalism, author of *And Their Children After Them*, winner of the 1990 Pulitzer Prize in nonfiction

Thinking Like Your Editor

How to Write Great Serious Nonfiction— and Get It Published

Susan Rabiner and
Alfred Fortunato

W. W. Norton & Company
New York   London

For information about permission to reproduce selections from this book, write to Permissions, W. W. Norton & Company, Inc., 500 Fifth Avenue, New York, NY 10110

The text of this book is composed in 12 point Bembo with the display set in American Typewriter Light and Medium. Composition by Gina Webster. Manufacturing by The Courier Companies, Inc. Book design by Dana Sloan. Production manager: Amanda Morrison.

Library of Congress Cataloging-in-Publication Data

Rabiner, Susan.
Thinking like your editor : how to write great serious nonfiction—and get it published / by Susan Rabiner and Alfred Fortunato.
      p. cm.
Includes index.
ISBN 0-393-03892-0
1. Authorship—Marketing. 2. Book proposals. 1. Fortunato, Alfred.
II. Title.
PN161.R28 2002
808'.02–dc21   2001044551

W. W. Norton & Company, Inc., 500 Fifth Avenue, New York, N.Y. 10110
www.wwnorton.com

W. W. Norton & Company, Ltd., Castle House, 75/76 Wells Street, London
W1T 3QT

1 2 3 4 5 6 7 8 9 0

To Great Books—
And the Authors Who Write Them

Contents

A Note to the Reader 11

Prologue: First, a little story . . . 15

Introduction 27

Chapter 1: Thinking Like an Editor: Audience,
Audience, Audience 39

Part One: The Submission Package

Chapter 2: How to Write a Proposal 61

Chapter 3: Wrapping Up the Submission Package:
The Table of Contents, the Sample
Chapter, and Supporting Materials 97

Chapter 4: Placing Your Manuscript with a Publisher:
To Agent or Not to Agent, and Other
Questions about the Publishing Acquisition
Process 120

Part Two: The Writing Process

Chapter 5:   A Question of Fairness and Other Limits
               of Argument in Serious Nonfiction   141

Chapter 6:   Using Narrative Tension   177

Chapter 7:   From Introduction to Epilogue: Writing
               Your Book Chapter by Chapter—and
               What to Do When You Get into Trouble   196

Part Three: From Editing to Marketing to Publication

Chapter 8:   How to Be Published Well   223

Appendix: A Sample Proposal and Writing Sample   239

Acknowledgments   269

Index   271

The book's the thing . . .

A Note to the Reader

The book that follows is written in Rabiner's voice. But it is the work of two people—Fortunato and Rabiner—who have spent a lifetime together talking about books and writing.

It worked out in our lives that Rabiner has dealt directly with authors, while Fortunato worked freelance on manuscripts. We continue very much in those roles even today, as we jointly run the Susan Rabiner Literary Agency. Because we wanted our book to echo the informal conversational sound of a meeting between editor and author, it made sense to write it in Rabiner's voice.

But as in our personal lives, where we can't tell where one of us leaves off and the other begins, the ideas in this book evolved out of long years shared turning manuscripts into books.

Thinking Like
Your Editor

Prologue

First, a little story...

Several years ago, while I was still editorial director of Basic Books, then the serious nonfiction division of HarperCollins, I went with two colleagues to a lunch meeting with buyers at Barnes & Noble. I had been especially looking forward to the lunch because I wanted an opportunity to persuade Barnes & Noble to change a shelving decision it had made on a title of ours just then being shipped to the bookstores.

Here is some background. At the top of our list that season was *The Physics of Star Trek,* a very entertaining book that also managed to teach some pretty high-level but fascinating physics. We had several early signs (a book-club sale, requests for excerpts from the book and online interviews with the author, a decision by Stephen Hawking to write the introduction) that this creatively conceived and executed book was a potential winner. Barnes & Noble apparently concurred in our judgment, placing the largest initial order for any title in Basic's history. So we were rather confident we were on the road to a best seller. Until it became apparent we had a little hitch, at least with Barnes & Noble, regarding where in their bookstores all these copies were to be shelved.

Apart from copies of favored books piled high on the "New Arrivals" table at the front of every bookstore, every title must also be shelved in a category location farther back in the bookstore. B&N had decided to shelve *The Physics of Star Trek* in the science section, on its face a perfectly reasonable place for a title loaded with hard physics. Except that I believed a stronger market would develop among trekkers interested in hard science than among science readers interested in *Star Trek*. Indeed, the sales pitch for the book was "the dream book for the techie in every trekker," and the editing, jacketing, marketing, and sales had all been designed to appeal to that audience, not to convert science readers into *Star Trek* fans.

So my job that day would be to persuade B&N that at least half of the copies to be stocked in the science section more properly belonged in the bookstore's *Star Trek* section. Yes, gentle reader, there is indeed a special section in many bookstores, often larger than the store's entire science section, devoted to the many novelizations, technical manuals, or whatever, about or based on the *Star Trek* series.

B&N, like Borders and, more recently, Books-A-Million, are referred to in the publishing industry as the "chains," short for the chain bookstores. For many years, you must know, hardly any of the oldtimers in publishing had a nice thing to say about them. They had, we believed, knocked the legs out from under the independent bookstores, those long-standing, cherished mom-and-pop book-shops that once dotted America's Main Streets.

We resented the chains for another reason as well. They intro-duced to bookselling what seemed a too relentlessly businesslike way of choosing which books to stock, how long to stock them, and where in the store to display them. As the chains grew in size, power, and influence, many editors viewed with anxiety a publishing future that increasingly closed off both the sophisticated and the not-easily-char-acterized book, or the book that had a well-defined but small audi-ence. Of course, pressure on editors to publish only those authors expected to sell really well is much older than chain bookstores. Publishing legend has it that the esteemed Alfred A. Knopf himself once asked his editors, "Why can't we publish only best sellers?"

By the mid-1990s, chain bookstore sales represented a staggeringly large percentage of all books sold. Chain dominance of the selling end, as well as other factors unrelated to retailing, such as the buyout of many small publishing houses by corporate conglomerates, made it inevitable that the once genteel publishing industry would have to become more businesslike. And so it did. For every project editors now take to their editorial boards, they must work up profit-and-loss projections—inputting production and other costs against hoped-for first-year hardcover and paperback sales, foreign-language and book-club sales.

Editors are generally not business geniuses, but most quickly figured out that these profit-and-loss projections tend to favor one kind of book—the kind that promises to establish itself quickly and sell well in hardcover over the first twelve months of publication. It puts at a disadvantage books whose initial potential is not clear, as well as those whose strength is "backlist," in other words, those that may never take off in hardcover but sell for many years in paperback. And so, notwithstanding the increasing presence of dour MBAs looking over their shoulders, editors began to look for creative ways to ease in and out of the mix of sales projection numbers those that would nudge toward the good side the profit-and-loss statements on books they wanted to acquire. They did so (and do so to this day) not to deceive, but because they truly believe that the decision about which books to publish is best made editorially, not financially, that is, by asking such questions as: It this an important book? Is this a book that my publishing house can publish well? So quite often it is the decision to acquire that comes first; then the creative math follows, as editors figure out ways to mute signals that they are predicting too large a first-year sale solely because they passionately want a particular book on their list.

The chains, however, entertain no such heresy on the subject of numbers. Publishing house sales reps can sweet-talk buyers about the brilliance of the author's writing style, the glitter of his reputation, or that this is the coming hot topic, and the chain buyers will listen and listen carefully. If buyers can be convinced that that information will have a direct effect on sales, they will certainly factor it in. But when it comes time to enter order figures next to titles, buyers too must do their numbers. Carrying the greatest weight are sales of the author's previous book (which is why this book will argue that authors should think very carefully about their careers from their very first book project), the publicity potential of this new book (which is communicated to booksellers by the willingness of publishers to spend their own money to send their authors "on tour," and, of course, by interest from the national television shows), and by how much "co-op" money the publisher agrees to give the chains to help them sell the book. Co-op money can be spent several ways— for example, to pay for print advertising by the chains or to obtain better placement of the book within the bookstore. If you see a book piled high on a special Mother's Day table, quite likely the publisher paid for that placement with co-op money. If you want Amazon.com to feature your book on its opening page, once again co-op dollars likely will smooth the way.

That's why I saw no difficulty in persuading the buyers to shelve *The Physics of Star Trek* in the *Star Trek* section of the store in addition to the science section. We would be speaking their language. The book had advanced a whopping 68,000 copies into bookstores across the country—suggesting that B&N was not the only bookseller to believe in it. Every day we were learning about new publicity breaks for the book and author. And we had been very generous with co-op money. B&N owed us—or so I thought.

Despite my beef with B&N on this one issue, I looked forward to the meeting for another reason. I had always considered it my misfortune never to have worked in a bookstore. I have long had a fascination with the entire business of books—how they are conceived, proposed, contracted for, written, edited, published, marketed, and finally presented to the public, to be read, enjoyed or not, and judged, favorably or harshly. I still spend many hours in my nearby chain outlet watching faces as people scan the New Arrivals table. I would enjoy exchanging ideas with these lucky folks who worked so close to the book-reading public.

These were my own thoughts that day as the three of us arrived at B&N's offices. Popping out of the elevator at the reception floor, we entered a small lobby. Glass doors separated the outer reception area from the inner offices of B&N. Flanking those glass doors were two huge line drawings, matched in style, each identically framed and hung. To your left was William Shakespeare; to the right, the modern Bard—at least to B&N's lobby designer—John Grisham. One of my companions, a quick-witted editor, looked from one drawing to the other and quipped, "Abandon all hope ye starry-eyed editors who enter here."

Things are seldom as black and white as we fear they might be. Our B&N lunch dates turned out to be intelligent people who clearly cared about books and about serious nonfiction, and who knew their books and their readers. (Today one of them is an editor, and her list is most impressive.) I learned a lot about bookselling that day. No one who met these two booksellers would argue that their job was just "punching in numbers."

Over coffee, I raised my complaint. Failure to stock *The Physics of Star Trek* in the *Star Trek* section as well as the science section would cost thousands of sales for both of us. Couldn't they at least shelve the book in both places? To my amazement, the answer was no, they couldn't. One of the buyers explained the problem.

As each publisher presents its new list to B&N, the titles are divided among the buyers, each buyer responsible for titles that will end up in one particular section of each of the chain's outlets; for example, the history buyer is responsible for buying, stocking, shelving, and selling all history titles, and the popular culture buyer has similar responsibility for all popular culture titles. Fiction, poetry, African-American or Jewish interests, business or gender studies, and so on, all the same. But some books don't slot conveniently into B&N's system or that of any other bookstore. For example, memoir is a well-established genre among publishers, but no memoir section exists in most bookstores. So depending upon how it is written, one memoir can land in biography, another in popular culture, a third in psychology, a fourth in parenting or even history. Cross-disciplinary titles present another problem. A book entitled *The Zen of Computers* could find its way into the computer section, squeezed in among thousand-page manuals about using Java Script in designing home pages. Then again, it might end up in New Age or science and technology.

An idea lies behind the system—clear accountability. Each buyer is judged by the performance of titles within his or her own section. Thus, when more than one buyer wants to claim a new release for his or her own, the problem is resolved, I learned that day, by a sort of "arbitration" (their word, not mine). Publishers are allowed no say in the process. Even more important, once that decision is made, the book will be shelved only in the winning buyer's section, as well as for a short period of time in the New Arrivals section.

In our case, despite good commercial arguments for double shelving, the book remained in science only. On this point, there was no moving anyone.

You will never convince me that in this age of sophisticated computers, having two buyers share stock—and credit for sales—on a particular title presents an insoluble problem. And three years later, when I sat in on a marketing meeting for one of my authors, now as an agent, I heard the marketing director say that booksellers were loosening up about double shelving. So the point here is not to berate the chain booksellers. Most books are shelved where sound logic dictates, and yet many still end up with disappointing sales. Others are not given an ideal place in the bookstore by editorial standards, and yet readers hunt them down and buy them. And bookstore buyers are not the only people capable of killing books. Publishers will admit among themselves to having slain more than a few by settling on the wrong title or jacket design, or by failing to exploit obvious marketing opportunities.

Nor do I tell this story to bemoan the fate of *The Physics of Star Trek*. We simply increased the amount of co-op money, assuring that lots of copies of the book would remain on the New Arrivals table far longer, allowing the book to establish itself. Of course, that worked because the book had such strong appeal within a core audience that shared information. Soon people came into book-stores asking for the book by name, allowing it to become a best seller despite the hurdles placed in its path by modern bookselling practices.

But for the typical serious nonfiction book, which will advance perhaps 5,000 to 7,500 copies into the bookstores initially, publicity opportunities are few and virtually no co-op money is set aside by the publisher. Even if lots of co-op money were set aside, such money would still not guarantee front-of-the bookstore display of the type we obtained for *The Physics of Star Trek*. That space is valu-able and limited: Booksellers will not devote any part of it to a title that cannot pay its keep there, no matter how much money a pub-lisher offers.

Rather, I begin with this story because it changed me as an edi-tor. I left that lunch more cynical but wiser, better able to serve authors by helping the house move books not only into bookstores but out of them. I understood for the first time why another book I had published just around that time, a controversial memoir written by a strong African-American woman, but critical of her ex-husband, an African-American icon, was doomed to weak sales once the decision was made to shelve it in African-American studies. It belonged in women's studies. The guilt bird perched on my shoulder still whispers to me that a different title, different catalog copy, and a different sales pitch to the bookstores might have brought that about. Or maybe not.

Did a proposed book's potential shelving ambiguity ever come up at subsequent editorial meetings? Yes. Ignoring problems doesn't make them go away. Then again, I never came close to advocating that books that do not slot conveniently into chain bookstore shelving categories be rejected out of hand. Or that all our problems would be solved if first thing we kill all the chain bookstore systems analysts.

But I did ask more questions of these books than I did of others—in particular, was there a way to focus the titling and market strategies so as to avoid an expected shelving problem? And I believed I was serving the author's interest in doing so. And in that lies a lesson for you.

Gone are the days when most publishers can justify publication of a book solely on the grounds that it "deserves" to be published. If you want a publishing house to take on your book and use all its extensive editorial and marketing clout to give it broad dissemination, you need to understand something of the road books must travel from idea to finished book, from publishing house to bookstore. No, you don't have to learn the publishing business inside out or lose sleep over bookstore placement. But if you want your work accepted for publication, and if you want to be published well, you must ask yourself questions about the book you want to write that are rarely if ever raised in writing classes or traditional writing books. Why are they not? Because they are not literary. Rather, they are about the audience for your book and how best to deliver a mes sage that will flow through to an audience willing to invest in your book.

This book will identify the most important of these questions for you and explain why they are so critical in today's publishing environment. It will teach you how to embed the strongest possible answers to these questions in your submission package, so your projects are accepted by literary agents and eagerly sought by acquisition editors. It will show you how to be your own best editor by subjecting your writing to these same audience questions. And in doing so, it will make your own book's journey into the bookstore and out of it much more likely to reflect a successful publishing experience. But in the process, your writing will change. For some this will be an exhilarating process; for others something to be resisted with every fiber of their beings.

And that's why I begin the book with this little story. And why I end this prologue by suggesting that if, after hearing of these new realities, you prefer not to factor in them in, you can't expect publishing to bend to you. Instead, you must seriously consider the alternatives. Fortunately, there are alternatives that may well meet the needs of many of you.

Years of receiving unsolicited manuscripts has taught me that a number of people spend a portion of their lives writing books with virtually no prospects for traditional publication. I suspect that deep down many of these authors—I use the word *authors* intentionally, for they are as much entitled to that designation as those who regularly turn out best sellers—know this. To their credit, they continue to write, I hope because they believe in the value of what they have to say. Or perhaps they continue to write out of a stubborn need to reject the judgment of others about how they ought to be saying it.

If all you want to do is write whatever you want, and in the way you want to write it, you do not need a publishing house to see your writing in book format. It used to be said that freedom of the press is a right reserved to those who own one. But today, more than ever, new technologies enable writers to self-publish inexpensively and effectively. There are companies that, for a modest fee, will help you print, bind, and jacket your book. They will also give you access to a list of marketing and publicity people who will help place your book in bookstores and bring it to the attention of the review media.

Or, if the lure of a printed book means less than the need to get your message out, you can skip publishers and bookstores altogether and place your ideas on the Web. Many of you may be familiar with the example of the novelist Stephen King, who serialized a novel on the Web, asking his readers to voluntarily send him a check each time they downloaded a chapter. Many did, though apparently not enough, or not enough to make all the problems of self-publishing worth his while; his next book was traditionally published. But unknown authors continue to use their Web sites to achieve instant worldwide dissemination of their work.

Publishers do not fear these alternatives. Indeed, they welcome them. Alternative forms of dissemination free up commercial publishing to do what it does best, and to do it with a diminished guilt about turning down good manuscripts for which they cannot envision marketing strategies that will assure these books a wide audience. The problem is rather that these alternatives have not proved themselves sufficiently appealing to authors. If my experience is typical, most writers still cherish the idea of traditional publishing. Maybe it's the outside validation, maybe the fact that the alternatives, in lacking the special cachet of traditional publishing, elevate traditional publishing even further.

But the price of traditional publication is that in selecting a topic and in determining how to put together a book on that topic, serious nonfiction authors who want to write for the general-interest reader must start to think not only about the book *they* want to write but about why readers will want to read what they have to say.

To make that transition they will need the help of editors. Many authors are eager for this type of help. Unfortunately, many editors are reluctant to come forward publicly with it, because they fear that if they talk openly the way they talk among themselves they will be seen as crass people who have lost their love of good books and see publishing primarily in terms of sales.

This book is an attempt to get past such posturing and to share what editors know with those who need and are entitled to it.

For those of you still interested, let's begin.

Introduction

I f you want to write book-length works of serious nonfiction and see your work published, this book is for you. It will draw on my twenty-five years experience acquiring, editing, publishing, and now agenting such projects, providing useful information on virtually all aspects of serious nonfiction writing and publishing.

In describing this business, I hope to open for public view much that has remained behind closed doors far too long. Aspiring authors need to understand: how to focus their projects so as to create maximum publishing house interest; why an acquisitions editor strongly prefers to, and in many cases will only, make a decision based on a proposal rather than a finished manuscript; what information editors must present to editorial boards and so want to find in a submission from an author or agent; when to employ the services of a literary agent and how to find a good one.

Even for those lucky authors who have already received an offer of publication, or perhaps several, important decisions await you. For example, how do you determine which of the publishing houses offering a contract is the best house for you? Is there ever a time when a university press is as good a choice as, or perhaps a better one than, a commercial publishing house? How do editors calculate advances, and what represents a fair advance for your book?

Also important are two questions you will have to face later in the publication process: How much editorial help can you reasonably expect from your editor? What can you expect a publisher's sales, marketing, and promotion departments to do to sell your book?

This book answers these publishing questions, as well as several others authors would not think to ask, because they are not familiar with the standards acquisition editors use in deciding which projects to sponsor at editorial meetings.

Receiving and accepting an offer of publication is only half the process. I will share what I have learned turning manuscripts into books for more than a quarter century—and that's a lot of manuscripts. I have helped many writers create powerful, compelling, and in some cases award-winning serious nonfiction, books that have been widely reviewed and have even changed the course of public debate. Others, sad to say, made a beeline for the remainder tables of discount outlets. I have likely learned more from my experiences with the second group than with the first.

The writing sections of this book may surprise you, for much of what they have to say contradicts a basic presumption of most general-interest writing books—that all writers, no matter their field, face similar problems in producing publishable prose.

When serious nonfiction editors talk about writing ability, they are speaking less about a skill at crafting graceful, image-provoking prose than about a range of skills particularly useful to a serious nonfiction author: to use language precisely; to manage data sufficient in size and persuasive enough in content to support an interesting thesis; to advance and defend that thesis through reasoned and reasonable argument; and, finally, to embed that argument in a dramatic and paced narrative so that the reader stays with the book through the final chapter. These are the writing skills I will discuss.

Some may ask: How will the writing advice in this book differ from that offered in scholarly writing books—those that teach graduate students dissertation or academic monograph writing?

This book is primarily for those authors looking to write serious nonfiction for the intelligent, general-interest reader, a subset of a category we in publishing call "trade" books. Let me define the term.

Trade books meet two criteria: They are sold primarily through bookstores (rather than direct mail), and they qualify for the steepest discounts to booksellers, an incentive for bookstores to stock such books. Virtually all books published by commercial publishing houses are trade books. A limited number of university press books, those with the strongest sales potential, carry a "trade" or long discount. The rest are categorized as "academic books."* These will carry high price tags, low print runs, and slimmer discounts to the booksellers, which explains why these books are generally available only in bookstores serving a university population.

Now let me answer the question. I was a university press editor for thirteen years and during that time published as trade books many scholarly books, including revised dissertations. But the acceleration of two trends in academia work to prevent many serious nonfiction books from appealing to those outside the author's own discipline, thus relegating them to classification as academic books. The first is that there is little cross-discipline agreement on what constitutes good writing, so authors tend to focus narrowly on satisfying the stylistic standards established by and for their own discipline. Only when it comes time to publish these books do these authors face the inevitable consequence that writing to such

---

* Some university presses maintain a third category called "academic trade." Do not be deceived. These books are still treated primarily as academic, short-discount books.

specialized standards precludes their work from being read by those in other disciplines, forcing their publisher to put a high price on their book to make up for a low print run. So until academia manages to establish universal standards, it will be difficult for one writing advice book to meet all the needs of all academics. Having said that, I must add that academics seeking to write serious nonfiction, even for an academic rather than a trade audience, will find much help here.

Second is the curse of coded writing; that is, the use of terms that only others in the discipline fully understand or would ever employ in their writing. Trade editors react negatively to the introduction of these terms because their use shrinks a book's audience. Trade publishing is interested in fostering the broadest possible dissemination of new ideas. Sadly, even if a brilliant argument lay hidden within one of these language-coded manuscripts, few trade editors would opt to acquire it; doing so would require a large commitment of time and energy to the daunting task of translating a mass of academic-speak into an accessible message.

Third, some topics of intense interest to academics have little power to seduce the general-interest reader, no matter how inclusively the manuscript is written. If this describes your topic, you are best served by publishing with a good university or academic press and by following the advice offered in books devoted solely to university or academic press publication.

I raise these impediments to trade publication not to demean the importance of scholarly books or the valuable role of university presses in publishing books meant primarily for the use and benefit of other scholars. I spent many satisfying years publishing such academic books. But many university press authors at some point in their careers (usually after they have been given tenure and feel they will not be punished for "going commercial") want to make the jump to commercial publishing. Or at least make their work suitable for trade-like publication by their university presses. This book will teach those of you so inclined what you need to know to make the transition, including how to pick topics with commercial appeal and how to turn academic writing into prose suitable for the general reader without dumbing down your argument. It will also teach you how to embed narrative tension in your writing, making your writing less abstract. Finally, for those not trying to break out of the university press mold but rather trying to break in, I will talk about revising a dissertation for publication.

This book is organized into four sections. The first, consisting of the prologue, introduction, and chapter 1, introduces those parts of the publishing process that you, as an author, need to understand. In particular, I discuss the fact that editors, while they may come into publishing with the mind-set and perspective of a writer, over time shift their perspective to that of advocate for the book reader. When editors ask themselves if there is value in a book, they do so on behalf of the ultimate intended consumer, the potential book buyer. This book will argue that if you want to receive enthusiastic support for your project at a publishing house, you must learn to conceptualize your book so that its value to some part of the book-buying public is clear to editors.

Part One walks you through every step in putting together a well-focused publishing submission package, one whose message resonates with an editor. I devote a great deal of time and attention to the submission package for three reasons.

As an agent I often receive unsolicited proposals from would-be authors to whom I must write back saying: "You may or may not have a book-worthy idea here. But based on the proposal you have written, I can't make a decision one way or another, because you haven't given me the material I need and publishers need to properly evaluate your project."

No author should be denied a publishing contract solely because he or she doesn't understand what to put into a submission package.

Equally important in today's publishing world, where most contracts call for the delivery of a completed manuscript twelve to eighteen months after a contract is signed, the bulk of the conceptual work must be done before, not after, one is put under contract. The best way to assure this is to have an extremely well-thought-out publishing submission in place as a master plan. I believe that a book that knows why it is being written, for whom, and most important, what it wants to say, is a book well on its way to successful publication. A colleague once described a proposal this way: "This author knows everything there is to know about his subject, except what he wants to say in his book." Such projects, even when they earn an author an offer of publication, start off severely compromised and rarely turn into successful books.

This section ends by discussing some of the factors you should consider in deciding whether or not to use a literary agent and if so, how to find the right literary agent for your work.

Part Two walks you through the elements of serious nonfiction writing, in particular the importance of fairness in argument. This book will introduce you to standards of argument I have not seen spelled out anywhere else, beginning with the premise that no matter how passionate you are about your position, you must treat competing theses with respect or risk losing your most valued readers.

It then moves on to the elements of narrative. Academic writing is often accused of being too abstract, often written without any sense of the need to hold the reader to the page. This section of the book will discuss those elements of narrative writing that can be employed in serious nonfiction without compromising intellectual integrity.

Next, it moves through a typical manuscript chapter by chapter, explaining why, for instance, your introduction is your single most important chapter, and why good introductions give away a book's entire argument.

In Part Three, I discuss what happens from the time you turn in your manuscript, through publication, to that glorious moment when you find it bound between hard covers, wrapped in an attractive dust jacket, and proudly displayed in bookstores in America's cities, towns, and malls.

I hope many of you have picked up this book before you've made a final decision on your topic. Why? Because I'd like a shot at shaping your project, by showing you the hurdles that various topics have to jump before being offered contracts for publication. If I catch you early enough in the process, you may be less resistant to making necessary changes in how you think about your topic.

I suspect that a number of writers will be reading this book after obtaining a contract, particularly those who may be having difficulty writing their manuscripts. If so, I urge you to read the book from the beginning, because solving your writing problems may require rethinking your project.

The second and third sections overlap to some extent. I was an editor long before I became a literary agent. Not surprisingly, I now use the same skills to shape proposals that I once used to shape manuscripts. Also, I have intentionally included certain ideas more than once, just for those of you who, despite my urging not to do so, may skip the early chapters because you came to the book with a contract in hand and are more interested in what I have to say about writing the text than about shaping a proposal.

Finally, a confession.

This book was long overdue at my publishers. It has been in the making for a decade and under contract for more than half that time. What held it up were changes in my own job—from editor to editorial director and then to literary agent—as well as changes in publishing. Long thought of as a staid industry, publishing has changed momentously in the last decade. As I suggested in the prologue, changes in how books are sold have forced changes in how books are acquired, edited, and published. As fast as I set down what you faced in getting your own project ready for submission, just as fast the process shifted under my feet. Many more revolutions may be down the road as digitization makes possible new means of printing, publishing, and distributing books. Jason Epstein in his *Book Business: Publishing: Past, Present, and Future* talks of a machine, much like an ATM, that might be stationed on every corner in America to produce any book on demand in thirty minutes.

So, I'd like to end this introduction by talking about a couple of these changes, which have attracted surprisingly little attention, even within the publishing industry, but which are of great importance to would-be authors. I refer to the computer tracking of inventories and its evil twin, "just-in-time" inventory. Consider what follows the second of three classes on the business of publishing. The first came in the prologue and the third will come in chapter 1.

Sales reps who started in publishing more than twenty years ago will tell you about a part of their job that no longer exists. In times past, after placing an initial number of copies of each book with each bookstore in his or her territory, a sales rep would return periodically to each store to take a physical inventory of stock, literally going to the shelves and counting how many copies of each of the house's titles were still there. The rep then made recommendations to the store owner regarding how many of each should be reordered to ensure that no customer would be disappointed, no sale lost.

The development of the computer and the bar code created real-time inventory control and ended that chore for the sales rep, taking one more book-loving human out of the loop. Today, as a checkout clerk rings up your selection, the computer uses the information coming off the bar code not only to price your purchases and add up your bill but also to decrease by one the real-time inventory of every title leaving the store.

But bar codes didn't just computerize inventories. They gave bookstores new information. Bookstores now know, to a certainty, store by store, hour by hour, the success of every book they ever stocked. They can also pull up the name of any published author and give you a profile of his or her former sales. In American business's propensity for sports jargon, this last became the author's "track record," later shortened to his or her "track," a term I use in this book.

You've probably already guessed where I'm heading. It was just a matter of time before these computerized inventory programs began to direct bookstore buyers regarding which titles to reorder, in which outlets, and in what quantities.

It doesn't take much imagination to play out the consequences. Bookstores began to order more initial copies of books that fit their profile of "high velocity" books and fewer of those books catering to narrower markets. Orders for many well-reviewed books, even winners of literary and industry awards, were scaled down; some even went missing altogether from some high-traffic outlets. Perhaps an editor's most poignant call will be from an author reporting that his mother walked through her local mall's bookstore and could find not one copy of her son's wonderfully reviewed serious nonfiction book.

Computer ubiquity gave birth to another far-reaching change in the relationship between publishers and bookstores, this time in the advance orders placed for new titles. Traditionally, bookstores took enough copies of a title to tide them over for the first three months of a book's hardcover life. And publishers have always encouraged them to do so by allowing the return of all unsold copies. But with bookstore space at a premium, real-time inventories possible, and an inventory philosophy colloquially called "just in time" stocking, bookstores began to take a three- to four-week supply. Real-time inventory also sped up the decision on moving a book from the New Arrivals front tables to the back of the store.

This particularly hurt serious nonfiction—which needs time to develop a review record and establish its audience—and led to a new destructive cycle. Because advance (prepublication) bookstore orders have always been used to determine first print runs, and because publicity and promotion budgets are pegged to advance orders, publishers were forced to lower first print runs and to scale back publicity and promotion. And then, because first print runs have always helped determine the book's price tag (larger print runs allow the spread of fixed costs, such as editing, design, and composition, over a greater number of units), inevitably the price of serious books eased upward. Because price is inversely correlated to anticipated sales, the cycle was self-perpetuating.

These computer-generated changes distorted other market forces publishers had once catered to. The influence on sales of newspaper and magazine book reviews was considerably reduced, especially when such reviews ran weeks after a book had hit the stores. Some bookstores will now return certain titles to the publisher before the major reviews run. An author whose previous book had won the Pulitzer Prize told me that he had worked six years on his next book and couldn't find a copy of it in the stores less than three months after its publication date.

Conversely, publicity, especially on television, can instantly spike a book's sales, so much so that even in serious nonfiction interested publishing houses may ask to meet the author in person. While the author goes to such meetings to assess the house, the house wants to assess the author's mediagenic qualities, that is, how the author will come across on the small screen in a few fleeting minutes.

One can just imagine the culture shock to those of us veterans of publishing's olden days. Consider the implications of this statement: a positive full-page review in the Sunday *New York Times Book Review,* the country's most influential print review medium, may or may not have discernible influence on the sale of a serious nonfiction title, whereas an author's appearance on national television will likely overnight catapult the same work onto most best-seller lists.

When I first wrote these words I thought the reader might hear them as conversational hyperbole. Since then, the *New York Times* reported on its front page that in the weekend after the book was featured on a television show, sales of Toni Morrison's nineteen-year-old classic, *Song of Solomon,* "soared by more than 3,000 percent at the Borders and Barnes & Noble chains."

Discouraging news? Not to the talented Ms. Morrison, of course.

While these changes have put new hurdles in the way of serious nonfiction publishers and authors, the good news is that they have not killed and cannot kill reader interest in good books. As long as readers demand the mental stimulation that comes from following an author from basic data to interesting and provocative thesis, publishers will continue to publish serious nonfiction. And there is no question the demand remains strong. As a literary agent who sells virtually only serious nonfiction, I can assure you that I can't get enough good serious nonfiction projects to meet publisher interest.

So the solution is not to give up writing the serious book you want to write but to understand the new realities and make reasonable adjustments to them. The next chapter will help you do just this. It's the closest thing to the sense of an editorial meeting at a commercial publishing house I can provide, apart from taping one and giving you a transcript.

Chapter One

Thinking Like an Editor: Audience, Audience, Audience

Every game is a numbers game. Of ten proposals that reach an editor's desk, eight or nine won't make it any further. And this is with an established editor, where literary agents know just what that editor is interested in acquiring. Many that survive this first cut won't survive the editorial board meeting. What was lacking?

First off, let's deal with a popular misconception: that writing style counts most, or even heavily, in getting a would-be writer past those first hurdles. In fact, the decision to offer you a contract is made on the basis of a submission package, not on a finished manuscript or even a substantial part of that manuscript. Why do I mention this? Because you must understand that how well you can write your book, indeed how good a writer you are, doesn't initially come into play. First an editor must determine if your project is, in concept and focus, commercially viable.

How is that determined? What factors do editors and editorial boards take into account? On your behalf, I've made up four projects. Let's see the reception each gets. By the end of this chapter, you'll have an answer to why so many projects earn their authors polite letters of rejection.

Project #1: You've discovered a cache of letters a little-known female artist of the nineteenth century wrote to her only sister over a twenty-two-year period. You approach an editor about writing the artist's biography, and to your delight the editor agrees to meet with you. You describe your fascination with this woman, her courage in the face of scorn by art dealers and fellow artists, how she managed to achieve some small success outside the major art schools of her time. A few minutes into the conversation the editor interrupts and says, impatiently, "Wait. Tell me why this is a trade book."

"She led such an interesting life," you say, "and there are so many nuanced contradictions to be explored in her relationship with her many lovers, her two husbands, neither of them supportive, and with the nineteenth-century art world."

The editor listens politely for another short while, then raises her hand in a STOP gesture and fires at you: "When was the last time her work was exhibited? Who owns most of her pieces now?"

You are crestfallen. Here you have discovered an artist who in an exhaustive and intimate correspondence detailed the source of her creative life force, and now the editor seems to doubt there is enough here for a book. "Isn't an interesting life enough?" you ask.

Project #2: You served on a team of lawyers that won a landmark case against a publicly traded company, the first award for damage to reputation ever won by a small firm to which work had been out-sourced by a company later found to be in violation of certain EPA standards. Everyone is pointing to your novel litigation approach as the key to victory. You have addressed the litigation session of the annual meeting of the American Bar Association. The audience of lawyers ate up what you had to say; members approached you afterward to tell you the case and your role in it would make a great book. You approach a friend's editor about telling the story of the trial and about the courtroom tactics that carried the day for you.

She responds: "Courtroom tactics? Sounds to me more like an article for *American Lawyer.*" But what about *A Civil Action*, you argue. That was a best seller about legal tactics. "The two books are really not comparable," she says, apologizing for her bluntness but declining to go further with you. But what *is* the difference? you are left wondering.

Project #3: You may be the world's best-recognized expert on women who kill. You have enormous data on the subject, as well as a new theory identifying which women are most likely to kill, why, and even how—which methods women favor. You have some brain scans that suggest that women who kill have differences in their hard wiring. Your work has appeared in professional journals, and when a woman in Colorado murdered her best friend, you were interviewed by *Psychology Today.* The interview was picked up and written about in *USA Today, True Crime Digest,* and, to your embarrassment, in *The Star.* You've published all your previous books with university presses, but colleagues tell you this is a much bigger book, and that you should try to sell it to a commercial publishing house as a trade book. You buy a book about how to write a publishing proposal and submit your proposal to editors at ten commercial publishing houses. Four months later, every house has written back rejecting you, most pro forma, but one saying that while your research findings are impressive and important, the project seems more suitable to a university press list. You wish you knew what factors went into the rejections, what seemed to be signaling no to so many experienced publishing people.

Project #4: You are a journalist who has written an article on the female biological clock. Your article also discussed just how close science has come to making the clock irrelevant, by making it possible for a woman to have a baby well into middle age. Another reporter thinks you should turn your work into a book. A friend of his has just been given a six-figure advance by a major commercial publishing house for a book about a group of Russian scientists who were asked to breed tamer foxes and ended up developing a new species of fox that seemed amazingly similar to dogs. You approach an agent your friend recommends.

The agent is enthusiastic, especially given your award-filled CV and the strong response to your article. Scores of women have written in to comment on what you said. The agent tells you to ask the magazine publisher to give you copies of all the letters to the editor, both those published and unpublished, so he can include them in his submission package to publishers. With his help you work up a proposal that expands on all the topics covered in the article but at his suggestion also promises a chapter on the moral, ethical, and sociological implications of older women having babies.

A couple of weeks later, your agent calls you. He thinks he has a young editor interested in the project. Unfortunately, that falls through when the editor reports that she could not gain the support of her editorial board. But the agent assures you that the project is still out at six or seven other houses. Four weeks later, your agent calls to say: "I'm afraid I have some bad news." Explaining that he just can't understand what happened, he lets you know that your book has been rejected everywhere. When you ask why, he tells you that many of the editors said they thought the material more suitable to a magazine article; others would not feel comfortable publishing a book on this topic unless it was written by a doctor or a woman and preferably by a female doctor. Still others just didn't "get" what the book was trying to do. The two of you are stunned.

And perhaps many of you reading this book are stunned as well. What *was* wrong with that last book project? And with the others?

Maybe you are muttering that you've seen books very similar to these in bookstores. And you likely have.

On their face, nothing disqualifies any of them as a trade book project. Each has something valuable to offer. But each also has a flaw that will likely kill its prospects for trade publication. If you've remembered the title of this chapter, you already have a good idea what that flaw is.

Before we examine these projects more closely, let me qualify what we'll be doing here. To those who think that any trade editor will publish an untested writer on the basis of a one- or two-paragraph description such as I used, be forewarned. A publishing submission, especially from a new, untested author, can run thirty to forty pages and is a much more complex affair. In the next two chapters I will talk about putting together a submission package that will dramatically increase your chances of getting offers of publication.

Second, despite what seems like a stimulating opportunity to play editor as we ponder these projects, this book is not written to make you a judge of project submissions. These short summaries are merely a device to get you thinking as editors think and to shake you out of the idea that writing for trade publication is about expressing your creativity. Rather, it is about producing something a broad range of prospective book buyers will recognize as good value, not just in terms of the dollars required to buy your book but, far more important, in terms of the time they'll have to invest in reading it.

Now, back to why these four examples fail. Each has an "audience identification" problem. In other words, the problem with each proposal is not in the idea itself but in the fact that my fictional editor looking at my made-up projects can't nail down the audience, or doubts that the audience mentioned by the author will find the book as appealing as the author believes it will.

Why is understanding audience in publishing terms so important? Talk to an author who has worked for years on a book only to find it languishing indecently on a remainder table in some bargain outlet store, and you will get an idea just how much authors care about sales. That's not the fate you want for your book. So forgive my tough talk as I maul these four projects. And, by the way, no need to wince for the author's pain. Remember, they are made up.

Here's a succinct guide to what commercial publishing is all about: Every decision about your book, from whether (or not) to make you an offer of publication, to the size of the advance, whether to edit it (or just let it go to the printer with a copyedit of what you have written), to how it is jacketed, marketed, advertised, and sold, will be based on answers to these questions:

- Does this project have a self-selecting book-buying audience?
- If yes, who makes up that audience?
- What will this book say of significance to those within this audience?
- Will this audience, once made aware of this book, go out and buy it?

Can't a book just be published and, based on reviews and friend-to-friend recommendations, establish itself as an interesting and important book and attract an appropriate audience?

Of course, everyone loves pleasant surprises, and both authors and editors always hope a book will prove interesting to a wider range of readers than anticipated. And, unlike scholarly books, trade books make every effort not to exclude even one potential reader. The most difficult trade book on quantum physics will have every term explained. So occasionally lightning (the good kind) does strike. But the books that have the best chance of succeeding with readers are those written with the needs of a well-defined core audience in mind.[*]

Let's get back to our four books and see how they fare when judged by these criteria.

What's wrong with the project about the female painter of the nineteenth century whose letters were discovered by the author? It certainly has a well-defined audience—people interested in art, artists, and the history of art. This audience is not only well defined but easy to reach. Art is an established section in most bookstores. There are endless art magazines where this book might be reviewed. If there is a good story here, an upscale magazine might take an excerpt from the book. In addition, there is always the slim possibility that publication of the book will spark renewed interest in the artist's work, which could in turn lead to an important showing of her most famous pieces, generating renewed interest in her life, and of course, new sales.

But if we are targeting the art world, with what are we targeting it? Other art-related books will be published that year. Why would a book review editor pick this one out of the pile? You don't believe,

---

[*] From my own experience publishing books in science, I have long believed that readers, by their buying power, have much more influence than they realize over the publishing process. It's easy to read this sentence and say, "Oh, now I get publishing. They want me to pander to some lowest common denominator." Not true. In acquiring books for the trade science market, I was always struck by the fact that trade book buyers were telling editors the opposite. Books about the hard sciences—math, physics, cognitive science—far outsell books about the soft sciences; high-level, highly theoretical books in math, physics, and cognitive science by far outsell dumbed-down treatments. When offered a high-level physics book, most commercially successful editors will grab at it, while they may give the author of a physics-for-poets book a terrible time.

do you, that every book review editor dutifully reads every book she receives and only then decides which to assign for review? Why, then, would she choose to assign this book for review? Here's one possibility. The artist's name and work are well known. Is that likely in this case? By the author's own admission, this particular artist has had no discernible influence on the river of art history. Her work was not widely exhibited in her lifetime, and prints of her work are not included in art books today.

In asking when the artist's works were last exhibited, the editor wanted to know if the subject's obscurity might be about to change. That, as I recall, was the case with Frida Kahlo, whose work was already starting to be recognized and sold when the publishing industry caught on and eagerly published her biography as well as books of her paintings. But this author is not suggesting that her artist is about to be rediscovered.

If one day she is rediscovered, described by the art world as another Mary Cassatt, an artist forced into a lifetime and then some of undeserved obscurity, there will be time and interest enough for several trade biographies. But the art world must first put her at least into the second- or third-tier pantheon before writers can attempt to elevate her.

So if not the art world, how about a market consisting of women who read biographies of other women? That's a very big audience, you tell me. With considerable competition, I add. But a possibility. But then, as the writer of such a book you must ask yourself what precisely about this particular woman's life is going to make this book stand out in the women's biography market? It's not as if there is a paucity of biographies of courageous women forced to lead pinched lives. For most of the past millennium, such lives have been more the rule than the oddity. Another factor: books appealing to this kind of audience must have a strong connection to the lives of women today. The constraints on the subject of the book must be similar to the constraints faced by the readers in their everyday lives.

In this case the connection is not tight. So let's go back to the only real audience, the art world. Perhaps we can strengthen the appeal of this project to its more natural core audience.

So, what else might we hang this book on? The one hint of an interesting angle is the artist's refusal to pander to any of the dominant schools of her time? Hmmm. Maybe. If there is a perception today among renegade artists that school identification has too much power to make or break an artist, and this woman was dealing with this very problem more than one hundred years ago, now we have something to shape the biography around.

Without belaboring the matter, let's surmise what an editor would like to have heard from this author in this situation. Let's say the author had come in and said:

> I want to write a biography about a completely unknown woman artist of the nineteenth century. I will not be arguing in the biography that the artist is more talented than art critics have judged her, or that the artist's work is suddenly about to be discovered. Nor am I saying that if you publish this book her work will suddenly be taken more seriously. In terms of how the art world assigns the term "great," I don't think we can make that case.
>
> But I regularly read the art journals and art magazines because although I am a historian by training, I also paint. And I know that one of the big debates today in the art world involves the power of art school identification to make or break young artists. [I'm making this up. I don't know anything about art school identification. —S.R.] Well this woman's correspondence to her sister refers to other letters of hers to the leaders of the great movements of her time, arguing passionately about the damage done to artists by such pigeonholing, about how they are stifling creativity, blah blah blah. I know when this book hits the art

world, even though this woman is an unknown artist, what she has to say is going to resonate.

Now you have a potential trade book. Why? Finding a cache of letters did not secure a publisher for your biography; the author's reasons for falling in love with the artist did not suggest much added value. But publishers are always looking for someone from within a community who can say: This is going to be an important book for my community and here's why.

Will you get an offer of publication? That will depend upon the quality of the letters themselves (how passionate and articulate they are and just how many deal with this particular problem), how interesting the rest of the life is, whether the art itself is second tier or fifteenth tier, and finally how good a biographer the sample chapter shows you to be. But there does seem enough here to pique an editor's interest.

Finally, let's say you were that author and you found those letters. Should you immediately approach a book publisher? Probably not. Publishers do not want a book to be the first ever expression of discipline-challenging ideas. The author would have held a stronger position if she'd written an article in an art journal about this woman and her work. Perhaps someone of reputation would come forward to shoot it all down as gibberish. But let's say instead that ten or so women artists write letters to the editor saying, "I can't believe that this woman who lived a hundred years ago is describing my own problem and feels about it precisely the way I do and so many other artists do. I'm dying to know more about this woman's life." You get the picture.

Let's move on to our litigation lawyer who won that *David* v. *Goliath* case involving environmental pollution. At that ABA meeting, he certainly had a rapt audience. In fact, members of that audience urged him to write a book. So didn't he do exactly what I am suggesting the previous author do? First test the waters with his core audience? Indeed, he did. And doesn't he meet my second test as well—he comes from within a well-defined community (lawyers) and he is addressing questions that they are eager to have addressed? Again correct. And as one of the litigators, he has a platform. So why did the editor abruptly turn him down? And, by the way, how *does* this book differ from *A Civil Action*?

There is a well-defined audience for this book, and the author has done many of the right things to persuade a publisher that what he writes will interest that audience. But in going to a trade publisher he is knocking at the wrong window. The publisher he should approach is not a trade publisher but a professional publisher, one who sells to lawyers, by direct mail, books that teach them how to be better lawyers. And my guess is the book he needs to write is *New Winning Strategies for Litigators, by the lawyer who won the famous David v. Goliath Case,* not *The Story of My Biggest Case.*

We may all be interested when someone wins a big case against the tobacco industry, or industrial polluters, but that doesn't mean that any sizable market exists for a trade book describing the legal strategies employed in winning such a suit, novel though they may be. Why not? Because trade books are generally idea books and the book this author can write is a practice book.

To give you a better sense of the difference, let's say this lawyer wanted to write a book for the general public called *How We Really Win: The Truth about How Lawyers Win Legal Cases and Along the Way Distort Justice.* In that book, he wants to talk about how a lawyer is taught to see evidence and argument that supports his side as favored truth; how he is taught to twist words, to make a lie seem like the truth and the truth like a lie. He decided to write this book because over the years, the more skilled he became as a litigator, the more he grew to dislike himself. Even though that book would talk about the same legal strategies, it would be a general interest book. Why? Because it appeals to the public in its role as citizens. Because an intellectual question guides the book; namely, how in our justice system did winning become more important than getting at the truth?

As for *A Civil Action,* that was a book about a lawyer who not only lost a case and brought down his own law firm in the process but also ran up against a group of clients who were unintelligible to the legal profession, because they wanted something beyond money as settlement for their terrible loses. *A Civil Action* exemplifies what publishing refers to as a character-driven work of narrative nonfiction; it is a "people" story. This kind of book is extremely hard to write without good narrative and dramatic skills. And only the very best of these books really make it.

Next, let's talk about the expert on women who kill. Isn't this the perfect example of a good serious nonfiction book? A credentialed author, an important topic, and potentially controversial findings. The answer is yes.

Editors and agents are always on the lookout for experts who have devoted their lives to the study of a particular topic. There may be nothing more pleasing to a commercial publisher of serious nonfiction than writing jacket flap copy that begins: "Based on a ten-year study by the leading academic in this field . . ." Such books are a pleasure to publish because they are filled with research to quote from and the author has the credentials to back up conclusions drawn from the data. To shortcut an editorial meeting discussion about an author's platform, to write the book he was proposing, JoAnn Miller of Basic Books coined the line, "This author owns the topic."

A sort of bonus for longitudinal studies is the second life that such books achieve in paperback, often in the course-use adoption market, that is, as books assigned to students. But just because an author has long studied a particular problem doesn't mean her results will translate into a general interest book. Why not? What's lacking?

Again we return to the question of audience. Who will buy this book? Perhaps you'll say women. The author's friend probably thought the way you did, which is why she believed this would be a big commercial book.

Confusion between a book entitled *Children Who Kill* and *Women Who Kill* creates the problem. The former has an easily targeted trade audience—women, in their role as mothers. The latter doesn't.

The difference is not solely related to a recent explosion of school violence. In *Children Who Kill,* the strong audience hook is not just that so many children have started killing but whom they kill and where and when—other children and on school grounds during school hours. So even if a woman had little concern about her own child's violent tendencies, she does worry that she might be putting her children in jeopardy just by sending them off to school. So this book's market is extremely large, for what mother wouldn't buy a book she thought might help identify ways to shield her child from violence?

But that's not the situation with *Women Who Kill,* unless the book argues that women are killing other women, or worse, children. My guess is that most women who kill, kill men. Any self-protection market would more likely be among men. But don't count on too many sales there. Few men read this kind of sociological treatment, and those who picked up this title in a bookstore might well put it down as soon as the flap copy made clear the writer was no misogynist male out to prove the Rudyard Kipling line that "the female of the species is deadlier than the male." The general principle here is that the people interested in your subject have to include, first, people who buy books, and, second, people receptive to your treatment and conclusions.

Watch this principle at work in other possible titles. Who is the audience for a book about Jews who kill, or about gays who kill, or about Hispanics who kill. Jews? Gays? Hispanics? Unlikely. And the market of anti-Semites, homophobes, and anti-Latino bigots who'd love to hear more about such books are not looking for a book you'd want to write or I'd have been willing to publish.

Obviously, defining the market for *Women Who Kill* will depend, to some degree, on what the actual findings say and whether or not the presentation is compelling. But my sense is that when all is said and done, we are really talking about a book for other scholars, and for prison officials, public policy people, and a smattering of psychologists. No woman I know would make a sociological treatment titled *Women Who Kill* a high priority on her shopping list.

I've already given you one of the tricks I use when I am not sure who the market is for a book—I hold all the elements about the project constant except one and see if doing so changes my opinion about the market.

I'd like to do that again, to afford you a better idea of how easily your subject can be finessed in order to find an audience. Let's say the author of this imaginary project comes to me seeking representation. I might suggest that we seek a publisher to take it on as an academic book. But I might also point out that she actually has two books; both could be spun off from this material and both might be of interest to commercial publishing houses.

Remember that the author said that other magazines were quoting from the *Psychology Today* interview of her. Those other newspapers and magazines weren't the *New York Times* but rather *USA Today* and *True Crime Digest* (a magazine name I've made up to serve my point). That tells me something—that an audience lurks among readers of true-crime stories, many of whom, by the way, are women, but not necessarily intellectual women. If the author wants to publish this book as a trade title, she might put together, perhaps with the help of a true-crime writer, a book of ten or so stories that would fall into this genre, ideally researching stories from the past so that there is some historical perspective on the topic. That book, titled *Women Who Kill,* based on her groundbreaking research, packaged for a true-crime market (perhaps as a paperback original or maybe as a commercial hardcover book that appeals to the Anne Rule market) might be enormously successful.

But a true-crime book is not serious nonfiction. Because it seeks a different reader, a different set of editors will consider it, judging its strengths and weaknesses against a different set of standards. When the manuscript is completed and comes in, its editor will strive to make it a good read for buyers of true-crime titles. Marketing for that book will be special as well, based on the reality that people who buy true-crime books will have hot buttons different from those who buy sociological or psychological studies. And with any luck, the bookstores will shelve it in true crime, not sociology or current events.

Let's say, however, that as a serious academic, this author is reluctant to go that route—often the case. Still, she wants to publish with a commercial publisher. Here's where I would go next to help her.

If enough of her research deals with women who kill their own children, this topic better lends itself to a general-interest book. Why the difference? It has appeal for a larger group of women and for the psychology market. I would guess that every woman who has ever borne and raised a child has worried if she has within her some aberrant trait that might lead her under extreme circumstances to kill her own children. This buyer is the same one who'd be interested in *Children Who Kill Children,* and for the same reason—to learn everything possible to protect her own children, in this case from herself. Further, the book would have the counter-intuitive aspect—from everything we know about evolution, the female of most higher species is programmed to nurture and protect her offspring, if necessary with her own life. What distortion, genetic or in their upbringing, causes some women's impulses to override the nurturing imperative? While a book like this doesn't start with a ready market, if done well it can tap into the broad women's market; I'd guess that at least some trade editor will figure out a way to offer the author a contract.[*]

And finally, we come back to the biological clock book. Surely many young women will want to read it, given the urgency of the issue for so many of them. Or will they?

This author mistakenly believes that a magazine audience for a topic guarantees an audience for a magazine-type treatment of that topic in book form. This is a mistake frequently made by journalists, so let's take a minute to talk this one through.

Any number of topics will attract us to a *60 Minutes* segment or even a long article in *The New Yorker.* And we enjoy the experience. But we won't necessarily buy a book on that topic. First, the topic may be too peripheral to our main interests to command so much time. But even where it is not, a serious nonfiction book is not a piece of journalism writ large. It is a different animal with different markings and a different role to play.

---

[*] An interesting note: Upon reading this part of the book, one of my early readers called to tell me that a book entitled *Women Who Kill* exists. She had read it and loved it. It was a history of women who kill, published by an academic press. A good use, as I've suggested, of this type of material.

I have often had to remind journalists that a book is not an article written to no tight word length. But the distinction is even more than that. In journalism, the details that underlie the event's newsworthiness put meaning into the event. The fire occurred at such and such a time in such and such a location and caused so much damage. Such details make up the meaning of the story; so many killed, so many injured, so many treated and released, so many Americans if the fire occurred abroad, so many home towners if at a resort location, so much property destroyed. The book business hates moving targets. By the time a book is published, the event will not be fresh in a reader's mind and will have lost its newsworthiness; indeed, other similar events will likely have overtaken it in terms of news value. Serious nonfiction book publishing strives to wring meaning out of an event, meaning that transcends its details. The justification for a book on a news story is that time and reflection and some comparative research have given the author a subtler perspective on either the event itself or how the event was perceived when it was news.

But it often happens that a journalist doing a story is left with lots of unused material. So why not sweep up the newsroom floor and turn it all into a nice fat book deal? Because the story is still a journalism story—its power still in the events themselves, not in the kind of distancing that introduces a new perspective. Indeed the story may be such that no great unanswered questions surround the event. Or a more distanced look at the event may, in fact, rule out trade publication, revealing the story as valuable only to technical or public policy people.

Why have I put this chapter on audience first? Not to discourage you but to educate you and thereby arm you. It is important that all who seek trade publication understand and accept this caveat: Editors will want to assure themselves of a viable market before they consider anything else about you or your work. You can predict their answers by asking these four questions of your own work.

- Is this a book idea rather than a long magazine piece? (That's where the biological clock failed.)
- Is the audience for this book a bookstore or general interest audience rather than a professional or scholarly audience? (That's where the litigator's idea fell down.)
- Am I correct in defining the audience? A book audience is not comprised simply of the number of people who'd find the title provocative. (See the case of *Women Who Kill*.)
- How compelling is what I have to say to the book's core audience? (That's the problem of the cache of letters author.)

But let's be positive. Let's say you are confident on all four points. Is, then, the road to publication marked by more hurdles your project must clear before anyone even considers your writing? I'm afraid so. Once a serious nonfiction trade editor has determined that the author is proposing a book for a well-defined group of reasonably well-informed generalists, the next question is: Does this author bring to the table, by training and intellect, the right sensibility to write serious nonfiction? How editors judge that will be discussed in the following chapters. Suffice it to say that while not every author can be the world's leading scholar on a topic, there must be a connection between the topic of the book and the author that will reassure publishers.

Trade editors, as opposed to university press editors, are not themselves experts in the fields in which they publish; while an occasional editor may have a Ph.D. in one field, he or she may be just as active acquiring books in other fields. What you can count on is that all editors who acquire works of serious nonfiction read serious nonfiction. And after years of editing history books or political biographies or literary biographies or science books and then reading the response of reviewers and comparing real sales figures with their own early judgments, they develop a data base about trends in writing history, or science books, or whatever your book is on. But they can't possibly know many of the really interesting questions that haunt each field.

So how do they decide to recommend a project for publication? As we move on, we will no longer be talking about failure, but rather about how to approach a publisher so that from the beginning your book's market is clear, its strengths and yours obvious. You do this through your submission package, the subject of the next two chapters.

Part One

The Submission Package

Chapter Two

How to Write a Proposal

The word *proposal* is often used as shorthand for the whole package of materials you must present if you want a publisher to consider your work. That complete package consists of a proposal, a brief (usually no more than two or three pages) table of contents, a sample chapter, and other supporting materials that might help your case, such as your CV, publicity about you and your work, and reviews of your previous books. This chapter will treat only the proposal itself, likely the most difficult part of the submission package to create. In the next chapter, I will show you how to put together a strong table of contents and sample chapter.

I urge you to read both chapters before working on your own proposal. I have learned over the years that some authors find it easier to write a sample chapter and table of contents, then come back to the proposal. Others find it helpful to go through a cumbersome process in which they start by creating a turgid table of contents—for their eyes only—and then extract from it the best material to include in the various parts of the submission package.

Before we begin, I want to underline my firm belief that you must put into your proposal the time and effort it needs. It's easy to slide into the idea that a proposal is a drain on valuable time that might better be spent on the actual manuscript. I hear this lament often, especially from those who have already written much of their manuscript and can't understand why editors won't read what they've written and vote up or down on the product itself. A word of advice to those of you harboring such thoughts: Don't even think of sending in your chunk of manuscript, hoping to pressure an editor into working in a way that better suits your needs than hers.

Other authors work to create the right kind of proposal, but view the process as merely part of the game; once it has earned them a contract, they never again consult it because, I suspect, it was not written with a sincere intention on their part to follow it. Authors who take this approach waste an excellent opportunity to think through the conceptual problems of their project *before* there is a delivery-date deadline ticking ever closer. Trust me on this one: Editors know what makes a good book. The questions an editor wants answered in a proposal are the same questions you must address to write a worthwhile book.

Still other authors fear proposals because they shy away from committing to paper the portrait of a book they may not be able to pull off. I've had several argue with me that they cannot really know their book until they write it. Editors understand this concern. They know—indeed, hope—that the book will change and grow as you write it. And they want you free to write your best book. But what if a plan that suggests itself as you are doing your research, or even after you sit down to write your book, doesn't take off as you hoped it would? Then they want you to have a sound and workable plan already in place to fall back on.

Still not convinced? Let me try this one: A better proposal will bring you bigger bucks and faster turnaround in the decision process. Yes, the stronger the proposal, the higher the advance *for the same book*. Why? As far as the publisher is concerned, it is not the same book. Granted, it treats the same topic, has the same author, uses the same data, and takes the same position. And ultimately, it may lead to the same book. But publishers presume that authors who know how to flash the strengths of their project have projects with strengths to flash. Or from the other side, that all authors would write strong proposals if they had strong material and the conceptualizing skills to draw their material together appealingly.

But, you may ask, don't some authors write weak proposals that lead to strong books? Yes, and editors fully recognize this. They also recognize the converse, that a project expensively acquired may disappoint. But they have to make their initial decisions based on your proposal, not on what may come along as you write your book.★

Getting a sizable advance means more than having a few extra dollars in your pocket as you research and write your book. A thin or scatter-shot proposal that depresses the size of the advance also triggers a depressed level of investment in advertising and marketing for the book down the line. At many of the major commercial publishing houses, key publishing decisions for your book will be made long before you turn in the final manuscript. Your title and subtitle, for instance, will likely be finalized; your dust jacket will be designed, catalog copy created, and the catalog printed; tentative marketing, advertising, and publicity budgets for your book will be established; the sales force will be estimating advance

---

★ This publishing logic can at times lead to a situation in which a publishing house offers a serious nonfiction author an advance so much larger than he or she expected that it intimidates the author, who now wonders if the house is expecting a much more commercial book than the author is capable of writing

orders, and based on these numbers your book's first print run will be determined.

These decisions are often made on the strength of your submission package, the most important element of which is the proposal. That's all the publisher has in hand until your manuscript comes in, is edited, copyedited, and circulated. So if your book proves more marketable than the book described in your proposal, it will have started out undervalued, underpublicized, undermarketed, and undersold. And it may not recover. Even if reviews start to come in suggesting a stronger book with stronger sales potential than your proposal promised, your publisher will be playing catch-up for quite a long time; those lost early sales are seldom recouped.

On the other hand, a proposal communicating just why a manuscript is being written, and the statement it will be making, generates its own in-house enthusiasm, eventually providing creative stimulation for the jacket designer as well as educating the publicity and marketing departments about how best to present the work to bookstores and the general public.

As to a rapid response, when I was on the editorial side, proposals that at a first skim appeared unfocused often sat in a pile next to my desk for weeks, even months. But I knew that I had to act quickly on projects with well-drawn proposals because they could be preempted within days (that is, taken off the table by one publishing house that comes in with a very high offer). I recall one editor close to tears as she told us about losing an excellent project. The proposal had come in on Friday and by Monday morning had been preempted by another publishing house. She sat in near shock, shaking her head and muttering: "Has it really come to this? When I get a strong proposal, am I supposed to call the agent over the weekend?"

In the old low-pressure, slow-motion publishing world, friends consoled authors waiting to hear from editors with the line, "No news is good news." Now, no news is bad news. Good projects are accepted or rejected quickly; weak ones languish.

Before I leave the point, one pub-biz war story from my new life as an agent: A senior editor, off on an editorial trip to Los Angeles, took a submission package he had received from me that morning, intending to read it while airborne. This was a much reworked proposal. I had even made the authors go back and unearth certain facts they believed they'd find but had not yet found. The submission was thereby delayed for months, which always vexes authors, but the final proposal had answers to important questions I knew would concern editors.

Its strengths must have shown, for as soon as the editor landed, he called my office to say he was in (meaning interested in bidding on the project); my office had to tell him that the project had already been preempted by another publisher. The editor reached me in FAO Schwarz by cell phone and vented his frustration for more than twenty minutes, as I tried to pick out a birthday gift for my young niece.

Let me be clear about this. The editor had been my friend for years, and I hope still is, but friendship had nothing to do with his ardor for the project. Rather, the proposal had given him the answers he wanted and the ammunition he knew he'd need with his editorial board.

Knowing what I know about the enormous advantages good proposals have over weak ones, I resolved as an agent never to send out a proposal without the elements an editor wants and needs. I had no excuse not to. I knew exactly what questions were going to come up at an editorial meeting because I had been there, done that. While I didn't expect that every editor would want to publish my every project, my goal was to have every editor treat my authors with respect and make a decision quickly. That's my goal for your work. A proposal that clearly communicates what the editor needs to know, rather than only what the author wants to say, engenders that respect. No author should have to play the supplicant when he or she can be in the driver's seat.

At the risk of motivating you ad tedium, I now repeat for emphasis the most important reason to write a good proposal, one I touched on above. It can help you write a better book, a much better book. Nearly as important, a good proposal will allow you to write your better book faster.

This chapter, while detailed, is not meant as a primer on proposal writing; it will not set out a first-you-do-this, then-you-do-that procedure. No "one size fits all" proposal will work for every project. Rather, this discussion will broadly treat what trade editors are looking for in a proposal, including the "Big Five" questions you may have heard about. And it will deal with the most frequent failings I have found in proposals submitted to me, as editor and then as agent, and make suggestions for avoiding or correcting such failings.

You have a lot to absorb in this densely packed chapter, so don't be discouraged if it doesn't all come together on a first read. It will after a period of reflection. At this point, some of you may want to go directly to the appendix, where I've included a serious nonfiction proposal by a first-time author. It elicited strong interest from seven publishing houses and won its author a very good contract, so you can be assured that it is not just my one view that it is a good example of a successful serious nonfiction proposal. Read it through, but don't start fitting your proposal into the model it represents. You don't have to do that and won't write the best proposal by doing so. My hope is that once you have read it, you will better understand what I am trying to communicate in this chapter.

Here are the questions editors say they want answered in a proposal. Don't take them as dogma; not every editor will require answers to all of them from every author.

THE BIG FIVE

1. What is this book about?
2. What is the book's thesis (many in publishing refer to it as the book's argument), and what's new about it?
3. Why are you the person to write this book?
4. Why is now the time to publish this book?
5. Who makes up the core audience for the proposed book, and why will they find it appealing?

You can find dozens of variations of these five questions floating around. Editors pass them out at writers' seminars and at academic conferences, and I would not be surprised to find a version on the Web. Know the five, so you have a touchstone as you read through the rest of this chapter. But remember, they are basic questions, designed to make the editor's job easier, not all-governing absolutes. Not every project is best presented by having the author answer all five questions in the proposal. And many projects raise several additional questions in need of answering.

I've numbered the questions for convenience, but do not presume they are listed in order of importance or that your proposal must answer them in this order. Which questions require more attention and their proper order should be determined by the nature of your project. Certainly, your proposal should not list each question and then follow it with a one- or two-paragraph answer. That would greatly diminish your proposal.

Why? Because a good proposal tells a story and is most effective when written as a short story, a little narrative tale of perhaps ten to twenty pages double spaced. Much longer than that and the editor suspects you are trying to synopsize your book in the proposal. Waste no sentences in the proposal. You want to leave the editor hungry to hear more about your fascinating topic, never that he's heard more than he ever wanted to know about the subject and now wonders if he has time to put his head on his desk for a short nap.

In picking up this book, you announced yourself as an author of serious nonfiction, but not necessarily a hotshot short story writer. Don't be intimidated. Good proposal writing remains more craft than art. As in all learning, you have to start from a point where you know nothing or little, to knowing a little bit more, then to where you seem to be getting a handle on it, before you get the confidence to say you have it figured out. It will come. Just be patient.

While your answers to these questions, or others you include, are very important in helping an editor judge your project, your proposal is offering a publishing house two commodities: your proposed book and you. Most editors will read between the lines of a proposal for evidence of an author who:

- Demonstrates real command of his material by showing that he is not afraid to make observations and draw inferences. Authors who come across as tentative, as qualifying everything they say, are probably better suited to university press publishing. At the other end of the spectrum lie those authors who argue by declaration, make broad pronouncements based on little more than their own credentials, or those of others they cite. These are generally not publishable at all.

- Knows how to pull readers into his world and make it come alive. Such an author also knows what to leave out. Painfully, this will be most of what he knows on the subject; a good way to judge any piece of writing is by the quality of the material deleted on the last edit. A good author is not afraid to take the time to explain the rules of his world but remains broadly respectful of his audience, never losing sight of the needs—and the reasoning power and other talents—of his readers.

- Has good command of the tools of rational discourse, displayed by precision in language, a sense for sound overarching structure, and good narrative skills. Publishers do not want the author to be learning these rudimentary book-making skills on their penny.
- Has a passion for her topic and a greater passion to leave her mark on it. Publishers want authors with a strong authorial voice. I've heard it said that a successful author is someone with something to say and a compulsion to say it. Maybe the word *compulsion* is too strong, but she surely must have a strong need to share with others what she has come to understand about her subject. While a serious nonfiction book should be scrupulously fair, it should not be neutral. If you are having trouble imagining a book that is not neutral, yet is scrupulously fair, see chapter 5, on fairness in argument.
- Knows what the published literature has already said on the topic.

Back to those Big Five questions.

Question 1: What is this book about?

This question is asking you to describe the topic of the book. Sounds easy, right? Here are the minefields to be wary of.

Let's say you propose a book on the impeachment of Bill Clinton. You would not begin by telling us that: "In 1999, President William Jefferson Clinton was impeached by the U.S. Senate for high crimes and misdemeanors related to his lying under oath about a relationship he had had with a White House intern, Monica Lewinsky, in a sexual harassment case brought by an Arkansas state employee . . ." and go on and on with all the details. As you would not open a proposal on JFK by saying, "I propose to tell the story of the thirty-fifth president, a man who was born to a large Irish Catholic family in Boston. . . ."

Let's go a little further with that new biography of JFK. If you really want to impress publishers, you would not waste a minute of your time—or theirs—answering question 1 in any detail beyond "I propose to write a new biography of JFK." You can safely assume that all editors know that a biography of JFK can be an interesting topic. They also know the answers to questions 4 and 5. Why is now a good time to publish? There is no bad time to publish a new JFK biography. Who is the audience? Certainly more than enough Americans to make it a potential best seller.

In fact, if you were to stubbornly detail the life and politics of JFK, including the highly visible place his wife and children have held in the public eye since his assassination, to argue that there is an audience for the book and that now, following the deaths of Jackie Kennedy Onassis and John Kennedy, Jr., is a good time to publish a new book on JFK, you would be making a case for why your final manuscript will need a lot of editing, a good reason for an editor to think twice about offering you a contract. So instead, your next sentence cuts right to the two remaining questions—What's new? and Why you?—thereby earning yourself the affection of every editor who will read your proposal.

But if the book you are proposing is not about a uniquely familiar figure or event, take time to describe what the book is about, whether that requires a page or ten pages. Your goal in answering this first question effectively should be to inform and seduce. Before edi tors can be interested in what you propose to say about the topic, they have to find the topic interesting. If later on in your proposal you find you have devoted too much space to this first question, go back and edit it down. But first get it on the page.

Say you are writing a biography of the painter Henri Rousseau or the philosopher Jean-Jacques Rousseau. These are reasonably well-known figures, but most editors would be delighted to have a little refresher course on either. Here is your opportunity to make your biographical subject come alive for us the way that he's apparently come alive for you. Ground us quickly by providing an overview of the man and his life but then, ideally in a page or two, or three, or five, if necessary, go right to those moments in the life that suggest why your Rousseau will make a compelling biographical subject. What makes a biographical subject compelling? What makes any life situation compelling—tensions, contradictions, unanswered questions.

Or let's say you propose to write a book about a relatively well-known event in American history, for example, the court case *Dartmouth* v. *New Hampshire*. Not all editors will remember that this landmark case had to do with the inviolability of contracts. So take the time necessary to remind editors when this case was decided, who the well-known actors were, and why it survived as a famous moment in legal history. Even though you are not yet ready to introduce your own contribution, you must suggest that there is more to the story than the facts themselves, which are, of course, available in any good American history text.

Thus you might write:

I propose to retell the dramatic and powerful story of *Dartmouth* v. *New Hampshire,* a landmark Supreme Court case of the early nineteenth century (1819). Even among those who know a great deal about the legal history of this case, the specifics of the complaint have long been forgotten.

The case began when the New Hampshire legislature unilaterally decided to amend a pre-Revolutionary charter it had granted to the college, and thereby place the school under state control. The trustees of Dartmouth refused to knuckle under. Instead they initiated suit, and eventually the case made its way to the Supreme Court. At issue was whether or not a state had a special right to break a contract if it deemed doing so to be in the best interests of the people of the state. Or did the U.S. Constitution protect a contract entered into between a state and a private institution of that state? These were the questions the Court would have to answer.

The case attracted two of the most important and colorful men in American history. One was Chief Justice John Marshall, who, together with his colleagues on the Supreme Court, would hear the case.

Arguing for Dartmouth was the eloquent Daniel Webster, a New Hampshire–born Dartmouth graduate. By the end of his life, Webster, like Marshall, would be a confirmed centrist. But just five years before *Dartmouth,* Webster had informed Congress, speaking on behalf of his new home state of Massachusetts, that Massachusetts did not intend to obey conscription, a federally mandated law, thereby challenging the power of the federal government to make decisions affecting the states. Now Webster would have to argue his case before the leading American force for centralized government.

In its time, the case was important because until Marshall, the relationship between the Federal government and the state governments was tipped in favor of the states. After Marshall, it clearly tipped the other way. But the case is important today, and worthy of retelling, because blah blah blah . . .

Especially where you are proposing a book about a complicated topic or one that takes time to describe, or one unfamiliar to editors—

cosmic ripples in the universe, the Bayeux Tapestry, a new theory of consciousness, the story of a little-known Greek sect—your ability to ground us in specifics becomes even more important. Here you may need several pages to position your story within a broader context—the world of science generally, or cognitive science, or the ancient or medieval world. With such projects, it is just as important that you demonstrate command of the general area of science or history or philosophy or religion of which your story is a subset as that you spell out the details of your specific story. Thus, if you are writing about cosmic ripples in the universe, we want to be assured that you can position your story within the larger, more generally known story of the Big Bang. We want to know that if you introduce technical terms, such as inflation, the energy of space, event horizons, local time, you understand the need to translate these terms, at least in regard to their impact on cosmic ripples.

Similarly, if writing about a little-known Greek sect, you want to come off as someone familiar with ancient Greek times and as someone unafraid to generalize, as in: "The Greeks, unlike the Romans, were not eager to . . ." But once again, never lose sight of the fact that you are presenting these facts and these generalizations toward one goal—to interest us in a topic that has grabbed your attention. Focus on what is grabbing you and let it grab us as well.

Of course, in presenting what the book is about, keep firmly in mind that editors are now waiting to find out what you, specifically, have to contribute to a book on this topic. That's the purpose of question 2.

Question 2: What is the book's argument/thesis and what's new about it?

This is probably the most important question of the five. It is also one that many authors have trouble with.

Some authors fail to provide a satisfactory answer because they do not understand the difference between what you are talking about—*your topic*—and what you are saying—*what you bring to that topic*. Instead of providing a thesis, they topic cover. In a minute I'll explain the difference.

A second group faces a very different problem. They understand the distinction between what you are talking about and what you are saying perfectly well. They cannot tell you what they are saying because they are asking to be put under contract before they have done enough research to have developed confidence in their thesis.

Let's deal with the first group of authors before we discuss how to solve the problems of the second group.

What you are talking about is your topic—dysfunctional families; gay life in New York, the Battle of Stalingrad, the discovery of the chronometer.

What you say is what you bring to the topic. Dysfunctional families: "Contrary to the popular view, family members did not spend more time together in the past, and they were not more supportive of one another than they are now." Gay life: "Gay life came out of the closet long before 1960." The Battle of Stalingrad: "New data contradicts the long-held position that Hitler's decision to order the Sixth Army to hold Stalingrad to the last man was really the turning point . . ."

Failure to understand the distinction will result in an author's providing this kind of information as his thesis: "This book will show how the Supreme Court's decisions on free speech affected campaign finance laws."

Well, that's just wheel spinning. Until we know exactly what this book will say about the effect of Supreme Court decisions on campaign finance laws, we can't evaluate how new or interesting your thesis is. So instead of saying, "this book will talk about how . . . ," your proposal needs to spill the beans, as in:

> **This book will argue that when the Supreme Court ruled in *Buckley* v. *Valeo* that laws regulating how private citizens might spend their**

own money to influence elections violated their First Amendment right to free speech, the soft money problems Congress is wrestling with became inevitable.

You won't be able to defend your thesis in the proposal, because you won't have the space to play out your findings in full. But your proposal should be clear about exactly what you intend to contribute to the debate.

Thus, continuing the previous example, you might follow up by saying:

By following cases from X to Y, as well as congressional debates on Z, this book will show how the language of the Court's rulings has put virtually all effective campaign reform in conflict with the First Amendment right to freedom of expression.

You suggest the material you will bring in to support your argument, but not the step-by-step progression of the argument itself.

Some authors foolishly conclude that if they fully reveal their argument in the proposal, no one will be interested in publishing the book. Just the opposite occurs. The more you provoke editors with a broadly significant thesis, the more interested they will be in acquiring your book, because you will be suggesting to them how the house can use your impassioned and provocative thesis to market and sell your book.

Other authors fail to spell out their thesis in the mistaken belief that a publisher will steal their ideas and pass them on to another author to use. I've never known this to happen. More important, a thesis is no better than the research upon which it is built. Is that other author going to go out and do the research you've already done to publish a book that will likely come out after your book is published?

The only situation in which an author might have reason to hold back on his thesis is where it has news value. But even here the answer is not to lock your thesis in a vault but to find an agent who can selectively take your project to the single best house to publish it. Then your interest in protecting your insights will be synonymous with their interests.

So if you know your thesis, spell it out in question 2. But, as I suggested earlier, many authors do not really know the overall position their book will take. How do they get around this problem and still provide a compelling answer to question 2?

First, you can give us key preliminary findings, for example, data or archival discoveries that suggest that the old interpretation is not as solid as it once appeared to be or that this topic is more interesting and worthy of attention than others have suggested. This is particularly valuable for people writing sociological books—books, say, about why families do what they do, or why criminals act the way they act—but it can be just as valuable for historians or those writing about business, politics, or law.

But if you lack even preliminary findings, here's another possibility. Don't try to fake the argument or thesis of the book with some weak commentary. Instead, approach the problem from a very different angle.

Editors want to know what your thesis will be for two reasons. First, they want to be assured that you understand the need for a thesis. They don't want to find themselves stuck with a book that merely regurgitates facts, telling us many interesting things but moving toward no overall point. In addition, editors want to be assured that your thesis will, when finally developed and refined, interest the general reader. Some scholars commendably devote years of their lives to very esoteric theses that, while useful to other scholars, cannot form the basis for trade publication. Still other authors attempt theses that are much too ambitious for any one book. Trade editors want to be able to weed out such projects.

So how do you assure an editor that your thesis will make a trade book before you yourself know what you want to say clearly enough to spell it out? By keeping in mind something that I have long believed. *"Every work of serious nonfiction begins with a question the author has about the topic and ends with an answer the author wants to provide."*

If you can't provide the answer (read thesis or argument), you can instead provide the question you will be asking. Revealing the type of question that interests you will give an editor insight into you as a thinker and help her understand the appeal of your book.

Here's how to figure out the question driving your book.

Begin by going over in your own mind how you first became interested in your topic. For example, let's say that ten years ago, while working on your doctoral dissertation on the history of cotton-growing in the South, you came across a little-known cotton plantation that was being run very successfully after the Civil War by former black slaves. You had never heard of this plantation and you wondered why not. Give this information to the editor right at the beginning of your proposal.

Or perhaps while preparing for a class, or working on a project for a foundation, you picked up a book in which you came across a reference to X or Y and you wondered how X or Y played so small a role in the industrial revolution or the rise of communism or in scientific research on quasars.

Again, in story form, start your proposal by telling us about your discovery and why that discovery stopped you cold and caused you to wonder about it.

Next, especially if after the discovery you went on with your life for a period of time, tell us what caused you to return to this topic and eventually to decide to write a book about it. What was nagging at you? Why did this topic continue to command your attention? What exactly do you want to know about the topic that is not already known? Figure all this out and you've figured out the question driving your book. That's the question to put into your proposal.

Thus, at the appropriate moment, you will likely find yourself writing something along these lines:

"This book will ask and answer the question: 'Why, given the state of blah blah blah and the influence of X, Y, and Z did such and such occur? Or not occur? Was it because of such and such or because no one really examined blah blah blah? Or was it that given the state of confusion at the time, blah blah blah?'"

You get the point.

How well you communicate these last two pieces of information—the question gnawing at you and why you find it compelling enough to write a book to answer it—will strongly determine the reception your project receives. To understand why, you need to put yourself in the shoes of editors who must decide daily which projects to offer contracts on and which to reject.

Have you ever wondered how editors gain the confidence to make decisions? How within one week they may be asked to evaluate a work of history followed by a high-level work of science followed by a literary biography followed by a work of cutting-edge psychology and then maybe a sociological examination, and through it all maintain their sanity? Especially as material gets more technical, which it does in science books, in books on economics or business issues, even in the occasional legal book, editors cannot decide what to publish based on an academic assessment of the scholarship. The scholarship is beyond the level of their expertise.

I recall discussing at an editorial meeting a project in which the author started his proposal with some early reference to the defeat of the proud American military in the Tet offensive of the Vietnam

War. Putting aside one's Vietnam politics, the battle known as the Tet offensive is now seen as significant because it was an unquestioned military victory for the United States that managed to become a public relations disaster.

Fortunately, one of us at the table happened to know this. But the situation disturbed everyone. What if we had published this book, only to have a reviewer point out the folly in its major presumption? Were there other books under contract with us that might subject us to ridicule? Serious nonfiction editors live in dread that they will publish a book of questionable scholarship—and be whacked in reviews.

In the world of university press publishing, every project under serious consideration gets sent out to an expert in the field. The editor has this evaluation to establish that at least the scholarship is sound, the methodology acceptable, and the conclusions drawn not outlandish. And yet, even in university press publishing, as Aida Donald, the former associate publisher of Harvard University Press confirmed for me, while the outside vetting process will determine the soundness of the scholarship, "the final decision to publish is made at the editor's desk."

How then is the decision made?

Commercial house editors try to protect themselves by looking at an author's credentials. (In a following chapter we will go into how to present yours.) Especially as material gets more and more technical, editors look for highly credentialed authors, to the consternation of today's Renaissance man. But highly credentialed authors get turned down by commercial publishers all the time, so having the right credentials is not enough.

At some point, editors must go with their gut reaction to you as a competent and reliable thinker. They will continue considering any project that intrigues them, but even if they become very interested in your topic, they need confidence that your book will be honestly presented and will add significantly to the topic. *The most useful clues they have are your book's question and your explanation for why it intrigues you.* If you doubt how much emphasis editors put on the question driving your book, just pick up any book and see how often the flap copy opens with a question. Why? Because just as the question your book poses determines the extent of an editor's interest in it, so too can it generate consumer interest.

This is especially important if you are covering previously trodden ground. Editors will want to know what was lacking in the existing interpretations and will be impressed with proposals that systematically explain the shortcomings of past treatments, provided only that in discussing such shortcomings the author does not come off as broadly and stridently condemnatory of those who do not share his position. If a proposal explains how *and* why the previous interpretation is no longer valid, we pay close attention, both to the explanation and to the respect with which it is delivered. If it tells us that new documents suggest a new interpretation, we look at what the author claims these new documents say.

Why then do so many authors fail to put this material in their proposals? Largely, I believe, because no one has ever suggested that for serious nonfiction they think in terms of *Every work of serious nonfiction should have a question. . . .* Instead, they have been told to think in terms of an all-controlling thesis, effectively straitjacketing their book before it has been begun.

Again, don't hold back on the explanation of why the question has come to dominate your thinking. Take the time you need to go back to the moment you first decided that this was a topic worth writing about. If you are really lucky, there may be a nice little story to tell in how you came to the subject, say a story that lights up a narrative opening to your proposal.

Let's imagine that author X comes to me to represent her on a book she wants to write about a mystical sect in ancient Greece.

Let's imagine she doesn't yet know her thesis. Even more discon-
certing, she doesn't yet know her question. In an attempt to encourage her to figure it out, I begin asking her questions she needs to ask
herself.

"Tell me about yourself," I say. She tells me she is a biblical studies scholar. "Okay, what in your studies brought you to ancient
Greece?"

Having done this back-and-forth with authors so many times, I
will not be surprised to hear a perfectly wonderful story spill out,
maybe about how she was drawn to mysticism or some other aspect
of ancient Greece. It has happened to me time and time again, as editor and agent. Even if she does not come forth with a charming tale
as she answers these questions, she reveals to me how her mind
works. If I find her reasons too academic, founded in a need to
organize and record new data rather than to communicate to others
the passion she feels for the subject, I will tell her so and suggest that
she write the book for a university press. But so far, let's say, I am
intrigued with the trade book hidden here.

So I go on: "What about this sect caught your attention? What
were they doing or saying that somehow contradicted what you
expected to find in an ancient Greek sect?"

Let's say she answers: "They were extremely modern in their
thinking. It's as if they had lived in the twentieth century and somehow were transported back in time. I was dying to know who they
were, where they got their ideas, what happened to them, why their
stream of history just dried up. After all, they were centuries ahead
of their time in their views on X, Y, and Z. I thought I knew all there
was to know about ancient Greece, and I'm telling you I am stunned
at how few scholars I have consulted have heard of this particular
sect. Even fewer know anything about their philosophy. I certainly
never came across their ideas before, and I thought I was pretty well
read."

Sound interesting to you? It does to me.

Now, how does this author write her proposal?

She can certainly begin by answering that first question in the Big Five, "What is this book about?" by writing, "In 867 B.C., in an area of Greece then known as . . ." and she may well do a good enough job addressing the rest of the questions to put together a reasonably fine proposal. But she is not playing to her strong suit. Because this type of book hangs very much on her voice (I am at ease about the reliability of her scholarship), the best thing this author can do is to tell her story first. So instead she begins her proposal by writing:

> In 1992, as part of a program doing research in the town of blah blah blah on the isle of Blah blah in Greece, . . .

or

> While reading about the ancient Blah Blah Blah blarians, I came across a reference to a religious sect who blah blah blah. This surprised me because . . .

While communicating her own spontaneous reactions to things she found, she carefully blends in fascinating facts about this sect, She might write:

> Most Greeks believed X, Y, and Z about the gods who ruled their universe, but this group believed M, N, and O. . . .

or

> Most Greek sects of this period did such and such with regard to the education of female children, but this sect did such and such . . .

further tantalizing us and intertwining the two—an interesting sect and the author as an interesting guide. Very quickly, she will have established the questions that will drive her book:

Who were these people? Why did their ideas not get greater currency in their time? Why have scholars barely mentioned their work?

Equally important, she will give us a window into her mind and how it works. If she has the right credentials—Does she read ancient Greek? Were her academic books well received?—and a distinctive authorial voice, this is a project that would intrigue most publishers. Remember what I said earlier. The best proposals tell an intriguing story and are more than robotic answers to a series of questions.

Will this project command a huge advance? It may well earn the author far more than she expected. Why? Because it is just the kind of marriage of story and author that editors recognize as being capable of breaking out. Once acquired, it will be viewed in house as a project that people want to get behind because the editor will find it easy to generate in-house enthusiasm. All she need do is circulate the exciting proposal.

Let's go to another example.

You are an independent scholar/science journalist. You want to write a book about two British scientists in the nineteenth century who influenced the course of modern physics, but you do not want to write a standard biography of either of them or even necessarily a dual biography. You don't know quite what you want to write. Okay, so now you start to grill yourself, but with the perspective of an editor in mind.

Would an editor care about the interesting link connecting the pair? Not at this stage of the process, because you don't have your driving question. Until you figure it out, delay your proposal. It may

take time to find your *stella polaris,* but don't rush off on a journey
to nowhere. Remember, you are not seeking a plausible scenario that
will con a publisher into making you an offer of publication. You are
trying to learn why you want to write this book. Perhaps you have
to do more reading about their lives. Then one day you wake up and
say, "I know why I am interested. Because they were two Scots."

Scots? Why is that important?

This time you know immediately.

"Because the common view is that England—especially
Cambridge—was the center of the scientific universe in the nineteenth century, because that's where Newton had been, and where,
supposedly, the traditions he founded were still dominant. But in
many ways Newtonian physics was stagnant in the nineteenth century, contributing little to the work that needed doing." (Remember,
I am riffing here; I know little of Newton's influence on nineteenth-
century science.) "The really breakthrough science was taking place
in Edinburgh, which had a different scientific tradition. Why have we
conveniently forgot that? And why did Scotland become so important a place for one brief period of time? Was nineteenth-century
Scotland to science what fifteenth- and sixteenth-century Portugal
was to global exploration?"

Can you imagine the fun proposal this author gets to write
once he has figured out the question driving his book? And you
can already hear his passion. In fact, because this is loosely based on
a project an old friend brought to me, let me add one more deli-
cious element. Let's say the author is an Englishman, and to boot a
physicist trained at Cambridge.

How does he write his proposal? He can begin one of a half-
dozen ways that will be interesting. Here are just a few.

**Just as Berlin, peopled by German and German-Jewish scientists, is
seen as the center of scientific inquiry in the early twentieth cen-**

tury, the great science of the late nineteenth century is usually seen as having come out of Cambridge. But the two most important figures in Western science during this period came not out of Cambridge but out of Edinburgh. . . .

Ideally this author will also embed in his proposal just why he thought there might be a book in these two scientists and how he came to understand what truly interested him—not the scientists themselves but the environment that produced them. As he does, we are offered a glimpse into his mind.

The message here is to be guided—but not intimidated or ruled—by the questions your editor wants your proposal to answer. If this author sits down to answer question 4: "Why is now the time to publish this book?" he has no good answer. If he tries to figure out the thesis for his book, he will again be stymied, because this is not a thesis-driven book. Rather it is a story of interest to serious nonfiction readers because it deals with intellectual collegiality and competition. It doesn't need a narrowly focused thesis, but it does need a question, and when the author has completed his research he must have an answer. Of course, here again, he must convince publishers that he can handle the narrative as well as the science, that he can, by the selection of a few choice stories and anecdotes embedded in the proposal or in the sample chapter, take us back to the Scottish intellectual world of the time, to help the editor relive that experience as the author unfolds it. And most of all, he needs to demonstrate by the way he writes, he thinks, and tells a story that he will be good company.

For neither the Greeks nor the Scots did our imaginary authors know the answers to the questions they posed. By book's finish, our writers will need to have married story and meaning or risk what one reviewer wrote of an author whose book was under review as I write this chapter: "If his interpretive gifts equaled his narrative ones, he might have produced a masterpiece." (Sunday *New York Times Book Review,* November 28, 1999, p. 23, *The Hungry Years* reviewed by Michael Kazin). But for the purposes of their proposals, all my two hypothetical authors needed was their questions.

Some are not that lucky.

I'd like to go back to the Kennedy biography we talked about in the last chapter.

But first, let me pause to answer a question that many of you, especially those of you who are academics, may have been asking yourselves ever since I introduced the word thesis, several pages ago. I say that every book must have a question and most must have an answer the author will provide. How does a thesis differ from this answer?

For the purposes of writing commercial serious nonfiction, they are close, but not the same. A thesis is the position an author reaches from an intelligent drawing together and analysis of all the data. But think of an answer as a thesis that has been subjected to one further question: And so? In other words, an answer draws out the implications of the author's thesis. This will determine for editors if the thesis is both significant and sufficiently interesting to readers outside the author's own discipline to warrant trade publication of the book. Here's an example of the difference.

Let's say you are a research psychologist. Your field is memory and you have concluded (your thesis is) that the amygdala (I did not make up the amygdala; pronounced *a-mig'-dala*, it is part of the brain, like the cerebrum or the cerebellum), not the cerebral cortex, plays the single most important role in the human short-term memory system (this gibberish I am making up). This may be an extremely important finding for the academic psychology market. It may well change the way all subsequent short-term-memory research is conducted. But does your research pass the "And so?" test?

In other words, how does this new understanding of the role played by the amygdala in short-term memory development change our understanding of ourselves? What's the payoff for the general reader?

If your answer must be "Science does not yet know; we'll have to wait and see," then, though I may applaud your research, your book is not for trade publication because it hasn't passed the "And so?" test. A trade book has to offer some answer valuable to those who lack a professional interest in the topic.

With a little thought, perhaps, you can play out your thesis until you get to implications of broader import. But you need to do that yourself. Few editors will do that for you.

Now, back to our JFK biography. The *only* reason to publish on this well-worn topic is to get a new interpretation. So question 2 is the most critical question in this author's proposal. He needs to have dynamite answers. So let's follow through that proposal to see how he can gain a book contract.

With this type of project, every editor will want to know the following:

1. Is it based on new primary research? If this book is strictly a new interpretation based on no new research, and you are a first-time-untested author, forget it. No publisher will put you under contract. Write an op-ed piece. And good luck in getting it published.
2. Assuming you have done primary research, just how important are your findings? So important as to be news in themselves? Must all subsequent scholars now deal with what you've found? If so, remember you can't just topic cover. You will need to spill the beans, even if it means working

out a confidentiality arrangement with a publisher so that your findings don't turn up in a news article, well in advance of your book. Here you might create a section in the proposal called, "What's new," and in bulleted form, you might write:

- That Kennedy was warned early on that . . . and still chose to send the Cuban émigrés, even though he knew that Castro . . .
- That during the midterm congressional elections, Kennedy called so and so into his office and promised that . . .

3. If the findings are truly new, based on new documents, the question will arise: How did you unearth what had eluded all others? Where did you find these documents? If in archives, why did no one else before you find them? Or if they were found but passed over, what made you see their importance?

4. If the documents are not groundbreaking but merely expand our understanding of one period of Kennedy's life or presidency, how informative are they on that period? Generally speaking, on a public figure as famous as JFK, even the discovery of any cache of documents may be enough to get you a contract. But it may not be enough to justify the time and labor exacted by biography. You may prefer to write a smaller book, one that pivots on your contribution, or even a magazine piece.

Of course, especially in this type of book, what you bring to the table as the author will be carefully examined. Your academic credentials, the breadth of your research, how your own political agenda, if you have one, will shape the research, and finally your skills at narrative; history as well as biography requires strong narrative skills.

How to begin such a proposal? It all depends upon what you found and how new your interpretation. If for instance, you were given access to documents that will completely change our view of Kennedy you might begin:

> On October 6, 1962, not two months before his assassination, John F. Kennedy went into his study in Hyannis Port, Massachusetts, and wrote a letter to Nikita Khrushchev, proposing a second meeting between the two, to take place on the isle of Crete. It appears that because of his poor performance at the Vienna Summit, he consulted no one but his brother Bobby before penning the letter. The letter did not survive, though the possibility of its existence has been noted; former White House aide Joseph McSomebody writes of overhearing a cryptic reference to it in a conversation between Jack and Bobby. It has been treated as little more than a footnote to history because the letter was never sent and the meeting never came off. Yet had this meeting come off, it surely would have changed the course of history. For according to a first draft of the letter, which we now know survived, Kennedy intended to propose nothing less than blah blah blah.

The meeting never took place. The letter was never sent. Nor were over twelve other letters, drafts of which, all written in Kennedy's own handwriting, have recently been discovered. Each was written, according to my source, while Kennedy was at Hyannis Port. Each was addressed to a world leader at the time. Together they reveal a portrait of Kennedy so at odds with the Cold Warrior he wanted the world to see that they raise a series of fascinating questions, not only about Kennedy's foreign policy but about why he would publicly talk and act one way and feel the need to test another side of himself in unsent letters. Do they reveal a man deeply conflicted about his own actions?

How did I find these letters and how do I know they are not frauds? First let me tell you a little bit about myself, so you know I am a serious scholar/political journalist/whatever.

But, let's say these letters only round out the accepted view of Kennedy. Then you have a more difficult problem in writing your proposal. Now you must tell us why a portrait of Kennedy made fuller in the areas covered by the new documents is enough to warrant a new book. You may not succeed. You are in the same situation as our science writer and our Greek scholar. It is what you bring to the topic that will determine the extent of interest from trade publishers. Still, your strong suit in this type of project is your research and your interpretation and so with less provocative materials you might simply begin:

> I propose to write a biography of JFK based on five years of research and the discovery of over 150 new documents. While these documents do not dramatically alter our interpretation of the thirty-fifth president, they do shed significant light on:
>
> a.
> b.
> c.
>
> These documents describe a man who was blah blah blah.

In addition to talking about what is new here, and your credentials to write this book, you probably will also have to devote some time to talking about the other major biographies of Kennedy, so it will be clear to an editor where your interpretation differs.

In general, the more the book hangs on the argument, the more fleshed out your answer to question 2 must be. However, keep the following in mind. This is the age of narrative. Commercial publishing houses are publishing fewer argument books than a generation ago, leaving the university presses to pick up the slack. In fact, these days, the old-fashioned sociological or economic or public policy study is probably best published by a university press. But the overall rule remains: The less the narrative carries the book, the more fully developed must be the proposal's argument. Thus, where an argument is the book's strong suit, a very good way to open your own proposal would be: "Ever since so and so articulated the thesis that phylogeny recapitulates ontogeny, biology has operated under the assumption that . . . This book will argue that despite the longevity of that position and the respect shown its originator, new scientific findings suggest that it is in error, that in fact . . ." Then, "Who am I, you may ask, to make such a challenge?" which takes you to question 3.

Question 3: Why are you the person to write this book?

If you are the world's leading expert in a field you have no problem here. In fact, open the proposal with your strong suit by writing:

> I have spent my entire life in pursuit of an answer to just one question: How do most of us make the most important decisions in our lives? I have written a number of academic books on this topic, but now I feel I have more than just technical answers. I feel I have a theory of decision making that suggests that . . .

You certainly don't have to be the world's leading expert to write a book on a topic. If you've spent years in archives, those years are your credentials. If you've written about the general topic for a newspaper or magazine, that's your credential. If you belong to the group you are writing about—women who have had breast cancer, men who have been accused of sexual harassment, women who have been accused of sexual harassment, victims of a terrorist attack—you don't have credentials, but you do have what is called a platform, and that might possibly be enough. Often the author's platform comes from some personal experience or professional role that has been well chronicled in the media. We find this in memoirs. Terry Anderson's platform came not from years of studying the Middle East but from his time as a hostage there. For political memoirists, time spent in government service often suffices. But there must be some connection between you and the topic.

But let's say credentials are not your strong suit. Can you do anything prior to the book to strengthen your right to be heard on the topic? Indeed, you can. Here are some suggestions.

At times it might be best to postpone trying for a book contract, and instead spend some time shoring up your right to be heard on the topic. For example, you might write and publish an article. And this article need not be written to your trade book target audience. The article's purpose is to establish you as a recognized authority in your subject area. Remember the woman who wanted to write a book about that relatively unknown nineteenth-century artist? An article in an art journal might be more valuable for her than an article in a more widely circulated newspaper or magazine. Why? Because a professional journal article validates you in the field. Even perfect silence following the article's publication in a professional journal is a form of validation. At least no authority scoffed at your position. Given that editors are never experts in their field, they like validation from recognized experts.

Not long ago, an author came to me with a book about how managers manage. I strongly urged him to do one or all of the following:

- Try to place an article on the topic in the *Harvard Business Review*; if you can't manage that, try other publications, work-

ing your way down until you find one that will accept your
work
- Teach a class on your theory
- Find a company that will let you test out your theory

Even if your book is not theory or thesis driven, you should
think carefully before seeking a book contract out of your field.
Here's the problem from the publisher's perspective. Two to three
months before your book is bound, jacketed, and sent to the bookstores, a preliminary paperbound version of the book, often called a
bound galley, will be put together. This early version will be sent to
a list of people, some of whom will like it, one hopes, well enough
to write a "blurb" (aka advance review) to be placed on the back of
the final book's jacket.

It is difficult enough to get a blurb when the author is known in
the field. Why? Because everyone is busy, most are honest, and the
blurber knows one should read a book before praising it. Colleagues
will put aside their own work if professional courtesy warrants it, but
it is another matter when the person from whom you will be
expecting a favorable quotation starts off knowing little about you.
When you are virtually unknown and your bio offers no real connection to your topic, it is almost impossible to secure validating
quotes. The blurber's reputation, after all, is at stake. The publisher
may find itself with a "naked" book, that is, a book with no blurbs at
all. Not good.

Now the sales reps must go naked to the bookstore buyers, with
no colleague recommendations to support the book. Unless the
book's findings are so incontrovertibly big, bookstores will take a
wait-and-see attitude. They may place an order but only in small
numbers, creating clear impediments to a successful launch.

An agent on a publishing panel with me earlier this year told his
audience: "I have never been asked by so many publishers to see the

author's CV as I have been in the past year or so. Who the author is seems just as important as what the author has to say." My thought was that only recently did this agent start to handle serious nonfiction.

Question 4: Why is now the time to publish this book?

Answer this question only if there is a timeliness to your project. If so, this question can open doors for you. For instance, on many strong projects, the author may be ahead of book editors, even magazine editors. Let me explain.

The ideal serious nonfiction author is someone highly respected, whether or not well known to the book-buying public. Let's say you are an expert on business organization; based on what you have observed and studied, the next big business book will be: What separates the startups that make it from those that don't? There's already a buzz among CEOs about this topic, and if you look at the best journals in the field, you will spot articles in which one, then another, then another expert inches toward this topic, offering the suggestion that whoever figures this out will have an important key to the future. But so far none of this has hit the public press. There has been only one article about it in the *Wall Street Journal*.

Here's how your proposal opens:

Within the next twelve to twenty-four months the question on every business leader's lips will be XXX. Because the topic hasn't yet hit the financial presses, even a devout reader of *Forbes* or the *Wall Street Journal* or even the *Harvard Business Review* may not know what waits just around the bend. But when the heads of the Fortune 500 companies get together, and when the most interesting people creating the newest companies in Silicon Valley talk shop, the conversation frequently comes back to this one topic. How do I know this? Because . . .

I propose to write a book that answers that question and tells the inside story of . . . I think I am way ahead of everyone else in realizing the power of this topic to focus attention because . . .

Question 5: *Who makes up the core audience for the proposed book, and why will they find it appealing?*

Here you should avoid laying it on too thick. Don't try to educate the publishing house on the enormous market that can be tapped for your book if only they'd do this and that. Marketing people know how to market. Doing as soft a sell as you can, set out who would be interested in your book, and what help the publisher can expect from sources within the audience. Let's say your book is about a squadron of pilots from the Vietnam War. These pilots have remained in touch all these years. One of these pilots, a close friend, has gone to bat for you, and many other pilots have agreed to tell you their stories. Indeed, you attended their annual dinner and gave a speech about the book you intend to write. And now you are getting letters from Korean War pilots, from pilots who flew over Bosnia, and so on. The major journal of the military airmen has agreed to profile you when your book comes out; this journal has one hundred thousand subscribers. Editors considering this project cannot know this unless your proposal tells them.

If your topic is specialized, but one with devoted followers, tell your publisher about these potential book buyers. Remember that many publishing marketers prefer targeting a small but well-defined and easily reached audience than a large audience of marginally interested readers.

Finally, in establishing the book's audience, you ought to distinguish it from other books already published on the topic. Don't fear existing competition. A plethora of books on the same topic confirms a strong market, perhaps ready for a new take. But if you are writing a new interpretation of the Battle of the Bulge, for instance, your proposal should make clear that you know the literature and that your book does indeed differ from previous books. Similarly, if you are writing about the Big Bang, you had better be able to set yours off from, say, those by Steven Weinberg, Stephen Hawking, or Kip Thorne, to mention a few.

That's it for the proposal, but please don't start writing. In the next chapter, we'll talk about two other important components of your submission troika—a table of contents and a sample chapter. Understanding the synergy among the three will help you organize a cohesive package.

Chapter Three

Wrapping Up the Submission Package:
The Table of Contents, the Sample Chapter, and Supporting Materials

Producing an outstanding table of contents and sample chapter takes time, but you are not being asked to reinvent the wheel. Each requires skills you have been honing since high school days.

Remember to keep your eye on the prize. Using all you have learned so far about how the publish-or-pass decision is made, fashion each part of the submission package to have maximum impact on an editor and an editorial board.

The Table of Contents

In a printed book, the table of contents usually consists of no more than chapter titles. Occasionally an author will decide, in consultation with the editor and book designer, to flesh out the table of contents pages with subheadings. For the submission package, the table of contents must be more detailed. A sound plan would be to follow chapter titles with two paragraphs, the first identifying the point of the chapter and the second highlighting materials that the chapter will marshal in support of the point.

You may well ask just how much time and effort you must put into a table of contents. When it comes to nailing down an offer of publication, I am often asked, isn't the sample chapter much more important than the table of contents?

Well, yes and no. Certainly, editors will focus more on the sample chapter than the table of contents, especially if the proposal has hooked them. An editor will usually be more prepared to undertake helping an author structure or restructure a book (the skill a competent table of contents demonstrates), than handhold as the author tries to create dramatic scenes that build narrative tension. While you cannot omit a table of contents, you will not be shot down if the one you submit is less than inspiring.

Still, there's a lot to be said for thinking through a chapter sequence that works, and for doing it now, before delivery-deadline angst is upon you. As with your proposal, those same strengths in your table of contents that helped earn you a contract can keep you on track as you research and write your book.

An author who produces a rather flat proposal will occasionally go on to produce an outstanding, although very long and detailed, table of contents, studding it with just the kind of commentary and insights that suggest a solid command of the topic. These are the very elements that should have been in the author's proposal. My guess is that such authors feel more surefooted within the discipline of a table of contents than with the option-filled job of creating a proposal.

So, if you are unsure of the strength of your proposal, or are blocked altogether and can't seem to write one that meets the demands set out in chapter 2, by all means go ahead and let a long, detailed table of contents pour out of you. Typically the final table of contents should run two to three pages, single spaced, with no more than two or maybe three paragraphs per chapter description. But certainly don't panic if the first draft runs much longer. This free-flow process may well yield some valuable nuggets.

Next, highlight all the charming stories, details, and important insights in your table of contents. Lift these and look through your proposal for places to insert each. As a first choice, check that section of your proposal that tells editors what the book is about. If you can't find a good location for these nuggets, create one. Call it "Highlights from the book" and just list them in bulleted form. See the sample proposal in the appendix to get an idea of how one author who first embedded just such interesting details in her table of contents shifted them to her proposal, where they counted for more in her attempt to get a contract.

Once you have removed all this good material from the table of contents, you may conclude that you have to start a new table of contents from scratch. If that happens, don't fret—it is actually what I hope will happen. Because now you are ready to accept the fact that a table of contents does not so much convey what's in the book as how it will be organized. It will be examined as your book's blueprint. That's why the final table of contents, no matter how well constructed, won't—and should not—be too flashy. It is not in your submission package to compete with either the proposal's sizzle or the dramatic writing of a sample chapter.

We'll talk more about how to structure your book later on. For now, this advice should suffice: Don't fall into the common trap of making the sequence of your research the sequence of your story. Though your proposal may effectively start at the beginning of your interest in your book's topic, the book itself should not trace your journey since that moment.

Regarding your chapter descriptions, keep this distinction in mind. Many creative writing teachers use the line, "Show me, don't tell me." But your chapter summaries should follow this very different rule: *Tell, then support.* Begin with the point the chapter is trying to make or the question with which it will grapple, then run through the material that supports your point. Don't try to write the book in the table of contents. A table of contents chapter description should look something like this:

Chapter 2: Rejection and Mother Love

Why are some boys better able to deal with rejection without becoming violent? This chapter will deal with this question, bringing in the study by Jones, et al., in which it was demonstrated that . . . as well as cases from my own work with juvenile delinquents.

    As an illustration of this denial phenomenon, the chapter will focus on the case of David Dunne, who came from a family in which the mother was blah blah blah and yet when asked to describe why he had lashed out at teachers and even classmates, he repeatedly described his violence as motivated by blah blah blah.

Again, the table of contents is where you communicate to an editor the sequence in which you intend to present your material, which first, which second, and so on, chapter by chapter. Here are some additional thoughts on putting together an effective table of contents.

1. Every chapter must have a title. In coming up with chapter titles, consider the purpose of the chapter. If it is a background chapter, use the subject as your title. If it is a chapter aimed at making a point needed to further the argument, use your point as the title. For instance, let's say you are writing a book on World War II and one of your chapters is a background chapter on the German military tradition. That's your chapter title: *The Germany Military Tradition.* But if this were one of

your argument chapters, you would try to express the point the chapter will be making. Thus, if it will argue that the oath of allegiance the German generals swore to Hitler before the "Night of the Long Knives" put Germany on a no-exit road to doom, your chapter title might well be: *Misplaced Loyalty: the German Generals and the Night of the Long Knives.* By the way, you might hold off coming up with your book's title until you have come up with all your chapter titles. One of these may well make or suggest an excellent book title.

2. Complex treatment, simple structure. The more complex a treatment your book requires, the more it will require intensified reader involvement, and the better it will be served by a simple structure. You'll have plenty of opportunity later, in your exposition, to display your innovative side. Until you become a skilled book maker, look to create a transparent organizational structure for the book itself.

3. As a last general thought, let me introduce a bit of taxonomy when it comes to chapter roles. There are basically three types of chapters: context or background chapters; chapters that further the argument and narrative of the book; and break-narrative chapters. Context or background chapters bring the reader up to speed on the topic and its tensions. Chapters that further the argument and narrative of the book are where you make your unique contribution to the topic. Break-narrative chapters pause the forward narrative movement to enrich the story with a broader understanding of the forces at play; these help pace a book, giving the reader a respite from a relentless narrative, while holding the rubber band stretched. They can be more reflective and wide-ranging than the straight narrative chapters; I often find them the most interesting chapters in a book. One key to writing the best possible table of contents is figuring out how many chapters of each category are

needed and where they go, so that the final manuscript is easily followed, well paced, and rich in insight and detail.

Let's see how this chapter organization works. You are writing a
history of the 1911 Triangle Shirtwaist Factory fire, a famous incident in which 144 seamstresses, many of them teenagers, died when
a fire broke out in an upper-floor sweatshop. The women could not
get to safety because to ensure that no workers left the work area to
take a quick smoke or other break from their work, the owners had
locked all the exits. Here is what I would consider a safe, if formu-
laic, model for this type of book:

Your first chapter could well open with a highly dramatic
scene—let's say the public display of the hundred forty-odd charred
bodies for identification purposes—in which you set the full extent
of the human tragedy, the *lacrimae rerum,* before the reader. Quotes
from witnesses or contemporaneous chroniclers of this scene could
make more vivid the public reaction at the time. But as strongly as
you will be tempted to include everything horrific, hold something
back for later.

Then shift to a context chapter. This would describe the stage upon
which the tragedy occurred, perhaps discussing turn-of-the-century
New York as a manufacturing center, the sweatshop conditions in most
factories of the time, the ILGWU's battles with the garment industry,
the limited worker-protection legislation that the labor unions had
been able to get through the New York State legislature, and other elements that made the tragedy predictable if not inevitable.

Five or six narrative/argument chapters would describe the hor-
ror of the fire itself, the fear and panic as some young women were
overcome, some burned to death, others crushed against locked
doors, while the lucky ones jumped several stories to their deaths; the
reaction of press and public, the calls for investigations; and finally a
chapter on the fire's legacy, hearings by the Robert Wagner, Sr.–Alfred

E. Smith commission that spawned new worker-protection legislation. Two or three chapters into this narrative/argument section of the book you might decide to end one chapter with a union leader testifying at a trial or hearing. Then, the next chapter could be a break-narrative chapter to discuss the first nineteenth-century attempts to unionize workers, the bloody history of the labor movement in America going back to the Pullman strike, and other notable milestones in the battle for basic safety rules in the workplace. Or you might write a break-narrative chapter about the generally futile efforts of reformers to lobby legislatures to enact legislation protecting workers. After each of these break-narrative chapters you would, of course, return to the narrative itself.

Such a chapter arrangement will work for this type of book. And it certainly would suffice for a publishing submission, though you should not accept mere sufficiency and let it go at that. It is my belief that the sequence of your presentation determines whether your readers will stay with you to the very end. You should care greatly that those who buy your book actually read it. So test several organization plans before you settle on the one that readers will have trouble putting down.

Just what is it that keeps readers reading? I have asked myself this question many times, and each time I return to the same conclusion. Readers stay with a book as long as it promises to answer still unresolved questions. Each chapter must give the reader a sense of a deepening, more complicated understanding of the competing forces at play—whether physical, human, societal, institutional, or intellectual. If at least some of these tensions remain unresolved, and if the structure of the manuscript promises to resolve them, the reader reads on. Our society whizzes through life. We suffer from a butt-in-the-chair deficit disorder. Consequently, everyone now reads with an eye on the clock and sour regret if a book doesn't reward the hours spent on it. If your reader senses that the book has gone as deep as it will go and can go no deeper, he'll stop reading or begin to skim. After all, we tell ourselves, do I really need another layer of data supporting the same point? So it behooves all would-be authors to do more than find a serviceable outline for their book. Good authors think deeply about tying the organization of their book to the specific intellectual questions the book will ask and answer.

Let me give you an example, from my own experience as an editor.

In structuring the book *The Rape of Nanking,* the author, Iris Chang, knew she had two main questions to address. The first was: What occurred? The second question: Why was the event allowed to disappear from historical memory?

She decided to divide the book into two parts. Part One of the book would tell the story of the atrocity itself, documenting the invasion of the city of Nanking by Japanese soldiers, and then move to the brutalization of the population in ways that far exceeded military necessity. Part Two would treat the factors that she believed had kept the story of the atrocity from being widely discussed.

Her main problem lay in how to present Part One, the events of the rape itself. Would dividing the categories of violence by type—individual rape, mass assassination of surrendering Chinese soldiers, brutality toward and murder of hundreds of thousands of nonpartic-ipants—prove to be a viable organizing principle? This plan made for effective storytelling. But it didn't sit well with Chang as the best approach, and she rejected it. Should she choose a fixed number of representative moments of inhumane treatment of fellow human beings and just concentrate on those? That was a possibility. The "rape" occurred over a period of six weeks. Could she tell the story chronologically, have six chapters, one for each week? Again, not a bad plan, but one that screened her from getting at what she really wanted to say. How then to organize the material?

In her case, the book's structure emerged when she reexamined the material she had. The Nanking massacre survived as an historical military event because it was witnessed by so many neutral noncombatants—Americans and Europeans living in the city who refused to leave despite the invasion by the Japanese. Further, while conversing with a relative of a high-ranking German official and businessman in Nanking at the time, she discovered his diary, kept through the early stages of the atrocity. This diary later became front-page news, and it seemed appropriate that she choose an organizational plan that made full use of her own contribution. In the end, she decided on an unusual, but in her case highly effective structure of roughly three background chapters matched to three narrative/argument chapters: one background chapter on the perpetrators of the rape (the Japanese military and the attitude of racial superiority it fostered in its troops), followed by a narrative chapter that discussed the actual invasion from military documents, in effect from the Japanese perspective. Then another background chapter on the victims—the Chinese—followed by a narrative chapter on what it was like to experience the rape, drawn from interviews of survivors and surviving relatives of people who had been the rape's victims—the Chinese perspective. And then a third background chapter on a fascinating group of non-Asians who had come to live or work in Nanking and refused to leave even when warned that the Chinese authorities could no longer guarantee their safety if they stayed. This chapter too was followed by a narrative chapter on the role these foreigners played both as independent witnesses and as Good Samaritans.

In essence, she told the story of what occurred three times, from three different perspectives, in what she referred to as the Rashomon style, after the plan used by the great Japanese director, Akira Kurosawa, in his movie, *Rashomon*. Why did this organizational style work so well for Chang? Because it got at the core of the problem as she saw it—that even today reactions to the atrocity vary, depending on the perspective and politics of the commentator.

It sometimes happens that from a commercial perspective the best way to get at an intellectual issue is through a human-interest story. Thus, when an author recently came to me saying she wanted to write about issues in genetic testing, I suggested that she find a compelling dramatic story in which genetic testing plays a key role and structure her book around that story.

While she must come up with a reasonably compelling story, both she and I know that the story itself is really a ruse—a vehicle allowing the author to get at the intellectual ideas she really cares about in a way that will engage the attention of the general-interest reader. The trick in structuring this type of book is to make sure that the intellectual chapters have as much prominence as the chapters devoted to the human-interest story. Let me give you a famous example of how one author did just that.

In his best-selling book, *Gideon's Trumpet,* written decades ago by the *New York Times* journalist Anthony Lewis, the author tells the story of an indigent in Florida, a man named Gideon, convicted of a felony, who wrote a letter to the Supreme Court asking the Court to hear his case on appeal. In Gideon's view, when the state of Florida failed to afford him counsel, it had deprived him of the due process of law guaranteed by the Sixth Amendment. The underlying event, the crime itself, was hardly worth a book. The real story lay in the case's path to the Supreme Court and the Court's ruling that an indigent defendant accused of a serious crime must be represented by an attorney at the state's expense. Here's how Lewis structured the book.

Every odd-numbered chapter takes the story a little further, from the commission of the crime itself, through Gideon's conviction, and then through the appeals process. Every even-numbered chapter breaks narrative and backfills on the fascinating legal and historical issues. For instance, when the narrative tells us that the Supreme Court agreed to hear the case, the book breaks narrative to provide a summary history of the Court itself, especially its role in protecting citizens against deprivation of federally protected rights by state police and courts. When the Court has to decide whether or not the Sixth Amendment's right of a defendant to "have the assistance of counsel for his defense" means that the state must provide one where the defendant is indigent, Lewis breaks the narrative to trace the history of Sixth Amendment cases. The book follows a narrative, break-narrative structure.

Which chapter arrangement is best for your book? Obviously, no one structure suits every book. In determining the best for your book, test each against the question you are asking, the answers you want to provide, and the particular contribution you are making to a better understanding of the event or topic. Then assess how many chapters a narration of the story itself will require, how much background information the story requires, and how many and where break-narrative chapters promise to enrich the story and add to the dramatic tension.

Now you are ready to write your table of contents.

Initially think in terms of no more than about eight chapters, plus an introduction and an epilogue. There is some flexibility in this, especially in biography, but for the purposes of writing a table of contents for your submission, try to stay close to eight. Of course, once you are under contract, feel free to talk with your editor, and hear him or her out on the prospect of some other arrangement.

Second, you don't need to explain what will be in the introduction or epilogue.

Third, create a first version of the table of contents as if every chapter is a narrative/argument chapter, that is, without any context or break-narrative chapters. See what kinds of chapters come out of this process. Then ask yourself the question: Are all these chapters simply bringing in fresh material to make the same point again and again? Remember that the reader must have a sense of progression to stay with the book, even if the progression from chapter to chapter is not always a straight line.

Journalists were once taught to organize their stories in a pyramidal form. The lead paragraph had to include the most newsworthy elements of the story in the most concise form possible. Each succeeding paragraph or set of paragraphs repeated the story in incrementally greater detail. This served the differing desire for detail about that story among the newspaper's many readers. The pyramidal structure is no longer as widely taught, because now most people first learn the general outline of breaking stories from television; those who still look to newspapers for news are looking for the story in all its complexity. But no matter what journalism schools now teach, the pyramidal form becomes a prescription for disaster in serious nonfiction books.

If as you read your chapter summaries you do not get that sense of progression, start again and rethink the chapters. What material will be bundled into each chapter and what order should the bundles take? Here's what on its face may seem a contradiction of my rejection of the pyramidal form: Many good books are layered—as they unfold, they reveal a more complex, more textured view of their subject. But they are not examples of the basic pyramidal form because simultaneously they are drawing you irresistibly toward the answer the author wants you to accept. The distinction is that layered books create a sense of progression, not simply of elaboration.

Fourth, ask yourself whether your first chapter demands so much backfilling of basic information that you can't get the narrative going. If so, list the information you must introduce before your reader can hop on the narrative. Pull that material out of your opening narrative chapter or chapters and plan for a separate context chapter. Because you generally don't want your reader to meet you in a context chapter, make sure your introduction has some narrative strength.

Fifth, now go through all the remaining narrative chapters to see if any of the later chapters will also have a context problem. Your story may twist and turn and bring in new settings, new issues, a new set of ideas to consider, a new cast of characters, new societal consequences for possible solutions, and some or many of these may require or benefit from context discussions. If the problem seems extensive, you may want to consider breaking up your book into two parts or even three parts, with each part opening with a context chapter.

Sixth, revise again, trying to hold to the goal of eight chapters plus an introduction and epilogue.

Seventh, ask yourself if this arrangement has constrained you too much in terms of your special focus. If so, will a separate break-narrative chapter, placed at the appropriate point, allow you to deal with that issue in an abstract way?

Eighth, revise again. Go back and second-guess your decisions. For instance, will an introductory context chapter make the opening to your narrative too thin and suggest a "this-occurred-and-then-that-occurred" presentation of the material to come? Would your background material work better if interwoven throughout the book in various chapters? Context pauses within chapters enrich the narrative, provided they do not suspend the narrative for too long or do so too often. As you look over your table of contents, ask yourself if the chapters, in the sequence you have them, create a sense of crescendo, either intellectually or in terms of an evolving story. No reader has an obligation to stay with your book, and may not, unless he or she is curious about when the next plot shoe will drop, or how you will resolve an intellectual quandary you have created. And an acquiring editor knows this.

Ninth, set the table of contents aside for a few days. If you don't find yourself sitting bolt upright one night with another arrangement that might work better, begin to trust what you have decided. If you do have such an experience, or develop an uneasy sense that you really need to sequence your chapters differently, don't ignore these signals. I find I can rarely help an author restructure a book until I have lived with the proposed arrangement for a while. Trust your own inner editor. Most of us are better at judging what we have done than in planning what we should do.

Tenth, be confident that if you invest sufficient time in the table of contents, and don't shut down your own judgment about it, you won't go wrong.

The Sample Chapter

Now you are ready for the fun part.

A sample chapter is not really a chapter at all. It looks and smells like a chapter, in that it usually runs about a chapter's length and has a beginning, middle, and end. But like no chapter in your final book, it succeeds by cannibalizing other chapters, stealing the best material in the book and presenting it in such a way as to showcase the dramatic potential of the book or the power of the argument, or the richness of the topic.

To help you conceive your sample chapter, let's give it a new name. Publishing refers to it as a sample chapter but to get you to think of it in terms of the role it plays in the submission package, let's think of it as a writing sample. It doesn't have to restrict itself to the stuff of one particular chapter in the finished book. It needn't have a title, although an appropriate title helps any piece of writing. Journalists who have written long magazine articles can often avoid submitting a writing sample, even if they are looking to become first-time book authors; they can submit published work in its place. However, if the material reads too much like journalism and not enough like serious nonfiction, requiring imagination on the part of the editor to see it as the stuff of book writing, be careful. You may want to submit, along with the previously published pieces, a writing sample based on the material in your book.

Does this mean that if you are an academic you can submit a sample journal article? Probably not, unless that article is written in the voice and style you will adopt in the book, a voice not laden with intradiscipline coded words and phrases. The voice should be inclusionary rather than exclusionary, one that will invite in a broad range of readers.

If you are going to create a writing sample for your submission package, here's how to determine what material should go into it.

First, from the three categories I've set out below, determine where your book would best fit. Much of what you should be learning from the samples I've created will apply to all three types of books, but some of it will be more narrowly useful to a particular category.

If your book has a narrative, one written in the form of a developing story, as, say, history books are, then even though an argument drives that narrative, look at the narrative model below for strategies.

If your contribution is the argument itself, use the model for argument-based books. Philosophy books, for example, are argument based; they promise the reader not new information but new analysis. But far more common are those books that make an argument based upon both the gathering and the analysis of a great deal of new data—books such as *Why Americans Don't Vote, The Overworked American, Lost Boys: Why Our Sons Turn Violent and How We Can Save Them.*

If your book is explaining cutting-edge research—this primarily describes science books—then your book is an explanatory book. Explanatory books have a narrative—one of my authors is currently completing a book on the journey through time of a single atom, from the Big Bang to the end of time. But it is his explanatory expertise that is creating a readership for the book, not the journey of the atom per se.

Narrative-Based Books

For narrative books, you will generally find it easier to create a writing sample out of material at the beginning of the book. Otherwise you may take too long explaining who is who, where's there, what's what. However, don't take this to mean that if you are writing a biography you would begin your sample chapter with the day the subject was born or, worse, with a long list of his parents, grandparents, and great-grandparents, and the occupation of each. Ask yourself this question: Is there a moment in your subject's childhood or even early adulthood that catches some distinctive aspect of the subject's personality, or seems predictive of the pattern of his or her life, or reveal the kind of inner conflicts faced later on in life. If so, begin with that moment. Here's an example, completely made up, of what I am talking about.

Devon Chambers could not have been more than five years old when it happened. And yet, forty-four years later, long after he had left the South of his youth, long after the South of his youth had been called to the court of history and judged severely wanting, he could not recall that one moment without first reassuring himself that that was then and this was now.

Perhaps it was the casualness with which his mother had pulled him aside earlier that day to tell him that soon Mrs. Harris was going to come by and take him somewhere, and he needed to be dressed in his Sunday best clothes. Why hadn't he asked where he was going? And why had Mrs. Harris taken him, not his mother?

It seemed like a long walk until the two of them turned down a long dirt path to a small building sitting at the edge of a woods. He remembered the sounds first, the sounds of women crying. And then the Hallelujahs, piercing the thick, moist summer air. He remembered the three steps he and Mrs. Harris climbed, her hand squeezing his tight, as she explained that they were about to enter a funeral parlor. And then the sight of row after row of black people, all dressed in their Sunday best, most with their heads in their hands, bent over, a few with their heads tipped way back, tears streaming down their cheeks, looking as if they hoped that the roof of that funeral hall would somehow burst open and let God in to relieve them of some of their pain.

And then he saw the man, lying in a box, dressed in Sunday clothes, his arms folded over his chest, as if he were asleep. Devon understood none of it. Why didn't the man get out of the box? Why were all the people crying? Why was he here?

As if she were able to read his thoughts as he thought them, Mrs. Harris dropped to her knees and cupped his face between her hands. "That man, lying in the box," Mrs. Harris said, tears in her own eyes, "was put to death because someone said he did something not nice to a white woman. We know the truth. He never hurt nobody. Your mama asked me to take you here not to frighten you but to make sure you understand that you must never, never be with white people alone. And certainly never with white women, no matter how nice and friendly they act."

Maybe it was the smell of all those flowers, or the hot summer air trapped in that crowded funeral parlor, but the next thing he remembered was being home, in bed, his mother sitting on the edge of his bed, telling him she was beside him and everything would be all right. He never knew how he got home.

Years later, he sat in the living room with his grown children, trying to explain why he had been so hard with them, why he had refused to let them become part of the modern world, why he had fought the fight long after others had given in. Not one of his four children so much as took his hand and said, "Don't worry, Father. We understand." By then too much had happened and not happened between them and him. As his eldest son, Marion Chambers, later recalled, "It was too late for my father. The man of whom John Dickson once said 'He helped thousands' had somehow lost touch with his own children."

Why open with such a story? Because doing so tells editors that you understand human emotions and that you know how to play out a poignant moment.

After this opening scene, move along as you would if writing a real chapter, except that you will be covering more ground than a typical book chapter covers. Embed the necessary background material, and do so with the confidence of an author who has no reservations about his command of his material. Deftly, start to introduce your interpretation. Quote directly from primary sources whenever appropriate but no matter what, don't download everything you have found, as so many academic authors do, by moving from quote to quote to quote.

Let me reinforce this. Scholarly books, for good reason, include everything the author has learned from his research. Their role is to make available for other scholars materials either buried in archives or widely dispersed among other primary documents. As a trade author, your primary obligation differs. It is to your reader, not to other scholars. Be cautious in selecting what to include and ruthless in deciding what to leave out. Trade houses want to hear the voice of an intelligent author guiding them through the material; they don't want plenitude.

As you work through the rest of the chapter, be aware of a mistake authors of narrative books frequently make in producing their writing samples: Instead of finding two or three or four key incidents in the period to be described, and building the narrative around these incidents, they include every piece of research remotely linked with the chosen time period. This communicates to editors an author's lack of control of his material.

If possible, the writing sample should end on a dramatic note. Here's one way to find the note. Ask yourself this question: If you were writing the book itself, what would be the next key event/decision/struggle in that subject's life? Perhaps a period of depression brought on by a mother's death, or a restlessness owing to his feelings of being out of sync with the rest of his family, or a change brought on fortuitously or tragically by events outside his control. If your book is not a biography, it might be an important next event in the story, a legal decision, a new leader on the scene, for or against, a major cataclysmic event striking at the larger society. Do not be concerned if in the actual book this moment comes much later. In the writing sample, figure out a way to get to that next narrative junction. Without actually covering the moment, foreshadow its importance. Then end the sample.

Thus, you might write:

> By the time he was fifteen, he had come to terms with the fact that his world would never be larger than the behind-the-railroads part of town where black folk lived. And then it happened. On the last day of school, just before junior high school graduation, all the students were brought together to the lunch room for an announcement. Something called Brown, a judicial decision by the highest court in the land, the Supreme Court, his principal now told everyone, meant that next year some of the black kids in the Theodore Roosevelt Junior High School would be going to the white high school on the other side of town. While the other kids were asking all sorts of questions about the white school, all he could think about was the man in the pine box.

Argument-Based Books

In an argument-based book, use the writing sample to showcase data that is compelling, varied, and bookworthy, and simultaneously to show that the author has something beyond the data to contribute. Little frustrates an editor more than being forced to edit a book that throws study after study at the reader but doesn't really interpret the material in a way that throws new light on it all. The legal expression "the weight of evidence" is just that—an expression. In a publishing submission, at least to a trade editor, weight alone won't do it. This often vexes authors newly out of school. Having spent their lives filling up exam blue books, they feel pressure to put it all down, to ensure a good grade. This is not where you demonstrate you know enough about your topic to write the book. Your proposal should have assured your editor of that.

So the skill in producing this type of writing sample is in taking one small aspect of your subject and making it come alive by establishing your authorial command. For instance, let's say you're writing a book about the psychological effects of rejection, and one of your selling points is that the way one deals with rejection depends on when one is first rejected. More specifically you will argue that the data shows that an adult propensity for violent responses usually follows a pattern of early childhood rejection, even when the pattern ends or is ameliorated by the age of ten. You have equally interesting data on how we deal with rejection when we are teenagers and adults. You also have some intriguing studies distinguishing the effects of parental rejection, rejection by lovers, rejections by bosses, blah blah blah.

Ideally, you would want to take the smallest possible piece of that first aspect of the story—minor rejections of children under the age of ten—and develop it into a fifteen-page writing sample. Don't even think about going to a twenty- to thirty-page length of a typical book chapter. It is at best a snippet and should be presented to editors as such.

Even in such a book, it is not a bad idea to begin with a dramatic story—though in this kind of book it would be called an anecdotal opening—especially one that suggests that your story has a strong personal component. You can, if it suits your point, end with an example that suggests that even if a child who has experienced rejection manages to get through his teens without displaying a tendency to violence, he can later on fall into a pattern of violent reaction to even minor slights. Suggest that an interesting distinction lurks here, but do not get into it.

In argument-driven books, the reader is always testing the writer's assertions against her own life experiences. In narrative-driven books, the author often draws a bye on this because these books tend to catch the reader up in the story, much as fiction does, so that the reader often accepts uncritically the author's data and the soundness of her argument. But even here, remember that your most valued readers, those whose judgment you should care most about, will always be your most critical readers. You may want to look at chapter 5, on fairness in argument, before you plan your sample chapter.

But argument-driven books never draw a bye. To the contrary, argument-driven books particularly tend to be highly interactive affairs. I have sat through heated editorial meetings where women editors lashed out at authors because they had described female behavior in ways that clashed with the editors' own perceptions. Always test your conclusions in terms of all the ways other reasonable people might hear them, then distinguish what you are actually saying from what a reader might be flash tempted to presume you are saying. Don't throw up walls against the very people who control the contract decision. "In your face" seldom works in a writing sample. A strident, lecturing tone in a writing sample is quicker than hemlock. It is very important that editors see the authors of argument-driven books as reasonable and respectful of the opinions of others.

Let me close by noting that it's always a bad idea to use your book itself to argue with academic colleagues, a worse idea to rehash old quarrels or avenge past slights. Using the writing sample to do so is even more self-destructive. We all have pigheaded colleagues, pigheadedly wrong on one point or another. Of course, you know just where and why they slipped up, and that only fearless and robust challenges can root out the error and put things right. But save it for your academic conferences.

Explanation-Driven Books

A typical explanation-driven book will be about science. But it might be about philosophy, legal decision-making, or economic theory. With explanation-driven books, of course, you are not necessarily favoring a particular line of reasoning (although you may have a preferred position), but rather trying to explain why the best minds in a field think the way they do about an intriguing problem or dilemma. You are explaining why one set of ideas (rather than another) gained currency at a particular time and place in our history, or has greater persuasive power than earlier dogma, or, though still speculative, offers the best hope for resolution of an extremely important but as yet still open intellectual problem, or though counterintuitive, is dispositive for one reason or another. Readers of such books want to understand not only the ideas but also the thinking that led to them. I used to tell authors of these books that readers would love to be microscopic flies on the inside wall of a great thinker's skull. So don't just give us the thought; give us the thinker too. In other words, tell us what you know about how the thinker came up with his or her breakthrough idea.

The decision about whether or not to offer you a contract will hang very much on your ability to explain such difficult-to-understand, often highly theoretical ideas without "going technical" on the reader.

What do I mean by the term "going technical"? Resorting to the technical language of your discipline, which is likely as unfamiliar to readers as the idea itself. Thus, if you are writing a book called *The Existential Dilemma,* and in explaining existentialism all you can talk about is phenomenology, you have gone technical on the reader. Instead, in fifteen or so pages, you tell the reader how the existentialist world view came into being, why it arose in opposition to the idea of essentialism, or blah blah blah. While doing so, you not only explain these terms but explain why these two terms emerged—during the course of what debates, over which issues. In this instance, I would want an author to position this debate in terms of a more general issue, let's say free will. In an explanatory-driven project, we want someone who will not only guide us through the particulars of a debate but tell us why there had to be this debate, why it arose in the first place.

If, in presenting a new theory of how life began, your writing sample drifted into the rules of organic chemistry, you would not endear yourself to editors. But if your writing sample instead discussed three previous theories of how life on earth began and explained clearly the flaw in each, and ended by suggesting a new idea that did not violate any of the principles elaborated in the three previous examples, then you would have written a more effective writing sample.

At this point, you might want to take a look at the writing sample included in the appendix. Once you do so, you are ready to get to work putting together your final submission package.

The Publishing Submission

In addition to the proposal, the table of contents, and the sample chapter, include your CV, any relevant previous writings, no matter how arcane, any publicity about you, even if not directly related to the book, and any other personal information that will help persuade a publisher that you are the person to write this book.

You are now ready to approach either a literary agent or an editor directly. You will have other decisions to make as well, including whether or not to submit your project to one house at a time or to many houses simultaneously. And you will also have to decide whether to include those university presses that are now aggressively trying to expand their trade programs. You'll find answers to all these questions in the next chapter, "Placing Your Manuscript with a Publisher: To Agent or Not to Agent, and Other Questions about the Publishing Acquisition Process."

Chapter Four

Placing Your Manuscript with a Publisher:
To Agent or Not to Agent, and Other Questions about the Publishing Acquisition Process

Putting together the proposal was hard work, but now you are ready to test the waters. For some few of you, the next step—showing your work to a literary agent or perhaps going directly to a publishing house with it—is pure fun. You can't wait to hear the responses. But for most authors (myself included) the next step is a bit too much like entering a beauty pageant. You parade; they—utter strangers—decide. For some of us, acceptance or rejection will not be just about our work but also about ourselves.

So how can I make this part of the process less painful for you?

First, by reminding you—especially those inclined to invest too much credibility in those who will judge your work—that publishing people are not all-knowing arbiters of taste, intelligence, or profundity, but simply people trying to earn a living. If you receive specific suggestions or comments from editors or agents, listen to them. Most are trying to help you. If rejection comes, don't internalize it. You are the same person you were before you sent out your work.

Second, by assuring you once again that the most important factor in determining success is a strong submission package. My hope is that you will use the earlier chapters of this book to help you produce such a package.

Third, by explaining how the process works, so you won't be fearful and tentative as you go through it.

Your question at this time will likely be: Do I need a literary agent to help me find a publisher or should I take a stab at finding one myself? Let's talk about the second option first.

Representing Yourself

Never cold-call a publishing house, hoping the telephone operator will direct you to an appropriate editor. Even if the operator does direct your call, you are not likely to speak with anyone higher than an editorial assistant. With many houses, you won't get past the main operator. These are the times we live in.

The same advice applies to sending an unsolicited proposal to a publishing house. Years ago, many houses had people on staff to read the "slush" pile—manuscripts sent in to no specific editor. They were treated respectfully if not seriously, and the occasional slush-pile manuscript did get published. Today, you are fortunate if your materials get into the hands of an editor's assistant, many of whom are just months out of college and may know less about what makes a manuscript publishable than you do.

Several months ago, when I was out of town without my telephone book and needed to speak to an editor at a major publishing
house, I called information and was given the listed number of the
publisher. I listened to a voice-mail message telling me that if I knew
the extension of the person I wished to reach, dial it now, but if I
wanted to submit a manuscript, here's where to send it, and, by the
way, I might expect a response in approximately six months. *Six
months!* Generally speaking, an agented project will be picked up or
rejected by most publishers within two to three weeks of submission. I think the message is clear. Sending in a manuscript cold is not
the way to go.

So when should you try to place a manuscript on your own?
Here are some situations.

If an editor approaches you—at an academic conference, by e-
mail, or in a letter or phone call—by all means respond to that editor. How would an editor know about you and your work? From one
of her own authors, who may have mentioned you to her. From a
magazine or journal article you wrote. Young, enterprising editors
often scan important magazines for new talent. Or finally, if your
name gets in the news. If you are quoted in *Newsweek* as an expert on
Islam and receive a call from an editor telling you he has been looking for someone to write a book on the Middle East, send your materials to that editor. However, if you receive this kind of call before you
have done the work of writing a proposal, be careful. Even if that editor were to offer a contract based on your journal articles or something else, he or she is not likely to make you as good an offer as you
might get if you took the time to prepare a strong submission package. Equally important, you do not want to be put under contract
before you are sure about the book you want to write.

Can you, on your own, approach an editor at an academic or
writing conference? Absolutely. And if that editor displays interest in
seeing your materials, send them on. Then again, if the editor seems

to be nodding to your words but thinking of other things, cut it short and move on.

In general, an editor who takes the time to seek you out, or hear you out, is a good editor for your project. If you send your materials, here's what to expect.

You will probably hear back within a month, if not much sooner. Let's say the editor writes thanking you for submitting your materials but declines to make you an offer. Or perhaps he suggests that you would be better served by first working with a literary agent. In both cases, your next step should be to approach a literary agent. Whatever you sent along just didn't cut it.

If the editor suggests a particular agent, call that agent. I have received numerous calls from would-be clients who obtained my name from one editor or another.

But if the editor calls back with an offer of publication, consider it seriously, especially if the size of the advance offered by the publishing house is not your primary concern. You can, if you want to, bring in an agent at this point to negotiate the contract. To me, that's a waste of money. While you may not get the most favorable terms from your publishing house, if this is your first book, don't worry about that. It is far more important to be with an enthusiastic editor who has a real feel for your project. You can take on an agent for your next book, especially if you want to shop it to other publishing houses simultaneously in the hopes of having the advance bid up.

Finally, there is one last situation in which you might approach an editor without an agent. Let's say that of the past five books you've read and loved, in three of the five the author thanks the same editor. These books are similar to yours in writing style, subject matter (both history, both science, both politics), and in the audience they are going after. In that situation, if you want to work without an agent, sure, go ahead and give it a try. But don't count on a fast response.

But in most if not all other situations, you would probably be wiser and safer working through an agent. The right agent can make sure your materials are in the best possible shape and knows the right group of editors to send your work to. It might be helpful to consider that when editors turn author, virtually all of them take on agents to represent their work. This book, for example, is agented.

So how do you get the best possible agent for your project? As in most of life, you get better results by expending more energy.

The first stop is your bookstore. Go to the section where the book you propose to write would be shelved—history, science, law, women's studies, gender studies, etc. Pick out seven or eight books that you admire, making sure to pick books published in the past five years. Turn to the acknowledgments page, which used to be positioned at the front of the book but now may be at the rear. Often, the author will acknowledge his or her agent. Collect these names.

Now locate those agents by going to the reference section of your local or university library and consulting a large paperbound book called *LMP (Literary Market Place)*. Under the category "literary agents," you will find a fairly complete listing of active agents. To be listed in *LMP,* a new agent has to demonstrate that he or she has placed at least two or three books within the past year or so and provide three letters of recommendation from editors. For most agents, *LMP* will provide you with the address, telephone, fax, and e-mail address. Some very good agents do not list themselves in *LMP,* or anywhere else, out of fear of being inundated by unsolicited proposals. If one of the agents on your list is not listed in *LMP,* do not remove him or her from the list. You'll just need to be more resourceful in tracking that person down; as a start, try the Manhattan telephone book.

Another possibility is the Web, at www.authorlink.com. Here again you'll find a list of literary agents. There are no requirements for being listed here, and agents are basically free to say whatever they want about themselves. See if the agents you've selected are listed here, and see what they say about themselves. Look for agents specializing in nonfiction and preferably serious nonfiction.

You might want to subscribe to *Publishers Weekly*, the trade journal of the publishing industry, or go to www.publisherslunch.com. The site is primarily for industry insiders, especially foreign publishers who want to know what is being offered by agents to U.S. publishers, but you'll find a section that refers to "new sales" or "new deals" that will include the name of the agent who made each deal. See if you find the names of agents on your list. You may have to go back a month or two or three to find your agent's name, because good agents are selective in what they take on and aren't dumping stuff on editors' desks every week. But here again you'll get a better sense of which agents are right for your book. You can also type an agent's name into a search engine, like Yahoo, to see what information comes up.

Talk to colleagues. Ask published friends for the names of their agents.

Finally, if you are currently publishing with a university press, ask your editor for a recommendation. Or, at that next academic conference, instead of approaching an editor about your book, ask him or her to recommend the names of some top-notch literary agents specializing in history or law or whatever your field may be. Most editors will gladly help you find an agent. And don't be surprised if they suddenly become more interested in hearing about your project. Similarly, if you've previously published in a magazine or journal, call the editor of the journal or magazine and ask him or her to recommend a good book agent.

Next step, either call, e-mail, or write to the agent. If you want to make a preliminary call—never a bad idea—you're likely to get the agent's voice mail. If so, do not leave a message such as: "This is Herman

Wise from Cleveland, Ohio. Will you please call me at . . ." or a variation on that, "This is Herman Wise from Cleveland, Ohio. I have a
project that I know will interest you. Please call me at (216) . . ."

Rather: "This is Herman Wise from the Department of History at
the University of X. I've put together a proposal for a book about blah
blah blah, and I am looking for representation. Would you please . . ."

Or: "I'm a freelance writer (but I do have my Ph.D.) and I've
written a book on . . ."

Or: "I saw your name in Authorlink and I am wondering if you
would give me a call. I'm a twenty-six-year-old stringer for the
Altoona, Pennsylvania, papers and I've been covering a story that I
think would make a terrific book. It's about an archaeological find
that suggests that . . ."

Or: "I am a twenty-six-year-old graduate of the University of
Pennsylvania who dropped out just before senior year to start a dot-
com company. The company went bust and I want to tell my story.
If you are interested, please call me at . . ."

If you are an obvious candidate to write a work of serious nonfiction, all you need tell an agent in a phone call is that you are an
academic writing about your field of interest, which is . . . Ditto an
experienced journalist. If your credentials to write the book are not
so wonderful, but your story is great, tell the agent who you are even
if you are Ms. Nobody, then speak briefly about the nature of the
project. Remember, good agents get ten to twenty calls a day. They
are unlikely to make a coy call the first one they return.

If you prefer to e-mail an agent, never attach your entire proposal, or worse, a few chapters of the manuscript itself. Give the
agent enough information to decide whether or not she wants to go
further with you, but do not jam up the agent's e-mail.

If you are going to use regular snail mail, you can send more. If
you have used this book to put together a submission package, send
that to the agent, though the agent may subsequently ask you to redo

parts of the package to make it more suitable for submission to editors the agent believes might be interested. Include a brief cover letter telling the agent who you are and what the book is about. If you want your materials returned, include a stamped, self-addressed envelope. If you just want a response, and a rapid one at that, include an e-mail address. Let the agent know that this is a multiple submission, that is, that you are showing this material to other agents simultaneously.

If you don't hear from the agent within two weeks, call. Find out how long it will take to get a reading. Don't be put off if the agent or his or her assistant honestly tells you that it will take three or four weeks or even longer. Good agents are always busy. But ask for a reasonable time commitment. If the agent won't give you that commitment, look for another agent.

Let's deal with the worst-case scenario first. All five agents reject your project. There are many possible explanations. The first is that the book is really too academic a treatment for a commercial market. You generally don't need an agent to approach a university press with an academic book, and good agents don't want to represent you unless they can do you some good.

The second, more troublesome possibility is that the idea was simply not well conceived. Most agents will not reveal this, because they fear getting into a long give-and-take with you over how you can correct the faults in the project. Try another three or four agents, but if you still get form rejections, go back over the first part of this book and rethink the project.

In my experience, most of the projects I turn down fall into one of the following categories:

- *No book audience.* The author has chosen a subject that lacks a large enough book-buying audience to support commercial publication. Many policy books fail on this score;

indeed, many lack any general-interest audience at all. Also, certain topics will not fly commercially because they are played out or because, time and again, books on these topics haven't sold well. Thus, it would be very difficult to publish a book on AIDS now—so many are out there—unless, of course, there was something startlingly new or important in the book. An example of a topic that would seem to have a book audience but does not is abortion; both sides are dug in on their positions and neither side wants to hear anything new.

- *Too theoretical.* This is an empirical age. Generally speaking, unless an author is well established, he or she must have some base of research. There are exceptions to this rule, but both book and author must be truly outstanding to get past most agents.

- *Outside the author's area of expertise.* Both as an editor and as an agent I see a number of projects from retired people, ex-lawyers, ex-CEOs, ex-engineers, buffs writing about a deep hobby outside their area of expertise. As an additional draw-back, these projects tend to be extensive think pieces, rather than data or narrative driven.

- *Academic in both topic and treatment.* Too many would-be authors restrict their reading to academic books and come to assume that what is of interest to the academy is also of interest to the general reader. In fact, trade and college audiences can be so different that a book that works very well in hard-cover may do poorly in the course-use adoption market; conversely, many of the serious nonfiction titles that sell modestly in hardcover are adopted by professors for their courses and go on to sell well for decades in paperback.

- *No argument.* The project reads like a rambling discussion on various aspects of the topic.

But let's say that fate is kind, and several agents express a strong interest in your project. How do you decide whom to pick?

The most important criterion is how many similar authors that agent represents. If he or she is active in serious nonfiction, you are probably in good hands, especially if the agent is placing such projects with major commercial publishing houses. If the agent worked inside a publishing house, that is generally an advantage, although some very successful agents have never worked in-house.

In any case, make sure that you are comfortable with the person you are focusing on. Remember, your agent is the person you will turn to when you and your publisher are at an impasse over the jacket design, or when you are frustrated by a paucity of publicity for your book. Especially given the fact that editors switch publishing houses much more frequently than they did in the past, your long-term publishing relationship is likely to be with your agent. Pick one you trust. Pick one you feel comfortable with. Pick one who clicks with you.

What do agents take in exchange for what they give? Most agents take 15 percent of everything you earn on book rights in North America. A few still take only 10 percent. For English-language sales outside the U.S. (that is, the sale of rights to publish the book to U.K. or Australian publishers) and for sales of the book in translation, most agents bring in subagents, who charge the agent 10 percent, so your agent is likely to charge you 20 percent to help cover this additional expense. The same percentages apply when agents bring in movie agents to sell movie rights. Some agents charge back to the clients costs for photocopying, mailing, and even telephone calls. Others do not.

Once an agent takes on the project, here's what will happen. Your agent may want you to further revise your proposal. If she makes that request, hear her out. Certainly do not say, "but I followed the advice in this book I read word for word." Why not? Because I often ask authors to redo their proposals and not infrequently they tell me that they followed the advice of so and so, or the rules passed out by such and such an editor at an academic conference. As far as I am concerned, if it is my problem to place your book with a strong publisher, I need to go out with materials I believe in. Every time an agent submits a project to a publisher, the agent puts his or her own credibility on the line. So I insist that authors do it my way or find another agent. Your own agent has the same right to ask for the materials he or she needs to go forward with confidence.

Your agent will likely have a chat with you telling you where she intends to submit your materials. Submissions strategies vary. Some will send your project out to twenty or so editors, covering every publishing house, and every editor within each division of these publishing houses who might be a good editor for the project. For example, right now there are four "big" publishing houses. They are Simon & Schuster, Penguin Putnam, HarperCollins, and Random House, which includes the old Doubleday publishing empire. At each of these houses, there are numerous imprints, sometimes referred to as divisions. Thus, a work of serious nonfiction can be sent to an editor at the Scribner division, the Free Press division, or the Simon & Schuster trade division, or even to editors at several of the paperback divisions. At Random House the situation is even more complicated. There are six publishing groups within the Random House complex and often several divisions within each publishing group.

In addition to the four largest publishers, there are a number of smaller but still highly important publishing houses, including the Holtsbrinck group, which includes Holt, Metropolitan, Farrar, Straus & Giroux, and St. Martin's Press; the Time Warner group, which includes Warner and Little, Brown; and the Perseus Books Group, which includes Perseus, Counterpoint, Public Affairs, and Basic Books. Other important houses include Houghton Mifflin, W. W. Norton, Walker, Hyperion, and Miramax Talk Books.

Certain of the stronger university presses publish trade books, and your agent may want to include two or three such presses.

As an alternative, your agent may submit to only three or four editors, those the agent believes are best suited to your project. If none of these editors makes an offer of publication, the agent will use the feedback to fine-tune the submission package and approach a second and then a third tier of editors. Once you've picked an agent, leave such decisions to the agent. Let her do her job. Go on with your life.

Let's go now to the publishing house, to the editor's desk when he or she receives the project. Here's what happens.

If the editor reads your materials and is not interested, he will quickly let your agent know. Some editors still write reject letters. Some agents request reject letters so they have something to show their clients. Others do not. I have long believed that reject letters are a waste of time. Starting out in this business many years ago, I was taught never to tell the truth in a reject letter, because it encouraged the author to come back and argue with you. In truth, editors don't always know exactly why they don't like a project. It just doesn't excite them. Yet they also know they are not infallible. So they make up something that won't be offensive and won't discourage the author too much, or embarrass themselves should the book go on to be a best seller.

If the editor is interested in the project, he or she must now get support for it. Remember, at most houses publishing decisions are made communally, especially if the project promises to command a strong advance. So an editor may choose two or three other editors, preferably senior people, to read your materials. These other editors will always see your proposal, will likely see your sample chapter and possibly your table of contents. If the book seems to have good foreign rights potential, the head of the rights department will also be given parts of the package to read, and may be asked to estimate the income that might come through the sale of foreign language editions. In addition, the editorial director and the publisher will look at every project.

At that point, depending upon the enthusiasm of those to whom the package was circulated (often expressed in brief notes back to the originating editor), the editor may put the project on the agenda of the next editorial meeting. Or, if the project is strong enough, the editor may go directly to the editorial director or publisher to work out a preemptive offer. A preemptive offer is like a preemptive strike. By offering a very large advance and possibly a marketing commitment as well—the publishing industry's version of an offer that can't be refused—one editor and one publishing house hope to take the project off the market before other editors have had a chance to bring it up at their own editorial meetings.

If this happens, your agent will call you, discuss the offer, as well as the strengths and weaknesses of the house and the editor, and help you make a decision.

If no preemptive offers are made, the project will be discussed at the next editorial meeting of each house. No matter how enthusiastic the editor may be about the project, without support at the editorial meeting, she will not go forward to an offer. A surprisingly large number of projects eagerly sought by one or another editor will die at the editorial board meeting. Why? Because it is in the nature of editors to fall in love with projects and the responsibility of management to ask the hard questions about appeal in the marketplace. But editorial meetings are not just about sales. The discussion may turn on anything and everything, including what others present think about the strength of the writing; the appeal of the narrative; the persuasiveness of the argument; the credentials of the author; how the book will fare against other books on the same topic (editors must keep up with what their competitors are buying); who the agent is for the project (an agent who regularly places strong projects will have his or her projects looked at more favorably), whether this author has future books in him that will be even more attractive to the publishing house; and finally is the author "mediagenic." Let me explain this last term, which I mentioned briefly in the introduction.

Mediagenic refers to an ability of the author to present himself or herself successfully on radio and television. Those few authors who have previously been on television will often splice together a tape of several of their appearances and include it in the submission package. Absent a tape, if a publishing house is going to make a substantial offer, they may want to meet the author in person. This doesn't happen all the time, but it does happen often enough that authors need to be aware of why the meeting is being called. Here's what management looks for when they ask to "meet the author."

In an age where electronic media appearances can have an enormous impact on sales, publishers want to know if this author is "attractive"—not so much in the physical sense; you don't have to be model thin or movie star beautiful. But you should be able to project yourself as likable and credible. You must also be able to project enthusiasm for the topic. Some authors are so nervous when on the spot that they will come to the meeting and spend the entire time never making eye contact with anyone at the table. Or they will mumble. Or talk so softly that everyone in the room must lean forward to catch what they have to say. Or be completely unable to distill their message into a TV-sized soundbite for those sitting at the table, which they must be able to do if they go on radio or television. At the other end of the scale, some come on as know-it-alls, arrogantly bombastic. Or defensive in answering simple questions. I would be less than honest if I did not say that in cases where the advance could be well up into six figures, the author's in-person presentation of himself and his ideas can often tip the scales, either way.

What happens next? Let's say that no one house tried to preempt or that the preemptive offer has been rejected. Now the project will go to "auction." Those houses still interested will bid against each other. Here again, all sorts of combinations exist for how an auction is conducted. Trust your agent to handle the mechanism of the auction without your input.

When the auction is over, you must decide which offer to accept. Generally speaking, unless your agent has set the condition that the project would go to the highest bidder, you will be able to choose the combination of financial offer, editor, and house that best suits your needs. At the end of this chapter you will find some help in making that decision.

What can you expect as an advance for your book? For good serious nonfiction, the range is too wide to give you a meaningful answer. I can only say that most works of serious nonfiction sold to commercial publishers sell in the range of $20,000 to $400,000. How do publishers arrive at an exact number? That's a book in itself.

You do need to know that the advance, no matter how big or small, is never paid in full on signing the contract. Rather it is doled out in portions. An advance of $50,000 will generally be paid out in two or possibly three portions, let's say $20,000 on signing; $15,000 on delivery and acceptance of the manuscript, and $15,000 on publication of the hardcover edition. An advance of $300,000 may be divided into three payments or five or six payments, depending upon many factors. So don't count on getting all that money up front. (Don't quit your day job.) You will receive only a small portion of it.

Now let me return to the most important decision an author must make: which house to go with when you have multiple offers. Most authors rely upon the information passed to them by their agent, who will likely know what other titles similar to yours this editor and this house have published. The agent will also likely have inside information on the experiences of other authors at each house, both her own clients and the clients of colleagues.

My best advice in choosing a house is as follows:

1. No matter how much money a house offers, go with a house that has a solid reputation doing your kind of book. Why? Because bookstores factor the reputation of the publishing house into their decision of how many copies of your book to take on their prepublication orders. A house that year in and year out successfully publishes biographies will advance more copies of your biography than a house that rarely does so.

2. Ask yourself whether or not your book has course-use potential. Be honest. If your book is going to be seven hundred pages, don't count on its being assigned by any but the cruelest of college professors. Or if its market is a graduate-level seminar, the numbers are so small that the course-use sales will be insignificant. But if you believe that this book will be assigned year after year, give extra credit to those houses with college sales forces, such as W. W. Norton, Houghton Mifflin, Holt, or aggressive paperback programs geared for the course-use adoption market, such as Viking Penguin, HarperCollins, and Random House/Knopf.

3. If you believe that the general reading public is your major audience, ask your agent about the paperback line of each publisher. Your agent will tell you that the house that publishes your hardcover edition can always sell your paperback edition to another house with a strong paperback line. That is true. But the decision about whether or not to do so rests solely with your hardcover publisher. And if your hardcover publisher has a strong record in paperback publication, it will not

likely be selling paperback rights to a house with a poor record of paperback publication.

4. If at all possible, personally meet every editor interested in your project. It is difficult enough taking criticism from someone you like. It will be much harder to hear criticism from an editor who intimidates you, or seems too full of himself for your taste, or too tentative for your straight-ahead style of working. At a minimum, try to speak on the telephone with every editor you can't meet face to face.

5. Finally, don't despair. A book that knows why it is being written, that is carefully thought out and well executed, can be published well by almost any publishing house. So don't agonize too much before accepting an offer from any reputable house. Should you be lucky enough to have received multiple offers, remember that you are trying to make the best of a good situation. The author who receives only one offer has less to agonize over, but you wouldn't want to change places with him. Do your best to make a sound decision. But after that, focus on writing the best book you can write. The other things will take care of themselves.

If things have gone well for you, you are now under contract. Congratulations. Your contract will take weeks to arrive and you probably won't see that check due you on signing until two months after the deal is closed. That's how publishing works.

Before we end this chapter and move on to the important stuff—how to write your book—let me spend a few minutes discussing the possibility that your best offer comes from a university press.

Perhaps you have already been published by a university press and really want to see what commercial publishing is all about. But you have also received a startlingly large offer from a major university press, much more than you were led to believe university presses offer. Your one experience publishing with a university press was not a bad one. In fact, it was quite pleasant. Should you give serious consideration to an offer from a university press that says it can publish your new book as well as any commercial publishing house and perhaps better?

The answer is yes. Many university presses are striving to develop programs that allow them to compete with commercial houses for certain works of serious nonfiction. These are works so important and prestigious that they will likely interest both academics and intellectuals outside the academy setting. Many of these university press trade programs are staffed with editors, marketers, publicists, and sales reps who previously worked for commercial houses and therefore know how to publish trade books well. So don't count them out. But do ask questions about their review process before you accept their offer. And make sure you are being offered trade publication. Many university presses have three standards—academic, academic trade, and full trade. Ask the question four different ways if you have to but confirm that you are being offered true trade publication, which should include a full trade discount to the bookseller. If not, go with a commercial publishing house.

Now you are ready to write that book. So let's move to the next section of this book: The Writing Process.

Part Two

The Writing Process

Chapter Five

A Question of Fairness and Other Limits of Argument in Serious Nonfiction

Earlier, I observed that every work of serious nonfiction should have a question it asks and an answer it wants to provide. How you get from question to answer, and whether you do so in a way that sustains reader trust in you as a credible guide to the topic, will depend upon your understanding of "argument." In common usage, the word conveys a sense of disagreement, of nonphysical altercation. But here we are talking about the process of leading others to accept our positions, attitudes, or even our mere inclinations about issues under discussion.

Despite the proliferation of high school writing courses and the steady growth of such courses in undergraduate and graduate programs, I know of none devoted to the limits of argument in writing. In fact, while argument is a term frequently heard in book publishing, it is not, as far as I can tell, commonly used in academia. You have your research and your interpretation of what you have found, adding up to your thesis.

Where then does argument fit in? Argument is what you use to pull everything together into a self-supporting whole that has meaning and coherence. But it must do more than simply document that this change has occurred or that that relationship exists. Good argument draws readers through the very thought processes that brought the author to the positions he holds. Moreover, as discussed, if you seek commercial publication you must relate your book's findings to an issue of significance to a broad audience. To do so, you must employ argument.

Yet argument is more than a set of expository or rhetorical skills. Like art itself, a successful piece of argument communicates somewhat more than it says explicitly. It stimulates readers to think in new ways not only about the author's topic but about other aspects of their lives as well.

While many tools of authorship help identify you to your readers, how you argue goes furthest in defining you. As you present your interpretation of the research, yours or that of others, especially the way you measure your interpretation alongside past or competing interpretations, you reveal to your readers whether you are someone fully to be trusted, as to both competence and integrity or, at the other end, so aggressive an advocate that the reader must be wary of everything you say.

Yet as important as argument skills are to serious nonfiction authors, I have never come across a writing book that treats argument as a skill the would-be author should work on. Instruction books tend to focus on the creative rather than rational aspects of good writing. But because serious nonfiction authors deal with the communication of ideas rather than emotions, feelings, and sensibilities, they must meet standards very different from those against which most other writing is judged. Fiction, for instance, is an expressive medium; both those who teach it and those who criticize it look to divine from the finished product the creative impulses that forged the work. Books that come out of investigative journalism seek to awaken outrage; the reaction of the author's next-door neighbor is as good a gauge as any as to the success of the project. A serious nonfiction author, on the other hand, must recognize that his most valued critics will come to judge his work almost solely on whether its major and minor theses are seen as intelligently posed, honestly tested, and credibly defended.

Further, professional reputation is of paramount importance to serious nonfiction authors, who see their careers hitched to how they continue to be perceived by their peers after publication of their work, rather than to how much flash the work itself generates. Even the desire for high sales, surely present with all authors, often takes a back seat in serious nonfiction publishing to protection of the author's reputation as a competent researcher, honest chronicler, and critical thinker.

As I talk about argument with my young authors, many say they associate argument in writing with a type of discourse long out of fashion—the deductively reasoned essay. Argument, I am often told, is what authors from another time employed to win over readers to the validity of their analysis *in the absence of data* to prove it. As one author put it, today one's data *is* one's argument.

Let me put this misconception to rest. While good argument is most effective when built on solid research, a piling on of facts does not an argument make. Absent an intellectual process that carefully marshals and positions these facts in support of a point, even the most thorough accumulation of data will come off as a boring recitation of all the author knows about the subject. This applies as well to books where the research yield is neither numerical nor tabular, such as, for example, most histories and biographies. The most intriguing tale, if told without an attempt to advance some insight larger than the story itself, quickly devolves into a MEGO manuscript (Mine Eyes Glaze Over).

doesn't matter whether you argue deductively or inductively, if you are trying to persuade someone to accept your take on a subject, you are making an argument. How well you succeed will depend upon the degree to which the argument you make in support of your conclusions is effective. And to be effective, it must be intellectually defensible. We have said that it is your argument that establishes you as a credible guide to the topic. Indeed, since few readers will check your facts, trust in your data as well as in your conclusions will swing on how trustworthy you come off in your argument.

In relating research to argument, think of your work as operating simultaneously on two levels.

In its early pages, your book will focus on presenting material in coherent and, if possible, compelling fashion—in other words, in setting up the story. Woe to the author who belittles the importance of doing this part of the job well.

But not too deep into the book, the serious nonfiction author must begin adding a running commentary on the presentation. Initially, these comments need not be far reaching. They may simply relate the material to some experience or set of ideas more familiar to the reader. Or to the contrary, the author may want to preclude the reader's jumping to an intriguing but inappropriate analogy. Or author musings may be introduced as foreshadowing, to alert the reader to the more important implications of what at this point in the book may seem inconsequential.

As the author gets deeper and deeper into her research, less and less of her time will be used merely placing data before the reader. A reader can digest only so many pages of facts, or straight narrative, before thinking: "Okay, I see the individual pieces of the picture. Now let's go somewhere with all this. What does it all add up to?"

Here demands on the author increase, and she must begin to sketch out a picture of the topic greater than the sum of the facts presented. She does this in many ways. First, she brings to the forefront those parts of the story that best illuminate the question driving the narrative. Simultaneously, she lets go of other threads that bear less on that question. As she gently begins to reveal her own thinking, by positioning the relevant parts of the research in one way or another, she asks the reader to accept certain interim conclusions that will later become the building blocks of the book's major conclusions.

Over the course of the book, this running commentary, this voice of the author putting his or her stamp on the research and extracting meaning from it, becomes the author's interpretation of the material. How—that is, by what reasoning standards—she introduces these observations, defends them, and allows them to build into a coherent, defensible, and ultimately persuasive statement is the book's argument.

Having defined argument as I have, let me warn once again that the publishing business is quite relaxed in its use of terms. Many editors use the word *argument* to describe the interpretation as well as the process through which the author strives to sell it to the reader. Further, if an editor asks, "What is this book's argument?" he may be looking to hear about its thesis. To minimize confusion, we will use the word *argument* in this chapter solely to describe the reasoning and persuasion processes, and thesis to describe the position the author takes on the book's issues.

Sadly, an editor learns early on that solid research does not always predict a satisfying argument interpreting it. A well-researched book may draw valid interim conclusions, all acceptable to the reader, but put forward an analysis neither intellectually challenging nor satisfying. All that research just to say this? the reader wonders.

Or the book may have the makings of a very interesting thesis, but an argument that fails to persuade readers to accept the significance of the author's thesis. Perhaps the author has stayed so tight to her research findings because she is still in student mode, afraid to think too independently on the page. Had she risked more, she might have had a very provocative discussion with her readers about the broader implications of what she found. Instead, she stopped short of the challenging statement she could have made. Her book doesn't quite seem worth the read. It is axiomatic that if you want to assume the mantle of authorship, you must simultaneously accept the onus of leadership, and be prepared to suffer the slings and arrows of outrageous critics. If in your daily life you are particularly sensitive to the criticism, "Who does he (she) think he (she) is?" you will have to work on a new persona for your role as author.

Far more troubling is the situation in which the argument is only tenuously connected to the very research it should draw upon. The research, while substantial, does little to support the author's thesis. The reader wonders why he is being given all this detail, while simultaneously growing impatient with an argument that has no grounding in the facts presented. Editors refer to this as argument by declaration.

Early on in my career as an editor, I asked a young author to explain just which parts of his research had led him to draw certain conclusions. He responded, defensively, "Why? Don't you agree with them?" I explained that I was not challenging the conclusions, but just wanted to know which parts of his data he saw as supporting them. He told me that he believed—or had been taught in school, I forget which—that if you got your facts straight, after that you could say anything you wanted. Not surprising, little of what he concluded had that sense of having come irresistibly out of the facts he had presented.

Later on in this chapter, I'll talk about what makes an argument both worth the read and persuasive. You may have guessed from the title of this chapter that I judge argument in good part on whether or not the author deals fairly with competing interpretations. This, more than anything else, will determine whether or not an author has me in his camp.

But we are not quite ready to get into what makes better argument. While I hope to have persuaded you that your data is not your argument, there is no getting around the fact that all argument begins with command of your subject matter. And in today's book world, that generally means with your research.

Indulge me while I make three points that may seem too obvious to warrant inclusion here. Experience has taught me that even the most intelligent and diligent author can lose sight of certain connections between research and argument.

1. Command

The indispensable predicate for effective argument is command of your subject matter. You will not be comfortable putting disparate elements together, distinguishing this from that, generalizing from specifics, and suggesting a new, maybe counterintuitive reading of the data unless you have done your research thoroughly and know what you have.

Many authors decide their interpretation too early in the research process and so narrow their search at the very time they should be opening it to the broadest possible base of information. They close off certain critical leads, often out of fear they will stumble onto support for competing interpretations. Having decided upon their thesis, they don't want to be exposed to information in conflict with what they set out to say. The research is just about providing examples.

Some, despite their best efforts, find themselves face to face with material they wish they had never seen, so they ignore it, hoping it will go away. Spare yourself grief. This is a research problem an author can't hide from. There is a sort of Murphy's Brother's Law in publishing: Whatever You Think You Know That Nobody Else Does

Will Be Revealed and at the Very Moment Most Embarrassing for the Author.

Other authors shut down the research stage prematurely because they find themselves getting tense as their research leads to complexity. Perhaps causality is becoming clouded, or blame broadening. They are afraid of losing themselves, and their thesis, in a maelstrom of conflicting data.

Research is always time consuming and labor intensive, and often frustrating. Fortunately, bookstores offer a number of books that communicate broadly acceptable standards. Moreover, my experience with college students I have taught and my own authors indicates that students, especially graduate students, are given a sounder footing in the uses of research, including established standards for attribution and citation, than in the limits of argument. What I am talking about here is an attitude, not research skills. Think of the transition from data to reader as a funnel, in which the wide end must be at the interface with your data, not the reader. If the other way round—for instance if you limit your sources of information, or reject information early on in the research process, when you should be most open to everything—what comes out of the wide end of the funnel is quickly spotted as diluted, stretched too thin, as having too much breadth for its substance.

This is not to say that you must use everything you find. On the contrary, you must limit yourself to material that bears relevance to the question your book is asking. Including material too peripheral to your story, simply because you found it and don't want it to go to waste, waters down your manuscript. A reviewer who wants to praise an author will often say she has an ear for the telling anecdote. If one anecdote after another tells nothing relevant, that same reviewer will likely say the book suffers from a lack of editing. So when in doubt, leave it out. There is an old Hollywood saying that you can judge a good movie by the quality of what was left on the cutting room floor. And you can measure the quality of a serious nonfiction book by the amount of good stuff that never made it from research to final book. Remember, however, the selection or rejection must be based on relevance to the issue, not on whether the data supports your own thesis.

Let me mention one other problem in regard to research. Some authors minimize the research period to maximize the time they leave themselves for writing, a more intimidating task for many. After all, writing skill, our culture has taught us, says something large about our very core, while research is nerd work. When such authors sit down to write their book and can't shape their material into a cohesive and coherent whole, their worst fear seems to have come true—that they do not have the creative writing skills to pull off the book. The more likely problem is that they lack either command of their material or confidence that their data truly and irrefutably supports their thesis. The computer people have their own expression for this: Garbage in, garbage out. No program can yield results more precise or reliable than the data that's plugged in. And your argument can be no stronger than the research upon which it is founded. Spend the time to do this part of your job properly.

You can't write your way out of a research problem that results in a skimpy, pat, or vulnerable interpretation. The clear solution is to go back and do more research. But human nature being what it is, most authors find it painfully daunting to go back to square one, especially with a manuscript delivery date marked on their calendar. So they end up struggling to protect a vulnerable interpretation.

Putting your data before the reader always threatens your control of it, but you cannot order your reader to view the data only in ways that support your thesis. It's like throwing a pebble out on a pond. The ripples go out in all directions, to all shores. You cannot simply say, "Follow only the ripple going to the north shore, because that's the only one that's important." Only a thorough command of your subject matter allows you to address those silent questions your reader will have about the other ripples.

What do you do when you get into this kind of trouble? First admit to yourself what has happened. Then let your editor and agent know you will not be able to deliver your manuscript on time and need an extension. A first extension on your contract of six months to a year is virtually never a problem. And some books delivered much later than that are still welcomed by their editors and published well. While I certainly would not advocate starting out with this escape hatch in mind, if you find yourself scrambling for supporting facts when you thought you were ready to write, remember that all you can pull out of a skimpy research hat is a scrawny rabbit.

2. All your conclusions must come out of the facts you make available to the reader on the page.

For every conclusion there must be a trail of facts available in the text. I mean on the page, capable of being independently evaluated by the reader. Why do I mention this problem? It comes about in one of two situations.

Some inexperienced writers, nervous that their readers will put down their book if they don't say something provocative in the first fifty pages, will attempt too-broad generalizations well before they have established a factual predicate for them. In essence, they let their argument run ahead of their facts.

As I suggested, your early chapters will be largely factual or narrative. Yes, you'll have small comments to make—interim observations giving context, distinguishing one thing from another—but don't worry if you haven't yet said anything novel or profound. Your readers will be satisfied with you as a guide to the topic if you use these early chapters to get them up to speed on the basics of the topic. In Chapter 7, I'll show you how to write an introduction that relieves you of pressure to impress your readers early on, by tipping them off to the fact that an interesting and significant argument awaits them if they patiently allow you do the necessary groundwork.

A second situation in which conclusions seem to rest on weak foundations results from an author's failure to respect his readers as his equals. In this case, I'm not talking about authors who make pronouncements as if their saying so makes it so, that is, argue by declaration, but about authors who have all the research needed to back up what they have to say but just don't have it on the page. As one author responded when I explained this to him, "Don't authors have a right to be trusted? After all, I've spent twenty years studying this topic."

The answer is no. What you say is only as good as the facts and analysis you present to support it. While your reader may be willing to cut a serious author some slack, he still has a right to test what you say against his own life experiences and against the facts you put before him.

Let me take this one step further. This same obligation to present facts comes into play when you quote others. Borrowing a respected authority's credibility to support your position can be useful or counterproductive, depending on how it is done. If I come across the line "John Fielding, the eminent epidemiologist, agrees that business causes 90 percent of all pollution problems in the United States," I am no more convinced that business causes 90 percent of all pollution problems than I was before you brought in Fielding. But if you were to write: "John Fielding, the eminent epidemiologist, conducted a twenty-year study in which he discovered that the vast majority of pollutants in the water, air, and soil in the period from 1965 to 1985 could be traced to perfectly legal dumping by industry of previously unidentified contaminants," I am much more willing to accept this information as supporting your position. Leaving out your own facts, or the facts upon which those you cite came to their conclusions, is asking your reader to suspend his own judgment and just nod in agreement with whatever you put before him. And that gives him good reason to put your book down. Keep in mind that the excitement of reading nonfiction lies in retracing with the author the trail that brought the author to his conclusions.

3. Your research is trying to tell you where your argument lies. You just have to learn to listen to it.

There is an old expression among doctors who train medical students in diagnosis: "The patient is trying to tell you what's wrong with him. You just have to shut up and listen." A similar statement may be made about research. It is trying to give you a picture of what really happened, so that you can tell that story in a more meaningful way. But if you confront it, challenge it, twist and distort it, instead of listening, you will never hear its full message.

During the research stage, some authors, especially those who have their thesis well established early on, may be disappointed with what the data seems to be telling them. Maybe the answer to their book's question is not what they presumed it would be. Or the answer the data supports will not likely change the nature of the debate on their topic all that much. But at least they know what the research supports and what it does not. One option here is to change the book's question to one that the data can answer.

It does happen that an author's research neither reinforces old interpretations nor openly calls out for a new interpretation. Yes, it has led to a treasure trove of great details, vivid scenes, sharper characters, a much clearer sense of the tensions and personalities of the period, or a better understanding of the forces at play during a certain period. But if you ask such an author what it all adds up to, you may get a long helpless stare. "What *does* it all add up to?" one author asked me. Some don't even realize that the research has to add up to something. "Can't I just tell a story, especially if it's an interesting one?" another author asked me. By now I hope all of you know the answer to that question.

Here is an example of someone pulling a very interesting interpretation out of a story that could easily have been presented as a narrow fight between two competing scientists of another time.

In *Boltzmann's Atom*, the author, David Lindley, quickly summarizes what his research revealed about the intellectual conflict between the protagonist Boltzmann, a scientist who believed that all matter was made up of atoms, and his nemesis, a scientist named Mach, who argued that until atoms were verified, that is, until their existence could be proved, science was better off sticking to what it could measure directly.

In his introduction, the author informs us that although the story's characters were preoccupied with atoms, he, the author, came to see early on that the debate between Boltzmann and Mach was less about atoms themselves and more about a new way of doing science. Essentially, the Boltzmann-Mach conflict was over whether or not scientists, whose task it is to gather hard evidence, can get a better handle on how the world works by testing possible mechanisms against informed but nonetheless speculative theories (in this case, the atomic theory of matter). In its jacket flap copy, the publisher went one step further, referring to this as the story of "the man who single-handedly invented twentieth-century theoretical physics."

It is much easier to listen to your research when it describes a conflict of another time and place. It is more difficult when we are talking about our own time and its debates, always highly colored by our own passions. Later on, we will talk about the pitfalls to avoid in those situations.

Let's say that instead of trying to ground your argument in your research, you decide to get very pragmatic and shortcut the process. Perhaps you say to yourself, I went into this topic because I believed that in the end I would be able to prove that X is really responsible for ... long-term poverty, or the failure of the U.S. to unseat Saddam Hussein, or that all politicians lie. And I still believe that, and that's the basis on which I am going to write this book. Or you say to yourself that from the beginning you were sure that the guilty people in your story are A, B, and C, and even if I can't really "prove" it, that's how I am going to write the story because my gut instinct tells me that's true and the rest is pettifoggery. I'll just pull out of my research enough stories and some data to write the book I know should be written, focusing on the data that supports what I know to be true. Following the murder trial of O. J. Simpson an embarrassing glut of such books managed to get into print. Many of these books were motivated by a gut knowledge that Simpson was guilty, and that his acquittal was an outrage. It should not be surprising, then, that in most of these books each and every piece of data presented supported the starting presumption.

This type of thesis–driven, rather than data–driven, manuscript comes with strong conclusions but weak argument, for argument is the data-arraying process that makes your conclusions inevitable. Let me distinguish between thesis-driven and data-driven books another way. In the latter, it is the totality of the data, not every scrap of data, that argues for the author's thesis. There is a sense of the argument confirming a broad natural thrust of the research. But in a thesis–driven book, the impression is of isolated bits of evidence being brought in only if and when they support the author's conclusions. The sole reason the author has chosen facts for inclusion is that they lend themselves nicely to a supporting role in this preordained interpretation of the material. A subtle distinction, maybe, but one that determines just which kind of reader will find your book tolerable and which won't.

Writing Argument

Now, surely, it is time to talk about argument itself.

Wherever most of us learn to argue, little in our formal educations alerts us to the possibility that argument habits we picked up informally may harm our writing. And that's an important part of the problem. I'd guess that the earliest exposure most of us had to argument came around the dining room table, as we observed our parents trying to resolve their conflicts with each other and with us, and as we, in imitation, tried to resolve conflicts with our annoying siblings.

Unfortunately, too many who have learned to argue around the house come to assume that contention and its cousin contentiousness are the natural processes of every argument. Worse, if our parents were below-the-belt arguers who said terrible things to each other and to each of us in the heat of family arguments, there's a strong probability that we tend whenever our ideas are challenged to reach for an "ad hominem" retort, that is, an attack not on the other person's facts or argument but on some personal vulnerability unrelated to what is being argued. If you grew up in this type of argumentative household, the very idea of juxtaposing "reasoned" with "argument" may seem lame, if not oxymoronic. Once you become an adult, argument crafted with just one goal in mind—winning—becomes the standard. Good argument techniques are those that win for us, allow us to have our way, get others to accept a resolution of a conflict that favors us. Or through any means, honest or dishonest, to win others over to our position on a current controversy.

I must concede a nasty fact about publishing: Every time a hot political controversy breaks into the news—confirmation of Clarence Thomas, charter schools or school vouchers, free speech versus decency advocates—commercial publishing dashes toward a certain type of book in which the author provides little new information or insight, but says precisely what everyone on one side of the controversy is already saying. Just about always, the author says it more aggressively, in ways that wound leading advocates for the opposing side. These books are often best sellers, possibly because buying such books becomes a statement of support for the cause.

Unfortunately, we are a stubborn species, highly evolved to resist having our minds changed. It has been said that there is no pain like that caused by a new idea. This may explain why too often those books that have the greatest appeal with the general public are not those that cause a reader to rethink his position but those that arm him for his next discussion on a contentious issue in the news—with colleagues, intellectual friends, or just Uncle Ned. But there is a price such a reader pays. If we are open only to material that reinforces our prejudices, our circle of friends soon narrows to include only like-minded people, with the other side's position less and less likely to be seen as having any basis in rationality. I worked with an editor at a very distinguished publishing house who regularly referred to the "good guys" and the "bad guys." We all knew precisely which side was which in any controversy.

So what's wrong with this type of argument, argument that reinforces with more apt phrases the favored side's position, while undermining by any effective means the position of the other side? Isn't that just what the adversary system is all about? Getting at the truth by allowing both sides to lie through their teeth? If it works for the legal system, what's wrong with applying such a successful model to public discourse?

The answer is nothing and everything. If winning is most important to you, nothing I say here will likely change your mind. Our society, however, is undermined when we fail to honor reasoned argument in public discourse. When we don't rely on it to inform the opinions of our citizenry, and thereby effect reasonable public policies that have reasonable prospects for success, the commonweal is ill served. An us-against-them spirit leads us to strive to place in positions of power or influence people who share our attitudes and tastes (or, if you like, read prejudices) and expect them to promulgate policies that advance only those goals that find favor within our own referent group. A person I know well, and love dearly, is fond of saying that *homo sapiens* is not a thinking animal, that the "sapiens" in his name derives from the Latin *sapere*, which means "to know," not "to think."

This taste for aggressive advocacy is reflected in the growth and influence of op-ed pages in most newspapers, and the increased presence on cable TV of confrontational political shows such as CNN's *Crossfire.* These shows do so much better in their ratings than say, PBS's *NewsHour,* and C-Span programming, which are generally more measured discussions, not marked by sneer, scream, and thrust.

What is my point in all this? That those who regularly buy and read serious nonfiction books are not a cross-section of the American public and tend to be much more interested in reasoned analysis. Authors who want to reach this market must recognize this.

Aside from the fact that some subsets of the general population have special attitudes toward fair argument, we must also take into account that all of us read with a special awareness of where we find the material we are reading. I have called this the "credibility calculus." To explain, let me use as an example the typical daily newspaper. We read the front pages of a newspaper expecting that the facts as known to the reporter will be set down relatively undistorted, with representatives of both sides of an issue given an opportunity to comment, the reporter acting as a sort of moderator. While television, with its immediacy, has become the medium the public turns to first for hard news, leading newspapers to provide much more magazinelike analysis on its news pages than they once did, most readers still assume (hope?) that what they read on the news pages has been put together with the aim of providing the complete factual story.

Not so when we read editorials. Here we adjust our credibility calculus with no conscious effort, assuming that we are being fed a point of view, though in editorials we expect to find a sagacious, almost paternal voice, rather than a strident advocacy. It is in a newspaper's op-eds that we expect, and arm ourselves against, attempts to bring us around, by any means possible, to the author's position. Further down the credibility line are the paper's advertisements, which we trust least and read most suspiciously. Ironically, of all the newspaper's material, only here are consumer protections against direct misrepresentation codified.

I have long believed that the absence of these lines of separation in television news reporting contributes powerfully to the lack of public confidence in television news. While some local stations run legends across the bottom of the screen identifying station-management editorials, no distinction is made between hard news reports and the advocacy pieces that network news divisions produce. For all the good that shows like *60 Minutes* do—and I can think of many individual shows that exposed and through their influence reversed hideous injustices— nothing warns viewers that they are watching not a hard news show but rather a presentation strongly edited to favor one particular understanding of the conflict chronicled. This is not to say that the producers did not come to the issue with an open mind, but only that once they determined where justice lay, the show was crafted was advance that position.

This lack of a clear division of standards between straight news and what might be called electronic op-eds was illustrated several years ago in the celebrated libel case brought by General William Westmoreland against CBS over a piece called "The Uncounted Enemy: A Vietnam Deception." While CBS's own internal investigation found the show's producer had violated many of the network's own guidelines for the presentation of news stories, CBS stood behind the show's conclusions as reasonable inferences to be drawn from the material the producers had to work with.★

As a demonstration of how far support for no-holds-barred

★ The case ended anticlimactically, when General Westmoreland settled for a vague and meaningless statement of regret. Under *Times* v. *Sullivan*, the case that federalized libel law, a public figure, which the general surely was, cannot prevail as plaintiff unless he proves malice, defined for the purpose of libel law as a reckless disregard not of fair play but of the truth as the author understands it to be. Thus, CBS did not have to demonstrate that the show's producer was fair but only that wherever he tipped the scales he did so to convince others of a truth in which he believed.

advocacy has taken us, let me mention another settled lawsuit and press reaction to the settlement.

A network produced a show charging that high-level officers in one of the tobacco companies knew of the addictive nature of nicotine and so were disingenuous when they argued that their customers were only consumers who consciously decided to accept the health risks of smoking in exchange for the pleasure it provided. Unfortunately, the show included the charge that the company "spiked" their product with nicotine. The company sued.

This case too was settled before it came to trial, with the network retracting only the one statement that the tobacco company had "spiked" its cigarettes with nicotine. The network withdrew none of its many other serious charges, for instance, that the tobacco companies favored tobacco strains that had more nicotine rather than less.

But surprising to me, the press strongly condemned the network for having caved in under the pressure of a lawsuit, even though the retraction dealt with only one of the many charges the show had made. Naturally, we don't want criticism of tobacco companies, or for that matter of any corporation, to be chilled by the threat of lawsuits. But do we really want to live in a world where someone who has said something that is untrue cannot with dignity correct the error without being accused of faintheartedness or fecklessness to a just cause?

Answering charges of unfair coverage, many in the media respond that no one can be neutral about important matters that have an impact on all of us. We all come to our work, whatever it is, with our own peculiar set of biases, programmed into us by all we have experienced throughout our lives, including both everything done to us and everything we have done to others. As true as this response rings, it does not address the charge. *Fairness in argument does not require that we purge ourselves of every emotion the issue being treated has ever provoked in us.* No matter how strongly we hold certain positions, we can present facts and analysis fairly, provided only that we come to the debate with a set of standards for fairness formulated before we are in the thick of it and are keenly aware of just which standards serve which side of the debate.

Often the unfairness will not even derive from a bias but from a belief that assuming capricious discretionary power is part of the job. An overly aggressive writer will often say that both sides are complaining, so he must be doing a good job. This is not necessarily true. Some judges are accused of being pro prosecution and others of being pro defendant, but it is with the worst judges, not the best, that criticism comes from every direction. If you go to a ball game and both sides are railing against the umpire, he is much more likely doing a bad job than a good job.

The broad acceptance of all this aggressive advocacy in the press causes a spillover into serious book publishing; I often receive proposals that would do honor only to a cross-examining attorney. And yet, whenever I have talked with people about this book, describing its contents, I am surprised at the number of people who have commented that the chapter of greatest interest to them is the one on argument. Or as one person said to me, "I would love to be able to read an op-editorial in the *New York Times* or a long article in a magazine such as *Commentary* or the *New York Review of Books* and have some better basis for knowing if this person has fairly earned my concurrence." So in full recognition of the reality that I may be vainly trying to restore a time and place forever gone, I will devote the rest of this chapter to rules that have guided me in working with authors over twenty-five years. I come with an advantage over most editors in that I entered publishing at a time when argument-based books were still being published and spent thirteen of those twenty-five years in university press publishing, where argument-based books are still common.

Readers of book-length serious nonfiction factor into their

credibility calculus an expectation of fairness far greater than they expect to find elsewhere. A sort of contract is presumed—the author does not have to hold the reader by the lapels in fear of losing him to an adjacent story, as he does in a newspaper story or television piece, and in exchange the author promises to lay out the story in whatever time it takes to get it fully right and in relevant context.

Let's establish that fairness does not require that you write a book such as President Truman's proverbial two-handed economist might write: "On the one hand this, but on the other that." On the contrary, I will never forget a sales conference in which a new editor was presenting his first book to the sales force, proudly telling them it was the most evenhanded, nonpartisan presentation of the facts he had ever read. He thought he was praising the book. He was actually pronouncing its death sentence. "That's a book we can't sell," the head of the sales force responded politely.

Your editor, booksellers, reviewers, and readers all want a book that takes a position. And argues it with gusto. Few readers will shy from a book that in making a reasoned argument is also funny, contrarian, and perhaps downright ornery in arguing its position. Still, a serious nonfiction author can't get around certain rules of fairness without paying a price.

If you don't make the best case for the other Side's position, you will sorely challenge your best readers to do so.

Let's say you are writing about the 2000 presidential election and want to make an argument that it was proper or not proper to count hanging chads. In an op-ed, you can get away with arguing that unless you do, "all the votes weren't counted," end of discussion. But if you write a book about this moment in American political history, you want that book to stand as more than a partisan, heat-of-the-moment bit of spin. That means you must present the other side's position at its best—not its weakest. It has been said that every man

is rational unto himself, and it's an important part of your job to determine and discuss fairly the rationale of both sides. It's not enough to
say the other side takes a position because that position serves its ends,
because your reader will say "Yes, as with you." If after you've presented to your readers the best, most reasonable case for why hanging
chads should *not* have been counted, you continue to believe they
should have been counted, go ahead and make your argument, as passionately and as powerfully as you can, demonstrating that the reasons
for counting them overwhelm the reasons for not doing so.

Again, fairness is determined not by your own lack of a position
but by the integrity and respect with which you deal with the other
side's position. It is always so tempting to undercut the other side, or
the competing interpretation, by presenting a weak case for that
position. But your contract with your reader requires that you make
the *best* case possible for the side you don't believe in.

Meeting this responsibility does more than protect your credibility with your reader. It also helps protect against a reviewer's criticism that you have overlooked some important part of the picture.
When the coauthor of this book taught our children to play chess,
he used to tell them they weren't to make a move until they had figured out, and written down, the other side's very best response to the
move they intended to make. To help them develop this mind-set, he
would have them play each other with each at the wrong side of the
board. If our daughter were playing white, she'd have the black
pieces in front of her and our son the white in front of him. This
gave each a sharper picture of the other side's rationale. And you
should do the same. Get up, in your mind's eye, and go around and
take a look at the debate from the other side of the board.

Failure to keep reminding yourself of the other side's rationale
can lead to being carried along by your passion to the point where
you polarize yourself and lose even the reader who came to your
book as an ally. While I was writing this chapter, I came across a

review of a book whose thesis is that serious damage is done to medicine by attempts to have it address political issues, for example, that women are underrepresented in trials for new treatments; that diseases that affect primarily men are better funded than those affecting primarily women; and that career opportunities as physicians and investigators are far less plentiful for women than for men. The author was fortunate in the reviewer she drew. Indeed, the review opens with a description of an incident in which the reviewer himself, acting as a member of a foundation board, had cast the sole vote against a grant for a program that promised to redress the built-in anti-women bias that pervades medical practice. As we would expect, the review is generally positive, yet toward the end of it we find this:

> Sometimes [the author's] enthusiasm for her subject gets the better of her, and she forgets—or prefers not to remember—that certain of the issues with which she deals would better be painted in shades of gray. . . . [H]er descriptions of biological differences in disease patterns read like feeble protests in the face of the experience of anyone who has trained in the teaching divisions of a large hospital. . . .*

Sadly, to make her point that too much focus on political goals might be compromising the independence of medical research, the author did not have to trivialize the very important concerns that had led others to seek redress.

Also troubling is the work of a scholar who puts all the facts on the page fairly, honestly, and even forcefully, and yet fails to bring his

---

*The review "Indoctrinology" appeared in the *New Republic,* February 19, 2001, p. 34. The review itself, especially in its opening, is a fine example of an author with a strongly held position struggling to put the position he opposes in its best light. Read it and see if this treatment doesn't increase the reviewer's credibility with you.

audience on board, not because he is insufficiently persuasive but because he is too dogged. Every piece of data is given a loyalty test. Those that do not serve the author's thesis are dismissed as worthless. In his argument he is so unwilling to concede anything to the other side, so tendentious, so relentlessly "on message," that after a couple of chapters the reader loses interest—or patience.

There is yet another reason you should be looking to strengthen the side you consider the weaker side, a reason that has little to do with fairness. I was recently working with an author whose historical manuscript dealt with the resistance of establishment scientists, under the aegis of the church, to certain new scientific speculations. The danger here was in dismissing as spineless toadies all scientists of that time, other than the author's hero. Yes, the establishment scientists had made a dishonest bargain with religious orthodoxy, which allowed them a certain freedom of inquiry as long as they respected an outer boundary determined by religious authority. But done as a battle between the good guys and the bad guys, the story is a hard write. A much better narrative is of scientists who late in life and career had to face the truth about the price they had paid for respecting that religious boundary, intelligent and learned people with a lifetime of professional and emotional investment in theories they knew in their heads, not their hearts, would soon be consigned to the dustbin of history.

We have said many times that serious nonfiction writing differs in substantive ways from fiction. But in at least two ways they are alike. The first is in the power of narrative tension to engage readers in all writing. This we will discuss in the following chapter. The second involves conflict as an ingredient essential for success. Real conflict, not phony-baloney conflict. The genius of Shakespeare's *Julius Caesar* is that the playwright's clear favorite is Brutus, who in the first act plunges a dagger into his best friend's side. If in fiction or drama the good guys are all good and the bad guys all bad, we dismiss the work as melodrama. If you don't create full-dimensional conflict in your nonfiction you run the risk of having it dismissed as polemic.

What happens when seeking out the best case for the other side starts eroding your commitment to your position? Occasionally, some piece of evidence you find so strengthens a competing interpretation that it threatens to undermine your confidence in your own thesis. When this occurs, you have two good options and a bad one. The first good one, of course, is to go back and reexamine the thesis. Better to do it yourself than have reviewers force that course on you. But a good thesis will survive a troubling piece of data. Thus, the second good option: Admit to your reader that you have not been able to accommodate this troubling piece of data fully within your overall interpretation and that you must leave the tension to another scholar or investigator to resolve. Serious readers understand that we do not live in a perfectly consistent world and appreciate such candor on the part of an author.

The bad option is forcing a fit with argumentative gymnastics. Indeed, some books seem to have a sense about them of the author relentlessly beating back challenges, on every page, in every chapter. These are unpleasant reads. If the full picture supports your thesis, minor inconsistencies can actually enrich your book.

The Uniform Applicability of Standards Rule.

Set reasonable standards against which to evaluate whatever it is you are treating. Then remember that those standards must be uniformly applied. What do I mean by that?

I went to college during the late sixties and was involved in my share of protests—free speech, women's rights, the struggle for racial equality. But unlike most of my friends, I had trouble committing myself on whether or not the United States belonged in Vietnam. By what standards was a nation ever justified in going to war? My father had been in the army in World War II; like so many of his generation he had willingly if not gladly allowed himself to be shipped overseas to save the world for democracy. What was the difference here? Was it heroic to protect democracy against fascism but not against communism? Some said that Vietnam was none of our business. Was that because in World War II we were primarily saving Europeans and in Vietnam those of another race? It became almost mantra to say that American servicemen were eight thousand miles away in a war they could not win. When had Mind Your Own Business become a liberal position? And when had a guarantee of victory become a prerequisite for trying? Such attitudes seemed more consistent with a conservative worldview than with an enlightened liberal view. It was said that the leaders of South Vietnam, our ally, were corrupt and undemocratic. Yet our World War II allies had been Joseph Stalin, one of the century's three most prolific mass murderers, and Winston Churchill, who proclaimed that he had not become prime minister to preside over the dissolution of the British Empire. The most persuasive argument against U.S. involvement held that we were destroying a country to save it from communism, but even here an inconsistency with standards we had applied to World War II jumped out. We had shelled France to liberate it, and even our enemies, Germany and Japan, whom we had bombed savagely, were now better off for having had their totalitarian regimes defeated.

It's not that the two wars could not have been distinguished—they surely could have been—but just that no one of the time was making an attempt to do so. Years later, by which time I was in university press publishing, I regularly received manuscripts essentially trying to argue a "just" war theory. In other words, they sought to identify overarching standards for when nations could morally go to war. It was comforting to know that others were troubled by the contradictions that had troubled me.

Another issue of controversy involving shifting standards, this one also with echoes from the past, involves free trade, including debates on NAFTA and the WTO. One side argues that opening the American market to goods manufactured under regulations very different from those that govern American manufacture threatens to weaken environmental and workplace protections, here and abroad. The other side holds that free trade has driven a great worldwide prosperity, that globalized trade, with multinational companies free to move their plants across national borders, creates broad-based wealth that trickles down to those within even the lowest economic strata.

You can take either side in the debate, but do recognize that if you argue that workers in developing countries are happy to have jobs paying three dollars a day, you risk having many of your arguments echo those made by opponents of workplace reform in the early twentieth century. In effect, you will be arguing that in the absence of unions and government regulation, workers considered fungible can effectively negotiate wages and working conditions with huge, deep-pocketed corporations. This position abandons the hard-won and broadly cherished notion that workers have a right to bargain collectively, and that government has a responsibility to set minimum wages and regulate workplace safety standards. You certainly can set out those factors you believe distinguish this time from that earlier time, but to protect your credibility you must take cognizance of this history. What you cannot do is ignore it as if it were irrelevant to the debate.

And finally, as I go over this chapter one last time before turning it in, a controversy is raging over pardons granted by President Clinton in the last hours of his presidency. While "Everyone does it" has never been a defense, not with your mother and not in any court of law, critics of the former president have a responsibility, and defenders a right, to put the matter in context by comparing Mr. Clinton's pardons with those issued by other presidents.

The difference between telling a lie and not telling the entire story is technical only.

An author invites trouble when what he writes is couched in such a way that those who know less than he does about the topic— presumably a heck of a lot of his readers—will come to an erroneous conclusion. Let me give you an example.

Recently I was sent a query for representation that included an analysis of the Supreme Court ruling that decided the 2000 presidential election. Within a couple of paragraphs I knew that this author's proposal had to be read skeptically, if I continued to read it at all. Here's why.

The opening paragraph stated that "by a 5–4 vote the conservative majority on the Court decided the election in favor of the conservative Mr. Bush." The author went on to report, accurately, that "these five justices took it on themselves to decree that the recount plan ordered by the Florida State Supreme Court was violative of the equal protection provisions of the U.S. Constitution, and that there was no time left to bring it into conformity."

I was concerned not by what the author said—true enough, if read carefully—but by what he coyly tried to get his readers to believe that was not true.

Those of you who followed the case closely know that seven justices, not five, found the state-wide recount ordered by the Florida Supreme Court unconstitutional. The five conservatives lost the support of their two more liberal colleagues in also deciding that there was no time for the Florida Supreme Court to devise a new recount plan that would be constitutional. So it may fairly be said that the five conservative justices in effect decided the election. But a reader would not know that the decision to overturn the Florida Supreme Court recount as it had been proceeding was 7–2 and not 5–4.

Now read the author's words again: "these five [conservative] justices took it on themselves to decree that the recount plan ordered

by the Florida State Supreme Court was violative of the equal protection provisions of the U.S. Constitution, and that there was no
time left to bring it into conformity." While true that the five conservatives came to both findings, the sentence is cast so as to create
the impression that it was five, not seven, justices who reached the
first finding, as well as the second.

Why did this disturb me? I was aware that there were several divisions in the Court's opinions, not all of them 5–4. Thus alerted, I was
only momentarily put at a disadvantage by the author's failure to put
all the information on the table. But what happens when this author
gets into areas I know less about? Why should I trust that he will not
do the same again and again, in situations where my ignorance might
leave me vulnerable to such language machinations? It will not be easy
to discover precisely when the author is engaging in such practices,
because nothing in his presentation jumps out as factually untrue. It's
just not the whole story. Here's a harsh but useful rule to follow: Any
attempt to cause others to believe something you know to be untrue
is a lie, no matter how defensible the words you have chosen.

Beware of Greeks bearing gifts.

Don't let your *Eureka!* reaction over the discovery of some bit of
new information that seems to be dispositive in your favor seduce
you into abandoning the skepticism with which you should view
any new information. As with most things in life, if it sounds too
good to be true, it likely is. One critic of President Clinton devoted
several articles and a book to trying to convince America that there
was something fishy about the death of Vince Foster and the investigations that concluded it had been a suicide. The pistol that killed
Foster, went one of the author's arguments, was found in his right
hand, positioned close to his head. This was unnatural, the author
argued. Recoil from the shot should have thrown the hand well away
from the firing point.

Then came the Trojan Horse. Somebody told the author that Foster was left-handed. Eureka! Triumphantly, the author went into print with the information, without the double or triple checking that such an important find warranted. When it turned out that Foster was in fact right-handed, every comment on the author's work thereafter featured the gaffe; inevitably the author's credibility was destroyed.

Here's another example. Several years ago I received a manuscript taking the position that the United States should not have dropped the atom bomb on Japan, a not unreasonable position to argue. As I read into the proposal, the author averred that the U.S. military thought that an invasion of Japan would cost only thirty thousand American casualties. No doubt some military person somewhere had written the words that were the basis for this statement. But I am just as sure that other military people produced other, much higher estimates, and that the author chose to use the thirty-thousand figure because it so well supported his position. However, those who know about the Pacific War, and about Japanese tenacity in defending Iwo Jima and Okinawa, inflicting casualties nearly that high in the defense of these off-shore islands, would find it incredible that conquest of Japan's home islands could be managed as cheaply. In effect, the statement was what Churchill once described as "the thirteenth chime which cast doubt on all that had preceded it." Sadly, questioning the propriety of dropping an atom bomb on unsuspecting civilian populations did not require this pragmatic calculation.

Do not assume that the presumptions and biases of your own informational network are universally shared.

Especially if you are in academia or the communications business, two sectors from which come many serious nonfiction authors, failure to observe this caveat can cause you to sound like an arrogant elitist to those outside your network and like a panderer to those within it. During the 1980s, I seemed to receive a proposal a week that opened with the words, "In this age of Reaganomics. . . ." I'm not sure just which message each author was trying to convey, but whenever I saw the line I heard: "I'm in the smart group, just like you."

You must win a reader over to your presumptions. Only after you have him on board with your givens can you try to take him to the next step. Many years ago, a heated clash broke out at a publishing panel between a panelist and a member of the audience over the issue of American and Chinese societies. When one of the two referred to the United States as an undemocratic society, the other expressed disbelief that his interlocutor could possibly consider the People's Republic of China more democratic. The debate quickly deteriorated into a contest in exasperation, neither side able to tolerate the other's position on this one point. It eventually became clear that the problem was one of presumptions. The person defending China defined democracy as serving the people, Lincoln's "for the people," while the one defending the American system saw the defining characteristic of democracy as free elections, Lincoln's, "by the people." Because the two were talking past each other, the confrontation went on and on, without making any progress. If each had understood the presumptions of the other regarding how democracy should be defined, a productive discussion might have ensued. The one could have argued that America's free elections were seriously distorted by corporate influence in the media and on both major parties, and the other that China's continuing poverty fifty years into communist rule illustrated how little the system had produced "for the people." The morale: Establish your givens and do your best to win concurrence on them before attempting to build on them.

Anticipate other possible interpretations for every piece of your data.

Take this as a reminder only. The validity of this rule should be self-evident. A good proposal I saw recently cited a government-funded study suggesting that kids who listened to classical music ended up with higher IQs, which the author saw as supporting a nurture-over-nature point he was trying to make. As soon as I raised the alternative explanation with him, that he could have the direction of causality reversed, he smiled sheepishly and promised he'd strike it.

Don't try settling a point by citing Webster's dictionary.

A dictionary is a chronicler of usage, not an arbiter. One author went a step further and cited "the first usage in the OED." The OED is "based on historical principles," meaning the first listed meaning of an entry is that implied by context in the earliest found usage, not the most important meaning.

The post hoc, ergo propter hoc *fallacy.*

This means, literally, "After this, therefore on account of this." It describes the faulty logic in attributing causation based solely on the chronological arrangement of events. Since B followed A, it was caused by A. Let's face it. We all, especially historians, use chronological sequencing to suggest a picture of what or who caused what and even, at times, why. "King John ascended the throne in 1350, accounting for the remarkable increase in the nation's prosperity in the latter half of the fourteenth century." The important thing to remember is that the temporal arrangement of events can suggest a causal relationship, but never prove it. Let your analysis concede this. Best of all is finding and citing the mechanism of causation.

Analogy.

Here again, the problem is that we try to make an argument device do too much. Analogies can be effective when used to suggest a relationship that we believe exists in an issue under discussion by reference to a well-recognized and broadly conceded relationship. But analogies can be illustrative only, and prove nothing. Analogies also come with a special caveat: They are extremely vulnerable to criticism if they reach for extremes, especially when they use as examples villains of history. For instance:

> The relationship between Smith and Jones was odd. It resembled the relationship between that historical odd couple, Hitler and Mussolini, in that the stronger of the two had greater psychological need of the weaker, rather than the other way round.

You can be sure that unfriendly reviewers will accuse the author of comparing Smith to that mass murderer Hitler.

Another example:

> In trying to understand why William Clinton risked such vehement criticism by granting those last-minute pardons, we must remember his truly remarkable record of never having been deserted by the American public, through scandal after scandal. Almost like John Gotti, the man reporters called the Teflon Don for his many acquittals, and who until he was finally convicted and sentenced to life strutted around town with an air of invincibility, Bill Clinton may too have come to think of himself as living a charmed life.

The author is not at all equating the offenses of the two men, only the perception of personal invincibility both came to believe in. But critics will surely say he compared Clinton to a convicted murderer.

Attributing motivation.

An author should exercise caution about attributing motivation to another without compelling evidence, most reliably from an intimate who has heard the person describe his own motivation. Egregiously, some fictionalized nonfiction will put words into the mouths of others. Attributing motivation goes one step further. It puts ideas into the heads of others.

There's also a logical fallacy that frequently accompanies the attribution of motivation. In current usage, the two words *motive* and *motivation* are distinguished in this way: *Motive* describes a valid reason to do something; *motivation* describes the impulse to do something. That a person has a valid reason to do something does not mean that he will do it, even less that if he has done it, he did it for that reason. Criminal prosecutors have trouble getting a conviction unless the prosecutor can establish motive. But of course establishing motive does not prove guilt. Every person who benefits from the death of another does not kill that person. In serious nonfiction writing, we usually know who did what. The error we find most often in manuscripts is a presumption that of all the reasons a person might have had for doing something, it was the most nefarious reason that motivated him.

My experience warns me that this last rule I now offer will cause many of you to be angry with me, for it has often provoked an emotional response when I have raised it with my own authors.

Respect the right of causes and movements to choose their own names for themselves.

People who call themselves "pro-life" on the abortion issue cannot abide referring to the other side as "pro-choice." They argue that the unborn fetus (or baby) has no choice in the matter. Pro-choice people, who selected their name to protect themselves from being seen as advocates of abortion rather than of a woman's right to choose, suffer as much when they have to refer to the other side as pro-life, preferring to describe it as anti-choice. Today we are very much aware that many social issues will be decided on the basis of who gains the language advantage, and so the more effective the name a movement has chosen for itself, the more likely that it will be challenged by the other side of the debate. Both these names are highly effective, and so each provokes anger and indignation from the other side.

However, civilized discourse requires conceding certain rights to the other side. And there is a long tradition of allowing movements as well as people to choose the names by which they will be known. "Nazi," for example, is an acronym for the German *Nationalsozialistiche Deutsche Arbeiterpartei,* "National Socialist German Worker's Party," hardly an accurate description of what Adolf Hitler stood for. But referring to them as "so-called national socialists" would have wasted a lot of energy better spent fighting the evil.

That's it for my favorite rules. You have likely seen every one of them broken, often by people you respect. But there is a practical reason that certain tactics that work elsewhere don't work in book-length works of serious nonfiction. A lawyer or television editor controls the flow of the material being presented. He can skim over uncomfortable information, moving ahead briskly to keep you focused on what is being said at the moment. But your reader doesn't have to get through your book at your rate. If he senses that you are being unfair, employing shifting standards, for example, he flips back and compares what you're saying now to what you said earlier. When he finds he missed nothing and figures out that you just fudged your way past some ill-fitting point, he will be forced to make a decision about you. Do it once and he may say, "Tsk, tsk." Continue doing it and you risk his putting your book aside and seeking out a more reliable guide to your topic.

If there is a theme to this book, it is that you are always writing to your audience. In formulating your argument, think of your audience as being comprised of three rough groupings. One is made up of those who come to your book sympathetic to the position you will be taking. At the other extreme are those with whom you are most in conflict. The middle are not yet fully committed on the issue.

You will have separate goals in mind for each of these groups as you write your book. You will get the most satisfaction writing to the first group, for it will provide you an opportunity to make yourself a hero within a group with which you are happy to be identified. Here you will get the most enthusiastic nods and maybe even a few amens. But just remember that you are preaching to the choir.

As to the second group, you'll have poor prospects for finding converts here, no matter how persuasive your argument. But fair argument will ensure that these people will come away from your book with a respect, albeit grudging, for you as a commentator.

Your primary target should be the undecideds, those marginals on the issue who are looking for guidance. It is this group, the least blinded by passion, who will hold your argument to the strictest standards of fairness.

If there is one overarching caveat that will help you fashion fair argument, it is that you should be wary of any situation in which you are tempted to elevate position over process. When the hottest issues of our time have been decided, or compromised, or overtaken by events, all that will be left standing are the rules by which we conduct public discourse and, through the enlightenment such discourse can provide, fashion rational solutions to pressing problems.

I hope this chapter helps you write more defensible argument. But on this issue, even more important than how your critics respond to your work is how you feel about it yourself. I have had authors tell me that their attempts to be scrupulously fair throughout their book left them with an improved feeling about themselves. Now that goes up as a win!

Now on to a fun chapter, one that deals with humanizing your book.

Chapter Six

Using Narrative Tension

Just about every business day, all over Manhattan, editors lunch with agents.

They do so because having lunch at trendy New York restaurants is one of the nicer perks of being in publishing. They do so to gossip, about their colleagues' successes and failures and about what is happening—or not happening—at publishing houses around town. But they also "do lunch" to do business—to see if a match exists between publishing sensibilities of this editor and this agent.

I became an agent in 1997 and almost immediately began receiving lunch invitations. Having been an editor for more than twenty-five years, I knew the routine of the editor-agent lunch, albeit from the editor's side. Or so I thought.

My confusion began when I opened my side of the conversation. I casually reminded these editors of what I assumed they already knew: that I represented mostly serious nonfiction authors.

"Oh," came the frequent response, tinged with surprise, discomfort, or even defensiveness. "But I do only nonfiction with a narrative."

At first, I was caught off guard, probably because I was still second-guessing my decision to leave the in-house side of publishing for agenting. Then I foolishly jumped to the conclusion that these editors were expressing a preference for a certain category of nonfiction book extremely popular these days, but one I rarely do. In publishing circles, this kind of book goes by the name "narrative nonfiction."

Narrative nonfiction books tend to be human-interest stories—man-against-nature, man-against-establishment, or man-against-man stories. Many have become best sellers. *The Perfect Storm, A Civil Action,* and *Barbarians at the Gate* are good examples of this type of character-driven book. The human struggle keeps you reading. All have fine background settings—the law, politics, adventure, the sea—and most have what I call break-narrative chapters, in which you learn some history, or something about sailing, or about the rough and tumble world of high-stakes business buyouts or lawsuits. But you turn the pages out of curiosity about how the story will play itself out. Will the sympathetic character or characters survive, prevail, prosper?

Had this genre become so popular, I now wondered, that it was crowding out more traditional serious nonfiction titles?

Then again, many of these lunch invitations came after I'd placed with a major publisher a well-publicized serious nonfiction project. Surely these editors knew before they asked me to lunch the kind of projects I represent. The confusion, I slowly figured out, lay not in my list of books but in my terminology. Many of these editors associated the term *serious* nonfiction with impenetrable academic tomes.

"What makes you think that serious nonfiction books do not have narrative?" I began to say in response, now jauntily defending my own list. "All my books"* tell a story.

----

* Those in publishing use a sort of imperial first person possessive. Editors and agents say "my author" and "my book" for any book produced by "my author." If two editors are chatting, and one says, "Do you know the title *Ring of Nonsense*?" the other might say, "Sure. That's Joe Blow's book," meaning not that Joe Blow wrote it, but that he was the editor.

And so they do. And so should your book. Even if you are revising your dissertation for publication at a small university press. Even if your book is an idea book, expressing the conflict between competing philosophies; even if your book is filled with statistics. Or difficult scientific concepts. Or economic theories.

Why, you may ask, should you write serious nonfiction as a story? At the risk of using a good line as a substitute for a real argument, I will suggest that the first job of any book is to get itself read. Unless you dismiss the value of having a readership, I know of no better way to lure and hold a reader than to tell a story. Doing so suggests to the reader that as deep as he is into the topic, another piece is still to come; that as much as she now knows, some missing element will complete her understanding. In fiction, narrative tension keeps the reader reading about people and events the reader never cared a whit about, waiting for resolution of a dilemma that can have no impact on his own life. In nonfiction, the author's burden is not as great. The people and events depicted are real, and the ideas discussed can have a dramatic impact on the life of the reader. Yet even in nonfiction, narrative tension remains a highly effective tool for keeping the reader engaged with the material.

There is a flip side to narrative tension. While it pulls the reader into the book and holds her there, it simultaneously imposes on the writer the need to get on with the story. It works to inhibit tangential meanderings and self-indulgent interludes that eat at a reader's time. Thus, for all its association with creativity, narrative tension is a very businesslike affair. And because of that, it fits hand-in-glove with argument, both directing a serious nonfiction manuscript toward a specific goal: having the reader concur in the author's take. The fit between the two is so tight that in good serious nonfiction you cannot always tell where narrative drive ends and argument picks up or vice versa.

While many authors initially feel daunted by the demands of

narrative writing, most eventually come to see narrative as a good friend. It works almost as a personal editor, telling you what to develop and what to let fall to the cutting room floor. Think back to good serious books you have enjoyed. Did you ever describe a nonfiction book to a friend by saying: "It's so good, it almost reads like a novel"? Why did you pick those precise words? Because there is something in us that loves a yarn. Our ancestors preserved their history in the form of stories—the story of our people, the story of our world. The Bible teaches proper behavior by telling stories about what happened to those who behaved well and to those who didn't. Stories compel in a way that reports do not. But exploiting that love of a good yarn requires learning to use narrative techniques.

Let me take a minute to answer the obvious question: If narrative does so much for serious nonfiction, why isn't all serious nonfiction written as narrative?

Much of it is. And you will find narrative interludes even in the most highly intellectualized books. So narrative is not alien to this genre. Too many of us, however, associate the need for consistent narrative solely with people stories—history or biography or, in publishing terms, character-driven stories. But using narrative techniques makes any project an easier write and can convert a sociological examination or an explanatory work of science or law or politics into a much better read. The difficulty is in knowing where and how to employ it.

I suspect that aside from a lack of awareness of the power of narrative to hold your reader, another factor explains the reluctance of many serious nonfiction authors to use narrative techniques.

Those following writing trends these days know that the line between fiction and nonfiction is growing disturbingly thin, a change that inevitably works against serious nonfiction. There is much talk in journalism about composite characters and questionable attributions. For the latter, a writer for *The New Yorker* was dragged into court, accused of having put quotation marks around words not spoken verbatim or not in the precise sequence presented to the reader. On this narrow issue, the court decided that as long as the material within the quotation marks represented substantially what the subject of the interview had said, the author's actions were not necessarily libelous. Not libelous and not the right thing to do are, however, two different things. Most of us continue to believe that the words within quotation marks should represent precisely what was said, and that when an author wants to paraphrase, he or she may not put the paraphrase within quotation marks.

This writer further served the dramatic needs of her story by taking several short interviews with the person she was writing about and combining them into one dramatic meeting. Of course, writers have been doing such things since well before the printing press was invented, but it is a sign of the times that when the full story was revealed the criticism of what this author had done was generally mild.

The case of Edmund Morris, the authorized biographer of Ronald Reagan, and his book *Dutch,* is far more troubling. Morris will be immortalized in the annals of writing for having been the first authorized presidential biographer to introduce fake characters into what Morris promised would be a substantial, scholarly book, and which everyone presumed would be a factually accurate presidential biography. Then, adding insult to injury, he created fake footnotes about his fake characters to make them more believable. The result was to further confuse his readers about where fact ended and fiction began.

Random House, his publisher, to its discredit, did nothing in the book itself to inform reviewers or readers about what Morris had done. After these questionable devices were discovered, a literary scandal erupted, with respected reviewers such as Michiko Kakutani of the *New York Times* and a chorus of others denouncing books that made these kinds of compromises with the truth.* Still, if the proof of the pudding is in the eating, it is hard to reconcile the uproar with the sobering fact that more than two hundred thousand people went out and bought the book after the inclusion of fake characters had been fully revealed and reviled, a telling commentary on the intellectual zeitgeist of our times. "It was a very good read," explained one of my publishing friends. All I could think of was the finger-to-the-wind observation of Professor Stanley Fish of Duke University, who once observed, "Now I no longer have to be right; all I have to be is interesting." (Two years later, Fish later repudiated that sentence, calling it "The most unfortunate sentence I ever wrote." He further commented: "The question of whether something is right or wrong is always the crucial question. . . .")

Of course, it is much easier to write dramatically if you can create characters, give them dialogue, put them on the scene, and have them recite lines you have prepared for them.

Still, almost a year after the *Dutch* brouhaha, Martin Arnold, in his "Making Books" column in the *New York Times* of July 20, 2000, "Does Nonfiction Mean Factual?" observed: "In recent years it seems that there have been more and more blowups over the question of whether book publishers actually care about the veracity of the material in the nonfiction books they publish."

It is understandable, then, that many serious nonfiction authors hesitate to use dramatic devices for fear of putting themselves on the

---

*Not all criticism was negative. Steven Weisman in his *New York Times* review wrote: ". . . a reader who surrenders to Morris's self-indulgent blend of scholarship and imagination will be led through a riveting story to a transcendent conclusion with a surprise twist. If there is a 'higher truth' [his quotes, not mine] justifying the book's technique, it is that Ronald Reagan lived in a world of his own fictions, far more extensive than the fictions of Edmund Morris. Who better suited to plumb a phantom subject than a phantom narrator?" This is a troubling justification. The failure of the subject of a biography to distinguish fact from fiction makes acceptable a biography that blurs the distinction. Will all seriously flawed public figures earn similarly flawed biographies? The logic loses me.

wrong side of the divide on this issue. Though some, to be sure, display no such reluctance. At least three or four times during my career as an editor, I have had to ask authors how they had obtained a particular detail in their manuscripts. In one case, the author had written about a coffee cup that rattled just before a plane crash in which all on board perished. When I asked the author how he knew about the rattling coffee cup, he said that he had learned that coffee cups tend to rattle whenever a plane reaches a certain speed and so just filled in that detail to "set the scene."

Whether coffee cups really rattled during this plane crash is not important. What does concern me is the slippery slope we may be putting ourselves on. First it's a rattling coffee cup, then a character who was never on the plane in the first place. Maybe even a character, as in the Reagan biography, who never even existed until conjured up by the author to help him get past a siege of writer's block.

So it is with some justifiable concern that many serious nonfiction writers hesitate to "tell it like a story." They fear putting the intellectual gravitas of their work in jeopardy and losing the approval of their peers that comes with absolute confidence that an author has not tinkered with the facts. Moreover, they rightfully shy away from anything that might diminish the seriousness with which the work will be received by the very people they care most about—intelligent readers.

A resistance to nonfiction as narrative is so ingrained in many authors that when I ask new authors who come to me for representation to tell me the story their book will tell (in other words, what the book is about), they either haven't a clue what I am asking for ("It's not a story," one author replied. "It's nonfiction."), or they start describing moments they will include, mistakenly believing that I am asking whether their book will have anecdotes.

So let's establish between us that despite my pleas to authors to tell it like a story, there remain many devices of fictional storytelling that cannot be adapted to nonfiction writing. You cannot introduce made-up facts or dialogue, no matter how trivial. You cannot put your words into someone else's mouth or attribute motive absent solid factual evidence of motive. If you present events out of chronological order, you had better make an argument that is not subject to refutation by anyone who takes the time to sequence these events, showing that event A could not have influenced event B because event A came after event B. You cannot divine what is inside someone else's head, although some leniency is shown toward phrases such as "Given that he was coming to the end of his time on the bench, and probably the end of his life, he *must have wondered* if somehow those decisions he had made about. . . ." You should avoid violating the rules of argument set out in the previous chapter, especially the rule that your argument must flow from the facts on the page, not those in your head.

Nevertheless, it is possible to use narrative techniques without falling into fiction. And there are very good reasons for doing so. Here are some of them.

Narrative works well with a question-driven manuscript. Once you have your book's major question and answer, you have key components of narrative: (a) a clear beginning and a clear ending; (b) a compelling reason to navigate your reader to that end; and (c) a clear sense of the key players or concepts who/that will come into the story, shaping how it can and should be told. As you think about moving from question to answer, think as well about how you might use elements of the "Triple C, R" of good drama: conflict, contention, confusion, and resolution. Most of us know instinctively what makes a good story; following your instincts about storytelling can make the presentation of your nonfiction journey from question to answer, from beginning to end, more seductive.

The problem is that most people confuse storytelling with its opposite—covering time. Covering time involves reporting what happened at each point in either the chronological time frame logical/argument sequencing, and no more. You don't foreshadow, that is, plant in the mind of the reader the thought that certain elements in your recitation, background to what is being covered at the moment, will come back to play an important role in the larger story. You plant no "hooks," leave no "cliffhangers." Nor do you use any other devices to intensify reader suspense over what will be coming next. As a consequence, you don't give the reader any reason to turn the page.

Narrative, on the other hand, relies on the presence of two simultaneously running stories to keep the reader reading. The first is the story of what is being described at that moment; the second, the story that will come together only lster in the book, out of pieces of each of the many real-time moments described. A skilled writer ties together strategically placed clues on an invisible string that we call narrative thread. In fiction and nonfiction alike the skill is in making the narrative thread functional but never blatantly obvious to the reader. While good narrative signals when a piece of an immediate story will play a role in solving the book's major mystery, it does so without giving away just how. By playing on the reader's natural curiosity, the author keeps the reader reading by speeding up the frequency of the clues as the reader gets closer and closer to the resolution of the mystery.

It is not even necessary that the reader be kept totally in the dark about the story's end. Millions of people saw the movie *Titanic*. All knew the ship would go down. People can be held in thrall waiting to learn just how the story will wend its way from the real-time moment to the expected conclusion.

Don't be afraid to go to a few good fiction or drama writing books to see what they have to say about creating narrative tension. Of course, many of their techniques will not be of use to you in producing nonfiction. For instance, a fiction writer can change characters or events to serve plot purposes, while you are stuck with your characters and facts. But while you may not be able to take all devices suggested in such books and apply them directly to your serious nonfiction writing, having a better understanding of how and why they work may help you find ways to introduce more narrative tension into your own work, while still not compromising your credibility.

It is important to note that storytelling techniques can be used to introduce narrative tension, even when the book is not structured as a story. Observe how a sense of more-on-this-to-come is created by lines such as the following:

> Economists focused intently on this particular aspect of his fiscal policy, but it appears that no one paid much attention to a briefly mentioned observation that . . .

Or:

> And yet it was this bit of encouragement that would turn out to have the greatest influence on Johnson, though it would take thirty years before it became apparent just how . . .

Or:

> It was a journey the group embarked on with justifiable trepidation. Only three of them would make it through the winter, and of those three, none would be men. It was the 1880s, and no one would have predicted that three women, all over the age of fifty, would prove to have better survival skills than their male guides.

That's the good side of narrative tension. The bad side is that it can be punishing to those writers who don't maintain tight control of the narrative thread. If at any point the reader gets confused about what's happening in your story, or feels as if it is going in circles, he won't stop to consider whether the problem is that he wasn't reading closely enough or that the author led him astray. He will simply stop reading.

If your subject matter is of such import that a great many people feel they must hear what you have to say, no matter how difficult they find getting through it, some readers will survive the lack of narrative tension and plow on to the end of your book. But most authors are not in that envious position. Their work needs to seduce as well as educate.

Which leads me to my second point about narrative. Earlier I talked about the fact that many associate narrative with character-driven books. I suggested that narrative also had a role in academic work that was not about people per se. And that remains my belief, with one qualifier.

Introducing narrative tension invariably humanizes any writing. On the one hand, it does so by encouraging the author to acknowledge and incorporate into his treatment, no matter how abstract or abstruse the topic, a sense for the fact that ideas emerge from the minds of human beings living in one social setting or another. The person who came up with any particular idea lived in a certain intellectual time and place and was responding to or building upon crosscurrents of thought within that world. In a moment I'll show you why this is important. On the back end, narrative reinforces the concept that ideas, again, no matter how abstract or abstruse, have the ability to change the human condition, either for better or worse. The good nonfiction writer does not allow his discussion to take place in rarified air, as if it did not say something ultimately about who we are, where we came from, why we value what we value.

It is the connection to the human condition that gives writing poignancy, and keeping this in mind helps an author use narrative techniques to great advantage. Good narrative is never written without a feeling for what it is to be a human being, that very special social animal. Note the difference between a manuscript that reads: "The intensification of market involvement in Los Legos, newly connected to Houston by rail, caused a cascade of dysfunctional socioeconomic consequences to the indigenous population of the small town"; and one that reads: "Once the last track of the railroad was laid between Houston and the sleepy town of Los Legos, the Mexican Americans who had lived in Los Legos for nearly three-quarters of a century were forced to accept that the society they had created no longer had a place for them in it." The first communicates a studied distancing from the human aspect; the second a feeling for the experience of the people affected.

It might be helpful if I try to illustrate the difference between projects that simply cover time and those rethought to improve narrative tension.

Let's begin with biography.

Most of us assume that biography easily lends itself to narrative. Yet inexperienced biographers frequently spend chapters covering the chronology of the subject's life, as if that were sufficient. This happened when X was in his teens; this was what he did in his twenties; these are the things he discovered in his thirties, which led him to win the Nobel Prize in his fifties. If the life was indeed rich and full, *and* if you are the first person to write a biography of this subject, or at least the first person in many years, so that the material is somewhat fresh, you may be able to pull your reader along just covering time.

But it is my experience that the compelling biography, the one that creates a certain satisfying sense that you understand the subject's life force, not just know everything about his life, only *seems* to come out of a recitation of the events of that life. More accurately, successful biography comes out of a telling of what I call the "mind story," the tensions surrounding the biographical subject at each critical point in his life, and how he dealt with them. When examined in the context of the unfolding life story, these tensions illuminate what he had to contend with/drove him to become a brilliant lawyer, a world-famous preacher, a Nobel Prize–winning scientist, the man who climbed a mountain no one else dared attempt, the brilliant anthropologist who . . .

The narrative thread, rather than being controlled by the chronology or facts of the life story, is spun out of thematic tensions, often seemingly inconsequential at each point in the subject's life but which can be shown to have persisted across time and a changing landscape of life experiences. The pattern within which the subject responded to these tensions provides the best key to how he was able to develop the special skills that made him unique in the way he was unique or gave him the vision to see something others had missed, or the determination to do so, or whatever. The answer must come not out of the real-life events themselves but out of the subject's response to those events over the fullness of time. What brings the subject most vividly to life for the reader is this pattern, what I call the mind story, the consistent or inconsistent way he dealt with life's challenges, from tension to resolution, in each moment of crisis. Sadly, some authors never realize that the mind story is there to be mined for exactly this purpose.

And that's not surprising. Figuring out a story line—especially a mind story line—is not easy, even for those writing biographies and histories, let alone those writing books without characters, human conflict, or a chronological framework. Even in writing biography, some subjects are just not revealing of the mental processes through which they resolved life crises.

Let me interject at this time that I am not saying that for a book to be structured in narrative fashion it must be spun out like a campfire tale, beginning with the earliest events and proceeding chronologically to later events. For example, not all stories, not even all histories, are best told in chronological order. It can make better sense for an author to begin halfway into the story and only later go back and fill in the earlier parts. At times certain parts of the story are just fuller; you know more about them than others, and so you have no choice but to structure your book around what you really know.

But just as you pull an argument out of the facts, you can usually find the threads of a story line within your data. Within certain limitations, it is almost always possible to improve the readability of your materials by weaving these threads into a humanizing narrative.

Let's switch genres and say you decide to write a book that explains Einstein's theory of special and then general relativity. This is the classic explanatory type of science serious nonfiction. You are not an Einstein biographer. You are a physicist. You know little more than a layman about Einstein's personal life. And you really don't care about the man behind the ideas, or out of what tensions in his life came his remarkable achievements. You care about science. You have held student-filled auditoriums spellbound explaining complex scientific theories. Now you want to put your explanations into a book, so that a broader part of the general public can understand these two groundbreaking theories. But how do you keep your book from sounding like a textbook? How do you create narrative out of a straight explanatory story?

Here's the covering-material approach. Part One explains the Newtonian clockwork universe, which Einstein's theories overturned, and its limitations. Part Two, Einstein's theories, carefully explaining exactly how they are better explanations for why certain parts of the physical world work the way we can observe them working. Part Three, how these two theories forever changed our understanding of time, space, and the fabric of the universe.

Once again, if there are enough people who just want answers to these questions, you may well be able to hold a solid audience without building in narrative tension. But most likely you are not the only person writing about this science, and surely the same material is available in textbook form. The serious nonfiction book buyer came to your book because he wanted something more. Will this approach sustain this reader through your material? Not likely.

So then, how do you build in narrative? Through the mind story. You do not begin with the limitations of Newtonian physics as an explanation of the forces at work in the cosmos, because at the time Einstein did his work, he didn't know, nor did anyone else, that there were limitations. You begin where the mind story (not where the science) begins—by identifying the specific problem Einstein had with the physics he had learned.

Remember, Einstein didn't just sit down one day and think, "Hmm, today I'll think about the universe," and just by accident have his mind drift to time and, poof, out came special relativity. He didn't say to himself, "The Newtonian clockwork universe could be improved if only I did such and such." Apart from the fact that this makes science seem like magic, it's not how new theories happen. There is always a provoking agent. There had to have been some very specific particular inconsistency, something that just didn't add up in some specific part of Newtonian physics, to cause Einstein to turn his attention to time, the key part of the theory of special relativity, rather than to some other aspect of the Newtonian worldview of the universe. You begin the story with whatever that something was. (Are you wondering what that something was? Fear not. In a minute I will tell you. It's a good story.)

Earlier in this chapter I said that narrative tension and argument work hand in glove. You might have come to this realization sooner had you paid more attention to the major question driving your book. Watch how you get to the same place from a different beginning.

Remember, every book has a question, even an explanatory book. So what's the question driving this book about special and general relativity? Is it simply "What's the theory of special and then general relativity all about?" Not good. That's the same question driving every textbook.

But if instead, in an attempt to humanize this story, you had worked your way back to the more interesting question: "What exactly caused Einstein to question the Newtonian concept of time?" you would have a question with a curious human mind at its center.

Now, while the story sets up the Newtonian clockwork universe, it really begins with the merging of electric and magnetic fields into the groundbreaking theory of electromagnetism developed by James Clerk Maxwell. For it is here, in this theory, that conditions emerged that suggested to Einstein an inconsistency between the observed wavelength of emitted light and the speed of that light. And in fact, if you look at the scientific article that Einstein published, in which he first stated the theory, you will see that it is subtitled: "On . . . electromagnetism."

Once again, with the right question you get the right start on your narrative.

Now, of course, the challenge becomes how to structure the story so that it reflects tensions common to the human condition. Again, go back to basics. What are the forces at play? What are the likely false trails that Einstein might have been lured down? Was there a roller-coaster ride of elation/despair, elation/despair? While you would be very wise to read an Einstein biography before you attempted your explanatory book, putting yourself in that situation and thinking about the likely pitfalls that would entrap any scientist will help determine what it is you should be looking for and even where you are likely to find it.

Once again, you find your narrative by humanizing your story. Scientific discovery is not about how science came to the present time, where it understands everything there is to know. It is about how scientists figured out answers to one set of questions that led them to look for answers to another set of questions, which led to the set of questions that scientists are wrestling with today. This is the ongoing story of which all science is a part. Leave curiosity out of the picture and you loose your human interest element. Leave out the special need of scientists to have all the pieces of the puzzle fit neatly together, and you loose your narrative tension.

Let me give you one final example of a manuscript that could not be structured as a story, but which could have been improved had the author better understood what keeps a reader reading. Years ago, I came across a sociological examination of the drug problem in twentieth-century America written by someone in law enforcement who had gone from one drug treatment center to another looking for what worked and what didn't work. The manuscript was organized on the basis of the order in which the author had visited these programs, with the author exhausting all the material he had on one treatment program before going on to what he had learned about the next program.

In discussing each center, the author treated the variables—the reaction of the community; the percentage of patients at each voluntarily as opposed to those there under court order; the number in full-time residence and those treated on an outpatient basis; the age distribution; and the rate of recidivism. He then went on to consider the same variables at the next center, until he had discussed all the centers he had visited. Talk about no narrative tension!

A much better approach would have been to take one class of patient and examine how this class fared within each program. Why? Because the reader is ultimately interested in which kind of program affords the greatest benefit for each class of patient. And the reader will quickly catch on to the way the manuscript is organized. As he is told about failure with a certain class of patient in one program, he'll be eagerly reading on to learn if this kind of patient did better in another kind of program.

The manuscript could have been organized into a compelling story had the author been more curious about how treatment regimens gain sufficient support to become incorporated into a treatment program. He failed to focus on the true beginning of his story. His research may have begun in these treatment program centers, but the story of each of these centers began in the mind of someone with an idea powerful enough to influence and change drug policy. Each one of these drug treatment programs came out of someone's vision. What disturbed that person about then-current drug programs that caused him or her to advocate changes? And did these changes prove to have positive or negative consequences for those who went through the altered programs. Again, organize around the mind story to find the human interest aspect that will help you create narrative tension.

For those who need further persuasion that an author who leaves the human interest aspect out of his manuscript will pay a price, let me quote from a review in the *New York Times Book Review*, March 4, 2001.*

> Segal deserves great credit for putting the history of Islamic slavery on the record in a carefully documented way. Sadly, the significance of the story is not matched by the skill of the telling. "Islam's Black Slaves" reads like a string of encyclopedia entries. Names of caliphs, emirs, sultans and slaves flow by in a relentless torrent. None remain as memorable characters. . . . We reach page 133 before encountering a full-fledged eyewitness description that brings the scene alive—a British officer's vivid picture of an 1819 slave caravan making the long, perilous trek across the Sahara. Segal quotes only a few such accounts, which is surprising because nineteenth-century Europeans wrote dozens of them.

---

* The review, by Adam Hochschild, is of *Islam's Black Slaves* by Ronald Segal.

Having made a case for the benefits of narrative tension, as well as the risks, let me end this chapter by conceding that no serious nonfiction book should be relentless narrative. There is other important work to be done. I believe it was T. S. Eliot who remarked that plot is the bone the novelist throws to the watchdog so he can go about his business. And so, in a similar way, the author of serious nonfiction uses narrative tension to keep his reader attentive, so that when he makes a case for his thesis, he has that audience.

It's now time to walk through a book, chapter by chapter.

Chapter Seven

From Introduction to Epilogue: Writing Your Book Chapter by Chapter— and What to Do When You Get into Trouble

Introductions

Have you ever found yourself in a bookstore watching a browsing customer pick up a book and examine it? I have, many times. Here's how it usually goes. First the customer opens to the jacket flap copy, reads a little of it, but never seems to read all of it. Then he flips the book over to the back of the jacket (what publishing people call the "back ad") and reads the blurbs, the comments of others who have read the book—all favorable of course. It's getting close to decision time. Either the browser slides the book back onto the shelf and moves on, or he finds a way to rest his belongings, so he can open the book and start to read. If the latter, he will most often go to the introduction. I've watched people stand and read a ten-page introduction, page by page by page, as if there were no one else in the

store and as if the hustle and bustle all around them were the
of a library reading room. What are they reading for?

The answers to three questions: What is this book about? How
did you happen to write it? How will this book enhance their
knowledge of your topic?

Your prospective reader would also like to get to know you a
little better before he commits to spending five to ten hours with
you. That's why publishers so often include a little picture with a
brief bio on the jacket back flap. But another kind of picture is
emerging in the opening words of your introduction, one based on
the ease and sense of confidence—or lack of it—with which you
answer these questions.

Of the three, the third—the payoff you promise for reading this
book—is the most important. To make this promise and complete
the transaction, you employ in the introduction the language of
exposition, not argument and certainly not narrative. As quickly as
you can, you state the major question driving your book and the
answer you will provide. But you don't argue the merits. That's what
the rest of the book is for.

Many authors operate on the reasonable but mistaken assumption that to hook the reader they must open with an anecdote. After
all, in the previous chapter I went on and on about the power of the
human interest aspect to engage readers. And that's precisely how so
many magazine articles open—with an anecdote. If you feel you
must open with a story, fine, but keep it short and then tend to the
introduction's real business—telling a serious reader what he will
learn substantively if he makes a commitment to your book.

With rare exceptions, the only story I would include in an introduction is the one about how you came to the book's topic, particularly if that story is quotable (by the publicity department, by
reviewers) and revelatory of the question that drove you to write the
book. For example, in the introduction to his superb book *King*

Leopold's Ghost, Adam Hochschild describes reading a book on an airplane flight and being pulled up short by a footnote that referenced a quotation by Mark Twain, "written . . . when [Twain] was part of the worldwide movement against slave labor in the Congo, a practice that had taken five to eight million lives. Worldwide movement? Five to eight million lives? . . . And why had I never before heard of them? I had been writing about human rights for years. . . ."

But then get right into the book's payoff. As I tell my own authors in discussing their own introductions, "Spill the beans!" And don't be coy about it. There is nothing more maddening than a tease introduction, one where the author talks around the topic, apparently in the mistaken belief that no one will buy his book if he gives away the payoff in the introduction.

Let's dispose of this misguided concern right off. There are always books we would like to have read but really don't want to read. One way or another, we try to learn enough about these books to discuss them intelligently. Browsing bookstores or library stacks may be a popular way to do this. But it is a self-defeating exercise to design your introduction to prevent readers who don't care to buy your book from figuring out its thesis. The attempt will surely cost you more readers than the few you could possibly gain. And the irony is that an introduction that boldly puts forth an interesting and provocative thesis may seduce that browser into buying it. Remember the *Titanic* example. An audience's attentiveness is not solely related to curiosity about the ending, but to just how the tale will be brought to that ending. A boldly stated thesis causes a potential reader to be ever more curious about how the author plans to get from here to there, and how he will defend that thesis along the way.

Let's go to examples.

In his groundbreaking book *Gay New York,* George Chauncey writes one of the longest and fullest introductions I've seen. Yet I have long thought it to be one of the best introductions I have ever read. Watch how in the very first few pages he lays out his entire thesis.

> The gay world that flourished before World War II has been almost entirely forgotten in popular memory and overlooked by professional historians; it is not supposed to have existed. This book seeks to restore that world to history. . . . In doing so, it challenges three widespread myths about the history of gay life before the rise of the gay movement. . . .
>
> The myth of isolation holds that anti-gay hostility prevented the development of an extensive gay subculture and forced gay men to lead solitary lives. . . . But . . . indifference or curiosity—rather than hostility or fear—characterized many New Yorkers' response to the gay world for much of the half century before the war. [Gay men] . . . forged an immense gay world of overlapping social networks. . . .
>
> The myth of invisibility holds that even if a gay world existed, it was kept invisible and thus remained difficult for isolated gay men to find. But gay men were highly visible figures in early twentieth-century New York. . . .
>
> The myth of internalization holds that gay men uncritically internalized the dominant culture's view of them as sick, perverted, and immoral, and that self-hatred led them to accept the policing of their lives rather than resist it. . . .
>
> Although the gay male world of the prewar years was remarkably visible and integrated into the straight world, it was, as the centrality of the drag balls suggests, a world very different from our own. Above all, it was not a world in which men were divided into "homosexuals" and "heterosexuals." This book argues that in important respects the hetero-homosexual binarism, the sexual regime now hegemonic in American culture, is a stunning recent creation. Particularly in working-class culture, homosexual behav-

ior per se became the primary basis for the labeling and self-identification of men as "queer" only around the middle of the twentieth century; before then, [gay men] were so labeled only if they displayed a much broader inversion of their ascribed gender status by assuming the sexual and other cultural roles ascribed to women.

Here's another example. *The Tipping Point* by Malcolm Gladwell is an idea/business book. What follows is an excerpt from its excellent introduction.

The Tipping Point is the biography of an idea, and the idea is very simple. It is that the best way to understand the dramatic transformation of unknown books into best-sellers, or the rise of teenage smoking, or the phenomena of word of mouth or any number of other mysterious changes that mark everyday life is to think of them as epidemics. Ideas and products and messages and behaviors spread just like viruses do. . . .

[T]hree characteristics—one, contagiousness; two, the fact that little causes can have big effects; and three, that change happens not gradually but at one dramatic moment—are the same three principles that define how measles moves through a grade-school classroom or the flu attacks every winter. Of the three, the third, epidemic, trait . . . is the most important, because it is the principle that makes sense of the first two and that permits the greatest insight into why modern change happens the way it does. The name given to that one dramatic moment in an epidemic when everything can change all at once is the Tipping Point.

There it is. The person who wants nothing more than to bluff sounding as if he has read the book has the thesis spelled out in the introduction. And yet there were enough book buyers, able to get this thesis right out of the introduction, who went ahead and turned the book into a best seller.

While we're on the topic of spilling the beans, let me digress a moment to emphasize the extent to which your publisher will use those spilt beans to contribute to the success of your book.

Editors use every chance they get to give away your thesis. They struggle to write flap copy that is not just topic covering—"the author talks about this and that"—but rather bean spilling—"the author argues that . . ." As in:

> **The author's explanation for the decline of leisure lies chiefly in the strong historic preference of employers for longer hours. This book shows how the demands of employers, growing unemployment, and ultimately the addictive nature of consumption form a seamless web. . . . —flap copy for** *The Overworked American* **by Juliet Schor**

On the back of the hardcover jacket, editors will lead off with the quote that of all those received gives the reader the most complete sense of the book's thesis.

One editor at Simon & Schuster told me that whenever he does a book with an extensive photo insert section, he tries to give away the book's thesis in the captions, knowing that browsers are so often drawn to them.

Finally, an introduction that spills the beans provides a resource for the marketing of your book. The publicity department will use your introduction to generate the material sent to the review media. Publicists will reread your introduction before they speak with review editors. In turn, review editors rely on introductions in the bound galleys to help them decide whether to assign the book for review, and if so to whom. And if your book is reviewed, don't be surprised to find words from your introduction sneaking into those reviews. Why? Because using an author's own summary of his thesis protects the reviewer against the accusation that he has characterized it incorrectly. Experienced reviewers know where to look for such summaries—in your introduction.

So for all sorts of reasons—to help your publisher publish your book, to make clear to reviewers why your book is important, and, most of all, to pull in readers—use your introduction to lay out the major question driving your book and the answer you propose. But don't try to do more than lay it out. Don't try to prove it superior to the standard interpretation. You have the rest of the book to do that.

In addition to spilling the beans, a good introduction gets into any problematic aspect of the book and answers presumed questions. Perhaps you might have to explain why, given the existing literature, there is a place for yet another book. Or how you obtained access to information not available to other researchers. Or why your book contradicts highly respected previous scholarship. The introduction is the place to raise and answer these questions.

Now let us turn to the one exception to these general rules about introduction writing—biography. Here a different tradition has established itself. Generally speaking, because biography is the nonfiction genre closest to fiction, in that it is much more about character than other forms of serious nonfiction, the introduction to a biography will generally be structured around a dramatic retelling of a single moment in the subject's life. It need not be a moment that produced great consequences. Nor does it have to be a public moment. But it should be a moment particularly revealing of those character traits the author believes to be predictive of the subject's eventually becoming the biography-worthy person he or she became.

An excellent biographical introduction (he calls it a "prologue") appears in Edmund Morris's *The Rise of Theodore Roosevelt*. There he tells the story of Roosevelt's inauguration day celebrations after his election in 1904, as he shook hands with the thousands and thousands of well-wishers who had come to the White House to greet the president personally. For most men this would have been an unpleasant and utterly exhausting public duty. For Roosevelt, as Morris so vividly tells it, the day was immensely satisfying, which helps explain Roosevelt's almost missionary zeal for connecting with the American people.

Let's now address the changes those of you revising a dissertation for potential publication must make in your introduction. Recognize that as your role has changed—from acolyte to authority—so too must your mind-set change. When you wrote the introduction to your dissertation you were the student trying to prove to the experts—your dissertation committee—that you had fully mastered the existing literature. Thus, much of your dissertation introduction was likely taken up with a literature review. "This is what so and so said on the topic, versus what thus and such said." That's over. Now you're the expert talking to other scholars less informed than you on this particular topic and to the general reader. Dump the literature review entirely. You don't need it anymore. Then, follow the rules set out above and do so with confidence. If a publishing house has given you a contract, you have earned the right to speak as an authority.

Similarly, if you are writing a work of sociology or economics, don't waste introduction time paying homage to Gramsci or to any other authority in whose footsteps you are trying to walk. Do not discuss the model in which your research is framed. That's dissertation stuff, not the stuff of trade books.

Chapter 1: Your Opening Chapter

You and your publisher have induced your reader to buy the book and read it. Now, how do you get your story going?

Some authors plunge into the story, and this often works just fine. But before you do so, consider one powerful alternative—the context chapter.

Earlier in this book, in the chapter on putting together a table of contents, I described three types of chapters: context chapters, which, as the name suggests, give context to the main thrust of your book; narrative chapters, which forward the story; and break-narrative chapters, which discuss related side issues. Many books can benefit from a context chapter before the narrative begins. Here's why.

Many authors underestimate the time it takes to establish background. But too much context in an opening narrative chapter creates narrative drag. As an editor, I was never surprised when I received a forty-five page opening chapter from a new writer. The cover letter would generally say, "I know this should be shorter, but I don't know what to drop."

The answer is nothing. You need two chapters. You need separate chapters to do justice both to the background material and to the narrative's opening. And you need separate chapters to develop the right pace for the book.

In describing a book's opening chapter, editors like to say that a good book opens at a nice, loping pace. Some use the words "less is more." They are telling you that you need to ease your readers into your book, not overwhelm them. In the first couple of chapters, the saturation point for most readers is low. The wise author provides a broad foundation only, even if it means leaving some details to be filled in later.

Let's say you are writing a book about a famous Puritan woman. Yes, we all know about the Puritan work ethic and that the Puritans were a Protestant sect that settled in the New England area in colonial times. But not much more.

So instead of plunging into your story, write an opening chapter about that Puritan world generally, about its religious beliefs, its values, its social structure, the way its people lived, and the

Puritan way of death. At the beginning of the chapter you might talk about Puritanism as a religious movement, generally, but as you get deeper into the chapter, move the reader closer and closer to the time, place, and characters of the story you are about to tell. So that by the end of the chapter you are not talking about Puritanism in general but about Puritanism in the Connecticut town of Y, in the year XXXX as it played out in the house of A, who happens, of course, to be the character your story focuses on.

Similarly, if you are writing about how dotcom businesses introduced broad-based stock options as a common form of worker compensation, spend a chapter educating the reader about the concept of corporate compensation schemes generally, about the sharp distinctions made in most businesses between the compensation packages structured for upper management and those for everyone else; talk about the difference between bonuses and stock options, about exercised options and what businesses call hanging options. This will prepare the reader for what you want to contribute to the subject, and why your contribution has social as well as accounting significance.

At times, the right context chapter calls for venturing out of the author's area of expertise. Doing so can be unnerving, especially for academics, but it can also enrich your book.

Recently I worked with an author writing a biography set in Scotland. Scotland is one of those charismatic places people wish they knew better. One part of Scotland, Edinburgh to be exact, is built on a once-active group of volcanoes. And the story was a geology story. Here was a perfect opportunity to write a fun context chapter.

Doing so required the author to do lots of reading outside his area of expertise, to allow him to talk about the revolt of Bonnie Prince Charlie, the intellectuals who constituted the Scottish Enlightenment, as well as the geological terrain of Edinburgh. No rule says you can't enrich a science book with a little history, or a history book with science.

Your First Narrative Chapter

The time has come to begin your book's story. Earlier I referred to good narrative needing two simultaneously running stories. I also talked about the importance of never losing sight of the human side of your story.

Here is one more piece of advice. Fiction people have a wonderful expression: Trust your story. The same applies to the early chapters of a serious nonfiction narrative. Let the story run for a while with very little interference from you. Do not try to shape the story to your needs. Use your research to educate your reader, so that when you start arguing for your interpretation, you will be challenging your now reasonably well-informed readers, not confusing them.

Section Breaks or Break-Narrative Chapters

In the previous chapter I described a science book that had three parts—the first explained the Newtonian clockwork universe; the second Einstein's theories; and the third, the effect of those theories on modern physics. That's just the type of book that benefits from section essays.

Section essays are two- or three-page minibreaks before the start of each section (some authors skip the first section essay) to give the reader the broader picture before the author gets into the fine distinctions he will make. Well done, they are a wonderful addition to any book.

Break-narrative chapters, on the other hand, break from the narrative drive of the manuscript to treat an important but tangential topic in greater detail. But they also work well in providing readers with what I refer to as a "freebie" education on an interesting side topic.

Several years ago, I edited a book by Dr. Robert Gallo, then an NIH (National Institutes of Health) AIDS researcher, on the scientific work his lab had done to make possible the first HIV blood test. In discussing the book with colleagues, friends, and others, I learned that many were curious about the NIH. "What exactly is it?" friends asked me. I, in turn, asked the scientists in Dr. Gallo's lab and was surprised that they too knew very little of their employer's history. So Dr. Gallo put in a wonderful break-narrative chapter telling how the NIH was created, all the good work it had done over the years, and the sad story of its one dramatic failure, when it allowed a batch of improperly deactivated polio virus to be distributed, infecting about eighty previously healthy children with polio. While I can't imagine that too many people would buy a book-length history of the NIH, I know that many enjoyed reading that chapter.

But Let's Say It's Still Not All Coming Together

I've probably made writing your book sound too easy. I know that for many authors just getting started is a nightmare. For other authors getting started is easy. But then halfway through, they hit a wall. And now a contract clock is ticking. What do you do?

First, recognize that you are not alone. One of my authors described spending nearly two months at his computer, hour upon hour, day after day, playing the same computer game, until he was just short of brain dead. Why did he waste all those hours? He kept telling himself that if he could just "left brain" it a few minutes longer, a fully coherent first chapter would effortlessly spill out of him first draft. Just like the genie obediently comes out of the lantern after a few good rubs.

It's not going to happen that way. Writing, as I suggested earlier, clarifies thinking, and until you sit down and try out various strategies for pulling off your book, the clarity will not be there. While you may not admit this to yourself, you somehow sense it. So you stare at a blank page wondering when, if ever, that clarity will show itself. That's also why you resist letting the few words that do manage to force their way onto the page develop into paragraphs and then pages of writing. You fear that you are not writing what is really needed, and so you self-censor and choke off approaches that might prove fruitful if you allowed yourself to put them on the page and work on them.

I wish I could offer a substitute for what editors refer to as the brute force method of getting started, but there is none. You must sit there and force out sentences and then paragraphs, no matter how off the mark you fear they are.

But here are a few tips that may help ease you through the process.

First, if you are having trouble starting, don't begin at the beginning of the book. Certainly don't begin with the introduction. Allow me one more chess analogy. José Raúl Capablanca, the great chess master and teacher, insisted that those chess teachers who started with chess openings harmed their students. The new player could not possibly understand the value in various openings until he understood the end game. In a similar way, you cannot write your introduction until you know exactly the book you are introducing. You tell your reader in the introduction how the book will end. How can you do that until you know the ending? In fact, writing your introduction before you write your book may box you into trying to write a book you cannot write. You may not be able to get there from here.

So where do you begin? Often, there is one chapter you just know you can write. It is likely a chapter filled with such obvious narrative tension that you've been thinking about writing it from the moment you decided to write your book. Write that chapter first.

This approach will not be without its problems, especially if you pick a chapter in the second half of the book. In addition to the psychological barrier to starting anywhere but at the beginning, you won't know what has been previously laid out. But this liability can be turned into an asset if it forces you to go back and review your original table of contents to determine what revisions need to be made based on your final research findings.

Or you can write the chapter as if everything your reader needs has been developed in previous chapters. Remember, you are not really writing a chapter of your book. You are in a break-out-of-the-block exercise, giving yourself the opportunity to develop your own voice and style and figure out how to lay in facts, comment on them, and move through time.

Don't worry if you never finish writing that chapter. Once you have broken out of your writer's block, you can set the chapter aside, finished or not. Or, if you prefer, go on and write the remainder of the book from that chapter forward. Then go back and write the first half of the book. You don't have to worry about writing the book in an order that seems to make no sense. If it gets you writing and causes you to come to the next day's work with enthusiasm, the plan has worked.

Don't be too hard on yourself if you produce just a few pages each day for the first several weeks. One of my authors recalled how she got herself started by setting a minimum standard for herself; she would not stop working for the day, no matter how many hours she had to sit at her computer, until she produced at least three new pages each day. "Three pages a day!" I can hear some of you muttering. "At that rate, I'll need a decade to produce a finished manuscript." You won't. Things will snowball once you get some momentum. But in the beginning, as long as you meet some minimum standard for the day, don't beat up on yourself. Give yourself a chance to find your writing voice and rhythm.

One last point on writer's block. Part of every author's problem is that he fears, maybe most of all, that he will not be putting out the best work he's capable of. Just know that on the day you turn your manuscript into your editor you have not lost all influence over it. After your editor has read it and given you comments, it will come back to you. Then a copy editor will make suggestions regarding grammar and style, and once again it will come back to you. At both of these stages you will have an opportunity to give it a final polish, if your editor and copy editor have not done it for you.

But what if your problem is not writer's block per se. It's not that you can't get started. Perhaps you were offered a contract primarily because you are one of the world's leading experts in your topic. Having read this book, you now realize that your book has no question it wants to ask and no answer it wants to provide. Just things it wants to talk about. How do you proceed?

In that situation you have two choices. If your subject matter is particularly exciting, go ahead and write what I call the "guided tour." In other words, go data bit to data bit, talking about what is new and exciting in your field. You won't write a great book, but you'll probably be able to produce something publishable.

The second alternative is to try to reconceptualize your book, to give it a provocative question to answer. If you succeed at this, use the advice in chapter 3 to help you write a table of contents that focuses only on those parts of your data that support your question and answer. You will discover that a great deal of what you know on the subject is left out. But what remains should fall into a coherent narrative.

Along these same lines, you might make your project more manageable by structuring it in a narrative–break-narrative format. Let's say for example, you are the world's leading scholar on daydreams. You are responsible for important research, and you have insights into how daydreaming colors personality, has an impact on the lives we lead, whatever. But beyond that you haven't a clue how to proceed. Everything you've written so far sounds very much like a popularized version of a text you wrote two years ago for graduate students.

Look for a single story you can tell. For instance, the story might be about a research project in which you discovered X. Is there enough there to follow the research project, step by step from conceptualization through funding through discovery? That at least gives you a narrative frame.

But that frame may not allow you to discuss rich aspects of your topic. That's where the break-narrative chapters come in. Every even chapter, or every second or third even chapter, take a break from the narrative and discuss in expository language broader issues related to daydreaming, for instance, daydreaming and sociability, daydreaming and intelligence, daydreaming and identity. The narrative chapters move the reader along and the break-narrative chapters allow you to put some meat on the topic.

And once again, *Audience, Audience, Audience.*

In Chapter 1, I advised you to define your core audience—those committed readers who regularly buy books in a particular field— and shape the proposal for that audience.

The same rules about core audience come back into play when you write your book. No matter how interdisciplinary your topic (climate and history) (medicine and sociology) or how wide-ranging your research, write your book to a core audience. Let's take a minute to go over this again because it will help you make hundreds of helpful little decisions.

If you are writing a science book, write for repeat science book buyers. You may desperately want nonscience book buyers as readers. And if you get really good reviews, or your topic has the sex appeal to attract a wider audience, you may attract this other audience. But you still write for the core audience. You won't turn off the non-core audience by writing for the serious science book reader. To the contrary, they want your book because it will help them think about science the way a committed science reader does.

What if you are writing a history of the city—do you define your core audience as history readers or urban studies readers? Here's a more difficult variation of the same question. You are by training a sociologist. Your book is about business and you would much prefer to write a book for the business market, a much larger market, possibly because many business people can buy your book on their expense accounts, than for the sociology market. Who's your core audience?

If you are addressing typical business-book issues, the core market is business book readers. But if I were you, I'd pick up a few business books to make sure I was correctly gauging this audience's tastes.

More likely, that you are writing about business is less important than the type of reader who will respond to your approach. If your book is getting at issues in the sociology of powerful organizations rather than how to be a better manager, you are writing for a sociology audience. Those business people with an academic interest in the sociology of powerful organizations may still buy your book. If they do, most will expect to read a sociologically informed analysis. So once again, shape the book to lock in the sociology market. It may be small, but at least it will be interested in the types of questions you ask and answer.

If your publisher knows the book business, it will position and sell the book to the sociology market and not try to pass it off as a business book. Again, writing your book for a core audience does not mean that no one outside that core audience will be reading your book. It's just that long experience has taught the publishing industry that compromising the appeal of the book within the core audience in a frantic attempt to broaden its market is a self-defeating endeavor.

Once you've defined your audience, you must define its level of sophistication. An important law book is likely to attract legal scholars, practicing lawyers, law buffs, political scientists, and a surprisingly large number of people who follow politics and law and have an interest in better understanding legal issues. So which among these readers do you write for?

The answer is that if you want to write serious nonfiction, and if you want your work to be taken seriously, you never dumb down. You always write up. Writing down runs the risk of having your book read like a young adult book. Assume a high reader level of intellectual sophistication, even though you suspect their knowledge of your particular subject may not be high. Fully explain, but do not simplify.

While you never dumb down, neither do you ever go technical on your reader. Every discipline has shorthand terms. Here's an example. Constitutional law scholars often use the shorthand term *incorporation*. It describes the special role of the Fourteenth Amendment, which, in essence, makes certain Bill of Rights protections (originally applicable only to federal government actions) applicable to state government actions. *Incorporation* became an important term in constitutional law because it evokes a series of cases, all of which turned on that concept. If you are writing to other constitutional lawyers, they likely know the ins and outs of those cases. Scientists have a number of shorthand terms, as do sociologists and philosophers. But unless you, want to limit your audience to your intradisciplinary peers, don't employ these terms without taking the time to explain the need for them. Educate your readers fully before you rely on intradisciplinary shorthand.

At times certain technical language seems to have been created not to serve an important technical need but solely to establish the author as an insider. Let's take the term *a gendered view of the eighteenth century*. All that term describes is a view of history from a feminist perspective. Those using the term are signaling that they are familiar with the wealth of literature playing out the consequences of having social institutions organized from a male perspective. You can't assume your reader has read what you've read. You certainly don't want her to feel diminished for not having done so. If you want to make a point about the differences between the experiences and treatment of men and women in the period, make the point directly. If your point is that this disparate treatment is part of a pattern, show the pattern. Then the reader can come to her own conclusions.

Line-by-Line

All this leads naturally into how you communicate what you want to say.

I include this section not to produce an all-purpose writing book. Readers with general questions about their own writing style should consult one of the many good books on grammar, usage, syntax, and idiom. But three interrelated writing problems common to serious nonfiction need to be addressed. They are: coded language; writing that tries to say too much in one gulp; and writing that suggests by its imprecision a less than precise mind.

Let's begin with the easiest problem to solve—coded language. Question: What's wrong with each of the following?

Each of these realms of cultural creation is now linked to . . .

Or this:

The popularization of spaces as a ritualized source of pleasure promotes a circumstantial and superficial . . .

Or this:

The rise to near hegemony of the ideology of . . .

Such language will produce an audible sigh in most experienced editors. Why does anyone voluntarily write this way? Several years ago, I worked on an excellent manuscript that was, unfortunately, sprinkled with these academic phrases, none of which contributed either to the book's scholarship or its narrative. I kept crossing them out, and the author kept putting them back in. "Tell me the purpose of them," I finally said. "To get tenure," he responded.

That's the only good reason I have ever heard for using this kind of vocabulary. Its subliminal message is "only authorized personnel read on."

For those of you who believe that academic publication (as opposed to tenure committees) favors this type of writing, listen up. There is enormous pressure on university presses to acquire bigger books, that is, books that have bigger audiences. If you want your book to be sought after by multiple university presses, write a book that can be read and enjoyed by any intelligent person. Put no barriers in the way of reaching a wider audience. At one time, reviewers, generally chosen from within the author's own discipline, bought into this game of using coded language to communicate that this club doesn't want you as a member. But now most reviewers criticize it as aggressively as do editors. Here is a paragraph from a review in the *New York Times:*

Mr.—'s book is less than nifty in other respects, however, especially in the way it is written: stodgily enough to make you think this author had pebbles in his word processor. His prose is burdened with an academic jargon ("spatial deprivation" applied to the condition of children living in trailers, "demographic dislocations" for the arrival of non-whites into previously white neighborhoods) that takes the juice out of his depictions, leaving behind dehydrated abstraction. —"The Red, White and Blue Plate Special" by Richard Bernstein, *New York Times*, Wednesday, March 14, 2001, p. E9.

Writing That Tries to Say Too Much in One Gulp

Read the following:

A recent skirmish has also developed on the flank—dissenting social scientists, grasping some of the tools of evolutionary theory, are calling themselves evolutionary psychologists and trying to wade into this debate more respectfully than did the previous neo-Darwinian combatants—where they are (perhaps reluctantly) admitting to the complexity of culture—and the variances we continue to see even in the best scientific models of behavior and how individual people actually behave—all the while promoting the merits of applying the tools of evolution to understanding human behavior at the aggregate level.

Most of the paragraphs in this book are shorter than this one sentence. This author needs to break up his writing into multiple sentences and make sure the qualifiers are all necessary. If they are included, they should be separate sentences.

A recent skirmish has also developed on the flank **of this debate.** Dissenting social scientists, grasping **(adopting?)** some of the tools of evolutionary theory, are calling themselves evolutionary psychologists. **They** are trying to wade **(step)** into this debate more respectfully than did the previous neo-Darwinian combatants. **Many admit** (perhaps reluctantly) to the complexity of culture **[no**

dash] and to the variances we continue to see even in the best scientific models of behavior. ~~and how individual people actually behave~~. **But most continue to advocate for an evolutionary understanding of** ~~—all the while promoting the merits of applying the tools of evolution to understanding~~-human behavior at the aggregate level.

Here is another.

The restoration of the monarchy, imposed under pressure—although some say the pressure was exogenous, especially that applied by the United States, through its insidious corruption of local figures by CIA operatives—still managed to thrive for a period of twenty years, producing some of the most important technological, at least from the point of defending the restored monarchy against its more aggressive neighbors, advances of the twentieth century.

You, reader, work on this one. Hint: the author has parenthetical mania.

And here is its cousin, qualifier mania.

The ascension ritual and the pledges of loyalty by the royal ministers have been seen by scholars, though concededly not by all scholars, to have been some sort of milestone on the road to world power—though certainly not the only milestone—and not to liberal democracy. Rather than a response to a popular desire to have a less autocratic regime—such a desire would have been difficult to express—the ritual was more an expedient concession to the king, who might otherwise have wreaked revenge on those who had opposed his ascension to the throne, though admittedly any attempt on the part of the king to do so might have thrown the country into civil war.

As they say in the war colleges, if you want to move forward, you cannot always fully protect your flanks.

Imprecise Writing

Once again note the difference between creative writing and writing serious nonfiction. In creative writing you may want to leave a certain ambiguity, to encourage the reader to use his own imagination to help the writer. Occasional poetic passages can enrich serious nonfiction, especially biography—*So the time had come and the time had gone, and with it the years to come. For the wall is high though the edge is thin*. But don't go too long without letting your reader know exactly what's happening. For the most part, imprecise writing in serious nonfiction creates the sensation of walking on sand, an irritating and frustrating sensation.

> **A broad group of employees have never had the opportunity to own and control this much future wealth, which represents the next wave of economic development.**

What, you should be asking, is the antecedent of "which?" At times this problem of an unclear antecedent can lead to unintentional humor. Witness the following description of an absentminded professor an author had in college.

> **By his second step across the front of the classroom, well before he reached his desk, he was already delivering his lecture. As he spoke he looked for a place to rest his hat and his briefcase. He placed his hat on the only open corner of his desk but then had no place for his briefcase, so he removed his hat from the desk and placed it on the chair behind the desk. Within a few minutes he wanted to sit, so he removed the hat from the chair and sat on it.**

On the chair or on the hat?

Here is another with that same sense of soft focus:

> By early summer they had managed to wrest control from him, but only kicking and screaming.

Who was doing the kicking and screaming?

Try one more.

> Having come so little distance in so much time, it finally occurred to him that he had to consider changing tactics.

This is the classic dangling participle. The implied subject of the introductory phrase must be the stated subject of the following clause. Grammatically correct is: *Having come so little distance in so much time, he finally faced that he had to consider changing tactics.* More precise is: *Recognizing that he had come so little distance in so much time, he considered changing tactics.* Why? Because it was the *recognition* that he had traveled so little distance in so much time, not his having traveled it, that caused him to reconsider his tactics.

I offer these examples not because I am a stickler for grammar or to make the point that you must be one to be accepted as a good writer.* While having a good grammar book at your elbow will be helpful to any writer, reading and rereading your own writing carefully to make sure it states exactly what you intended, and only what you intended, offers the best guarantee that your writing will not create the sense of a fragmented mind. This should be your major concern.

---

* As you may have noted, the title of this book, *Thinking like Your Editor,* is grammatically substandard. But *Thinking as Your Editor Does* just didn't have the same ring to it.

Epilogues

Once you have told your story, offered your interpretation, and defended your thesis, the last decision is whether to include an epilogue. Though by no means necessary, epilogues can be extremely valuable in bringing the reader up to date on information that is not part of your narrative, especially when events have run ahead of your main story. Before you decide to include one, make sure you have something to say that will interest your readers, not just you and your colleagues. If you decide to write one, write it in the style of the introduction, as explanatory writing, not narrative.

From here on in, you're on your own. Good luck in writing your manuscript. The time has come to move on to the last chapter in this book—how to be published well.

Part Three

From Editing to Marketing to Publication

Chapter Eight

How to Be Published Well

Y̲ou've turned in your manuscript. You're probably both eager and nervous to hear what your editor thinks.

There may well be a long delay before you hear anything, so you'll have to be patient, even if you've made real sacrifices to meet your own delivery deadline. And it may take even longer before you actually receive an editorial letter or an edited manuscript. For when your manuscript arrives, it rarely finds your editor's desk empty. And herein lies the problem.

For the year or so that you've been writing your book, your editor has also been busy, signing up new projects, editing others, and helping to publish yet another group. And while editors must learn to juggle many competing roles, most have difficulty starting a new editing job while still in the middle of one not yet complete.

So here's your first lesson in how to be published well. Start off on the right foot with your editor. When you are ready to turn in your manuscript, send your editor an e-mail, saying "I've put it in the mail today. Hope you like it." Then turn your attention elsewhere. (In a moment I'll give you a long list of things to do in this wait-and-see period.) Do not ask your editor to give your manuscript a "quick read over the weekend." Do not call the editor if you don't hear from her in a week. If you don't hear from her for a month, do not assume that she hates your manuscript. And never, never tell an editor that your schedule provides only a limited window of opportunity to go over her comments and make changes. It is not your place to schedule your editor's time to suit your convenience; given the fact that you signed a contract that requires you to go over the edited manuscript, then the copyedited manuscript, as well as what are called "first-pass" pages, you'd be wise to keep your own calendar flexible, rather than boxing off dates.

Why the tough talk? To start you off right with your editor.

Editing, like writing, requires large blocks of time. And that's one thing successful editors have too little of. In fact, publishing house offices are generally such bustling enterprises these days that most editors make no attempt to edit during the nine-to-five workday. Instead, they will take your manuscript home and sit down with it after dinner (or after they have put their kids to bed) or on weekends, until they are far enough into it to be able to justify working at home for a couple of days to finish it without interruption. Now do you get the picture?

So how long should you wait? If you haven't heard a word in a month, send an e-mail. "I'm wondering if you'll be able to take a look at my manuscript soon." If you don't get an answer, don't panic and don't bristle. Although you seem not to have received an answer, you've gotten one. That editor has not yet found that clear block of time needed to deal with your manuscript. Be especially considerate if you have turned in your own manuscript six months to a year late, throwing the editor's schedule off. Nothing upsets an editor more than an author who has requested additional time, been given that time, and probably more time after that, and then starts nagging the editor the week the manuscript hits her desk.

Eventually your turn will come. What kind of editing can you expect? That depends on four factors—how much work and what kind of work your manuscript needs; whether your editor feels he or she can make a contribution to your manuscript by editing it; whether you communicate a receptivity to editing (editors are listening very carefully for signals from you about how aggressively they can go at your manuscript); and finally, sad but true, how important your book is on her list.

Here's what happens from the time your editor gets to your work. Your editor will read your manuscript and form an initial impression. The first question he or she will ask is: Is this manuscript publishable in its current form?

For instance, let's say you've turned in a thousand-page manuscript and you are under contract to write a 350-page manuscript. You tell your publisher that you really feel you can't do justice to your topic in fewer pages. You may be right. If your editor agrees and can convince management to accept a much longer manuscript, no problem. But if not, after a couple of suggestions, the manuscript will be returned to you for cutting. When you resubmit, it goes to the bottom of the pile.

But if your problems are more severe—let's say you have a very weak structure, or no strong argument appears to be driving the book, or the book seems to be drifting rudderless—your editor may be up against some hard choices. Editors will do a great deal of work on a manuscript that is even three-quarters of the way there, but they will not start from scratch. And for good reason. There is no way to do good editing on a manuscript that doesn't know what it is trying to achieve. In that situation, the editor can opt for either of two decisions. The first, and more benign, is to suggest that you use the remaining portion of your advance (or some part of it) to hire the services of a freelance editor. The second is to suggest you try to place your manuscript with another publisher.

Let's consider each separately.

Freelance editing does not come cheaply anymore, as well it shouldn't. The cost of such help can run from $7,500 to $25,000, and more, depending on what has to be done. For most authors, there will be at least this much money still available in the unpaid portion of the advance. If you find yourself in this situation, you would be foolish to focus on how much money goes to the freelance editor. Think instead about what that freelancer can do for you: allow your book to be published and allow you to keep the money already given you on signing and any other money due you above the freelancer's fee, as well as royalties should the book sell.

More troubling is the situation in which the editor feels he cannot go ahead with the project. If that happens, you are entitled to a letter from your editor specifically telling you what's wrong with the manuscript and giving you an opportunity to correct the problem. But you are more likely to get real help in a telephone call, because it is far less time consuming for an editor to tell you verbally what's wrong than to put it in writing, especially these days, when such letters may have to be approved by legal departments. But if the editor thinks you will either crash under the bad news or react defensively, he or she will simply clam up. Or talk solely to your agent. Or talk only in the most general terms to you. So keep your wits about you. If you find yourself in such a situation, you will wish you had taken on a literary agent to represent you. First because your editor is less likely to pull the plug on you if you are represented by an influential literary agent, and second because that agent is in a better position to negotiate with your publishing house for time you need to revise the manuscript and/or place it with another house.

I don't want to make too much of this problem, though the possibility is one every author faces. The vast majority of manuscripts put under contract are accepted as delivered. But if you have dramatically changed the project from that described in your proposal, or you simply can't fulfill commitments you made in the proposal, your editor has the right to say this is not the book I contracted for. If your manuscript is at all publishable, a good agent should be able to place it with another publisher, although possibly for a smaller advance. My guess is that something less than 5 percent of projects given contracts are not accepted when completed and delivered.

But let's look at the bright side. Most likely your editor will be basically happy with the manuscript, at least in terms of its being a solid first draft. How will you know? She will tell you. But don't expect gushing praise. Your editor may be many things to you, but she is not your mother. Busy editors have no time to stroke your creative psyche.

Now, what kind of editing can you expect? A lot depends upon how your editor defines good editing. When I worked on a manuscript, my primary concerns were those expressed in this book—to make sure: solid argument skills drive the narrative; each chapter has a point and that the point of the chapter contributes to the overall point of the book; that the manuscript as written highlights the newness and breadth of the research findings.

But down the hall from me were editors who were much more concerned with the beauty of the writing. Line by line, they would painstakingly recast phrases and sentences. Would I have done the same on their manuscripts and would they have revised structure and argument on mine? I'd like to think so, but I also know that editors do the work they do best and feel most comfortable doing. And that varies from editor to editor.

The second factor that determines the type of editing you receive is how confident the editor is talking about your topic. Recently I had a situation in which a first-time author I agented turned in a manuscript that didn't make clear what it was trying to achieve and why these goals were important. The editor correctly identified that the manuscript was not working, but didn't know enough physics to dig in the way an editor must, aggressively querying the author with probing questions. The author felt he had not received the help he was entitled to, especially as a first-time author, and the editor regretted that he could not provide that help. In this case, a compromise was worked out, with outside help brought in. If you find yourself in such a situation, where the editor says that your project is not working but can't really help you revise it, you may want to talk to your agent about hiring freelance help. Or about moving your project to another house and editor, even if it means taking a smaller advance. This is why, earlier in this book, I advised you to take into consideration more than simply the size of the advance offered you before signing a contract. If your editor does not have broad experience working on manuscripts like yours, she will have little to offer if you get into trouble.

Let me also say that it is much easier for an editor to say why a manuscript isn't working than to figure out how to correct it. The first is obvious from a quick read. The second takes both time and a lot of mulling over. So if your editor comes back to you saying he or she has read the material and needs to send you an editorial letter, but that editorial letter doesn't arrive for several additional weeks, don't assume the editor has lost interest in you. She is thinking about your project and holding off writing that letter until she has a firmer idea how best to make the book work.

There are certain situations in which editors will do little or no work on the delivered manuscripts. Unfortunately, probably 30 percent or more of manuscripts fall into this category, which is why so many authors feel they are not getting enough editing. Here are some of those situations.

You've done a competent job. The manuscript is what it is, is basically good, and editing won't dramatically increase its value. In that situation, most editors will simply pass the manuscript on to copy editing. You should take pride in having done a good job.

Or, you've written the book you promised to write in your proposal. While it is close enough to what your proposal promised and so can't be rejected, it is not very good. Your editor is not really excited about it. In this case, some editors will make a perfunctory attempt at improving the manuscript. But few will really dig in. Here's the rationale: If you were not prepared to put more time into making your book as good as it could be, why should your editor expend his or her own valuable time trying to make it work?

Finally, there are certain manuscripts, often bought from powerful agents for a great deal of money, that have to be published, whether they work or not. This is especially true when the author is a very important person and the agent is breathing down the editor's neck. But if editing won't improve the manuscript, smart editors won't waste their time trying to do the impossible. Many of the authors who are most angry about not getting editing fall into this category.

If you want your editor to go at your manuscript aggressively, tell her that you want her to do whatever she thinks necessary to improve the manuscript. You may still not get editing, for one of the reasons outlined above. And if you do get exactly what you asked for, you may not be pleased. Those first three chapters that come back to you—to test whether you really want editing—may have numerous new lines added by your editor, paragraphs moved about, and pages slashed, as well as queries embedded throughout the text.

Your first reaction will be shock. After all, this editor raved about your proposal. And gave you a big contract. All very true. But your proposal wasn't for publication, and there is a big difference between writing twenty good pages of a proposal or writing sample and putting together an entire book. There are certain elements of pacing and narrative, as well as how you lay in an argument, that experienced editors can improve dramatically. If you let them.

If your manuscript does come back with extensive editing, try to accept most of the changes. Generally speaking, editors know what they are doing. And if they find that you have rejected too much of their work, they will back off and do less on the rest of the manuscript. Or move on to the next project.

A frequent complaint of authors is that in trying to tighten up prose, editors will occasionally edit out a fine distinction the author was trying to make, or in some other subtle way change the author's meaning. If this occurs, don't assume the editor was taking a cavalier attitude toward your work. What likely occurred is that the fine distinction you were trying to make was not clear. While you may not want to take the simplifying changes your editor suggested, you do want to go back to your original and rework the text, so that what you intend to say is absolutely clear. Or you can always "stet" a change and explain in the margin why the editing didn't work. But don't get personal and don't get huffy.

If I can leave you with one last message about how to get good editing for your manuscript it is this. Editors respect hard-working authors. They respect authors who give them their best and then graciously accept criticism. Some feel that far too many authors take the money and then produce second-rate books. Your best protection against being ignored by your editor is to produce a book that excites your editor, one with rich research, a clear argument, and a good narrative.

Now let's return to all the things you can do while waiting for that editorial letter or comments embedded in your manuscript. This is no time to slack off.

If there are illustrations in your book, make sure you have a permission for each illustration (credits) and a caption line ready to go. Don't attach captions or permissions to the illustrations. Create a caption manuscript and then type each caption sequentially—from 1 to 10, for example—keyed to a number you put on the back of each illustration. The same goes for permissions. In addition, if you have quoted extensively from any source, make sure you have all your text permissions ready for copy editing. If you don't know how to go about obtaining these submissions, ask; someone in-house will set you on the right track.

Next, prepare what publishers refer to as "front matter." You will have to tell a publisher whether or not you want your book to contain a quotation page (or epigraph), a dedication page, and an acknowledgments page. If so, begin to prepare the copy for each. If you haven't already prepared a table of contents page, do so now. Remember, the table of contents in your book is very different from the table of contents in your submission package. If you don't recall the ways in which they differ, review Chapter 3 of this book.

Third, ask yourself if you really have the best title and subtitle for your book. If you are not sure, your publisher will throw your book into a "title" meeting, where editors, senior and junior, publicists and marketers sit around a table brainstorming, trying to come up with a title that will resonate with the book-buying public, all based on a smattering of information about your book. Title meetings can be hilarious events, especially as everyone becomes creativity-weary, the primary symptom of which is a contagion of giggled absurdities. Generally speaking, you don't want a title committee to title your book.

So let's talk a minute about what makes a good title. I always look for one that goes to the heart of the dilemma driving your book. Let me give you an example.

Recently I worked with two authors writing a work of narrative nonfiction. Theirs is the story of the 1925 dog race to bring diphtheria serum to an isolated Alaska town in the middle of winter, when no planes flew and the water route was frozen over. The working title was *The Serum Run*. But that's what I call a "topic" title, not a dilemma title. Later on, the authors came up with a much better title: *Icebound*. (After we placed the project with a major house, another book, about a doctor who discovered she had cancer while trapped in a research project in Antarctica, was published as *Ice Bound*.) Why was *Icebound* such a good title? Because it described the dilemma of the book—that ice closes off the sea route to Nome, Alaska, nine months of the year, and the outbreak occurred in the middle of this icebound period. In the other book, the dilemma is similar, even though it takes place at the opposite pole.

Similarly, the sample proposal in the back of this book began with the working title: *Henry Ward Beecher: A Biography*. It is now called *Breach of Faith*. Why is this a better title? Because the question driving that biography is how could Henry Ward Beecher, a religious leader whom so many people trusted, violate that trust by having affairs with members of his congregation?

In addition to reworking your book title, you might also go over each and every chapter title. Use what you have learned in this book about the disparate roles of chapters. If you are writing a context chapter, the subject matter can provide the title; if you are writing a narrative chapter, the title should revolve around the point the chapter is trying to make. If you revise any titles, be sure to revise your table of contents page.

Now you are ready to help your book get off to a good start by creating a little buzz about it. How do you get that buzz going? By making sure that influential members of the core audience know that your book is coming.

So, for example, if you are writing a work of history, try to get yourself on a panel discussing your topic at the next OAH or AHA meeting. When you are announced, the moderator will tell the audience that you are the author of a book on the topic that will soon be published. Or if a prominent character in your book was connected with an institution, try to hook up with that institution to see what they may be prepared to do to help talk up the book.

Identify influential people in this field, people whose opinions matter. Write to these people telling them about your book and asking them if you can include them on a list of people to whom your publisher can send prepublication copies for an early quote to be used for publicity purposes. Ideally, you should be prepared to deliver to your publisher a list of about ten people with whom you have previously made contact and who know something about your book.

Look through your book and see if one chapter might be suitable for excerption by a magazine. Don't think about the major magazines. Your publisher will know how to get to these magazines. But there may be a small but extremely important magazine devoted to your topic—a magazine that goes to members of the military, or is published for sailing devotees, or history buffs. Identify those magazines and read several issues to help you determine the type of story they accept, and the word length they prefer. You might also see if they take opinion pieces.

Finally, if your book has newsworthy elements to it, take a minute to put together a bulleted document highlighting either the news value of your book or its most important findings, which your editor can make available to sales and marketing departments. In other words, now that you know your book, identify for yourself and for your publisher why this book is going to have appeal in the marketplace. Doing this will also help you fix your eye on the prize— making your message accessible to the broadest possible audience—as you await your editor's comments and prepare to decide which to accept and which not.

When the marked-up manuscript or editorial letter arrives, confirm how much time you have to make the suggested changes. You and your editor may decide to rush your book onto the next list or hold it off for the following season. (A publishing "season" can be as short as three months or as long as six months, depending on how many times a year that publisher releases new books to the bookstores.) In discussing this with your editor, overestimate how much time you will need. Once an editor puts your book into the seasonal catalog produced for the sales reps to deliver to bookstores, your book has effectively been scheduled for publication. You don't want to leave a hole in your publisher's list.

When editing is complete, your manuscript will next go to copy editing. The job of the copy editor is to style your manuscript for the printer and to eliminate errors of grammar, usage, punctuation, and spelling. But some copy editors will do much more work. They will edit sections of the manuscript that still seem loose or ambiguous. The copyedited manuscript will be sent back to you for review. Authors tell me that many of these copy editors are highly skilled at tightening up prose without altering meaning. You have the final decision regarding how much editing to accept. Be open-minded.

After copy editing, you will receive a typeset version of your manuscript. You cannot rewrite your manuscript once it has been typeset. At this stage you can only make minor adjustments and correct errors introduced by the printer.

Between editing and copy editing, or between copy editing and printed pages, you will likely hear about or be shown catalog copy. Catalog copy is the copy that is prepared for the sales reps and the bookstores to announce each season's new listings from your publisher. Your editor or an in-house advertising department usually writes the copy, though some houses ask the author to write a first draft. Here's what you must know to write good copy.

Catalog copy is not addressed to the ultimate book buyer. It tells booksellers why they should stock the book. How do you write good catalog copy or judge if what your editor shows you is good? You have to imagine that you are talking to the buyer at Barnes & Noble, or Borders, or an independent bookstore, not the ultimate consumer. They want to know who is going to come into their store looking for your book, and why this person is going to want your book and not another book on the same or a similar topic. Catalog copy is not the place to reveal to booksellers either your argument or why you wrote the book. They want to know why others are going to be interested enough to buy your book and who those interested others are.

Here are some tips about what to include, should you be asked to write catalog copy. If there is an anniversary tied to your subject matter coming up—the sixtieth anniversary of the bombing of Pearl Harbor—put that in. If there is a special affinity group who will be particularly interested in your book—kite fliers, the sixties kids, elite college graduates, ex-wives, children of divorce—put that in. If your book first appeared as an article or on the Web and caused a stir, put that in. Or if your book is extremely similar in appeal to another book that was a best seller—after *The Rape of Nanking,* I must have seen ten books, not all about China, whose publishers described them in catalog copy as "the next . . ."—put that in.

Finally, if there is a newsworthy element to your story, make sure that is included.

The only other copy some houses will ask you to write or look over is flap copy. Here you *are* talking to the ultimate consumer. Primarily you want that person to know that there is something here they haven't heard before and can't find in another book. Good flap copy hooks the reader in the first sentence. Go with your strong suit as in: "Based on ten years of research . . ." or "Here is a book for anyone who has wondered . . ." or a provocative question: "Will humans survive the twenty-first century?"

Here are interesting first lines from the flap copy of two very successful books, one a narrative history, the second a business book.

> The ordeal of the whaleship *Essex* was an event as mythic in the nineteenth century as the *Titanic* disaster was in the twentieth. (*In the Heart of the Sea* by Nathaniel Philbrick)

> What if the real power of the Web lay not in the technology behind it but in the profound changes it brings to the way people interact with business? (*The Cluetrain Manifesto* by Rick Levine et al.)

Last, you will be given an opportunity to comment upon your jacket design. What makes a jacket effective? I have always looked to have it meet two requirements. First, the type needs to be legible from a distance. Sound basic? I've seen jackets where the type could not be read from more than arm's length.

Second, a good jacket communicates to the core audience that this is a book that will interest them. Bookstores will turn a particularly attractive jacket face out rather than spine out. But more important than the artistic quality of the jacket is that the jacket reinforces what the title, flap copy, catalog copy, introduction, and the book itself must make clear—who the audience for this book is. The artistic quality of the design must appeal to the core audience for the book. For instance, an avant-garde jacket would not be appropriate on a book appealing to a highly conservative audience.

Don't despair. Despite all these hurdles a finished copy of your book will soon be in your hands. As an editor and as an agent, I have always experienced a certain lift when that first copy of a book I have ushered from proposal to finished book is in my hands. As the author, you will experience an even greater lift.

The final questions this chapter will answer are: What can you expect from marketing and publicity? And how can you work with the bookstores to make your book a success?

You don't have to worry about your book being sent out to prominent print reviewers. Most publishers will send out two to three hundred advance copies of each new book, to make sure it is in the hands of all the major media. But your publisher may ask you to provide the names of smaller, specialized magazines that might review your book.

In addition, a press kit will go out to TV and radio shows pitching your book. The press kit will contain a letter from the publisher's publicist, suggesting why this book might interest viewers or listeners. If interest develops, you will find yourself doing lots of radio phone-ins and perhaps a television show or two.

Some authors will be put on tour; that is, they will be sent to three or four or even ten cities where advance publicity has been arranged.

Will your publisher take out an ad? Perhaps. But don't expect an ad in the *New York Times*. I believe most publisher ads are taken out not to sell the book but to communicate to the rest of the industry the luster of the publisher's list. Which accounts for why so much book advertising is done for books that are already best sellers, and so little for those that need sales. I have never met someone in merchandising or advertising who believes that publisher ads have a profound effect on book sales.

In addition, some of the money that your publisher will spend with booksellers will go toward ads the bookseller places. These seem to be more successful than ads placed by publishers, maybe because they include a convenient place to go out and make the purchase. For most works of serious nonfiction, strong reviews are still the single most predictive factor of the success of a book. They can't create an audience where one doesn't exist, but if there is a strong market or a seducible market for your book, good reviews may induce book buyers already in the bookstore to stop and pick up a well-reviewed book.

If you walk into a bookstore and don't see your book, what should you do? First check out the bookstore. If it's a mall store that carries mostly light reading, recognize that this bookstore is not going to generate sales for your book, even if copies were piled high on a front table.

But if you walk into a bookstore well stocked in hardcover editions of serious nonfiction and your book isn't there, find the manager during a quiet period and ask her about it. Give her a good reason to stock your book. For instance, if it's your hometown bookstore, and you know that your local paper will be running a profile of you, tell the manager. She is there to sell books. Just give her a reason to sell yours.

Similarly if you know that a review is coming from a major magazine or newspaper, tell the manager. You might also offer to autograph copies.

Let me end this chapter with yet another statement about booksellers and book buyers. Remember the story with which I opened this book, about my problem with how a bookseller would be shelving *The Physics of Star Trek*? It just so happens I've become friends with the science buyer I met that day, who is now, as I mentioned in the prologue, a very successful science editor. We recently talked about the business of bookselling. As I listened to her spirited defense of booksellers, I realized that just as I feel the need to tell writers that they must take into account the needs and tastes of the book's audience, so too have booksellers been trying to tell editors and publishers that the decisions they make about which books to stock are dictated by respect for that same audience. If this is a price we have to pay for living in a democratic society—where the general public and not some government agency decides what we publish—who would have it any other way?

Appendix

A
Sample
Proposal
and
Writing
Sample

Breach of Faith: A Biography of Henry Ward Beecher

In the fall of 1986, while still a sophomore at Amherst College with a job in the college archives, I was asked to research a series of exhibits the college planned to present on, of all things, notorious alumni. My first assignment was the Reverend Henry Ward Beecher, class of 1834. I had taken quite a few courses in American history by this time and thought I was fairly knowledgeable, but I had no idea who Henry Ward Beecher was or why he was so notorious. I did know his father's name, however. Like Cotton Mather or Jonathan Edwards before him, the Reverend Lyman Beecher was the last of the famous Puritan ministers, a fire and brimstone Calvinist who preached a harsh form of obeisance to divine will.

But Lyman Beecher, it turns out, was also the father of a large, outspoken, and eccentric family who, for two generations, loomed larger than life on the American stage. As a family, the Beechers possessed a reputation and influence that equaled that of any of the great mythic clans of American history, including the Adamses, the Jameses, the Roosevelts, and the Kennedys. They seemed to fit no ordinary categories—"This country is inhabited by saints, sinners and Beechers," one common saying put it.

As I dug into the archives, Henry Ward Beecher soon began to emerge as the brightest star in a family filled with stars. Like his father, he became a minister. Indeed, all seven sons of Lyman Beecher would become ministers. But Henry's reputation would transcend even the enormous respect typically showed men of the cloth, particularly in that period of our history. More accurately, Henry Ward Beecher would become the closest thing in his age to a media sensation. Newspaper clippings pointed out that on an average Sunday a sermon by the Reverend Henry Beecher drew over 3,000 people to his Brooklyn Heights church. The flow of tourists coming to hear him preach was so great that the papers regularly referred to the Manhattan-to-Brooklyn ferry as "Beecher Boats." Beecher would also write a best-selling novel; he would tour the nation as an ardent abolitionist and as an advocate of the rights of women and workers. By the end of the Civil War, Abraham Lincoln declared Henry Ward Beecher the single most influential person in America!

And yet, three things, in particular, took me by surprise.

The first was the content of Henry's religious message. Remember, his father was Lyman Beecher, the standard bearer for an unforgiving Old Testament judgmental God. And yet, in his sermons, as well as in his articles and even in his private letters, Henry comes off much like a peace-and-love hippie. He would become the most famous minister in America, with a message of forgiveness, empathy, and tolerance. Beecher's audiences were as entranced by what they nicknamed his "Gospel of Love." Contemporary pundits, on the other hand, had more difficulty with exactly what this message meant. They debated whether his greatest rival was the philosopher Ralph Waldo Emerson or the showman P. T. Barnum.

Even more surprising was Henry's private persona. There was something irresistibly modern about Henry Ward Beecher that broke every dry stereotype of history. He was openly funny, and irreverent, with a wicked talent for satirizing anything pompous, hypocritical, or narrow-minded. He was a vivid storyteller with a poignant sense of life's ironies, who often drew his material from his own personal foibles. Although written over a century ago, his words were somehow as intimate and self-revealing as if they were yesterday's gossip.

But there was also something less easily accounted for—a certain cynicism about Henry that came out from time to time in the statements and actions of family, friends, contemporaries. Was this the source of notoriety? There were indications in the materials I read that Henry danced more than once on the edge of public disgrace, only to extricate himself at the last moment.

Chalk it up to youth, but by the time I finished my first day of research, I couldn't get enough of Henry Ward Beecher. I was spellbound by both his letters and his life—and dying to know what exactly he had done to acquire his infamous reputation.

I would soon learn.

Henry's notoriety is usually traced to one extraordinary chapter of his life. At the pinnacle of his career, when he was widely acclaimed as the most beloved man in America, Henry was accused of seduction and adultery. Under political fire for her own sexual promiscuity, Victoria Woodhull, the famous suffragist and the first woman to run for the United States presidency, publicly charged the beloved and loving Reverend Beecher with secretly turning the Gospel of Love into a justification for Free Love.

Henry, it seems, had been carrying on a clandestine relationship with Elizabeth Tilton, a young member of his church and the wife of Theodore Tilton, Henry's best friend and occasional ghostwriter. According to later testimony, Elizabeth Tilton first confessed the affair with Henry to her husband in 1870. Theodore immediately confronted the minister, but then agreed to suppress the scandal when it became clear that if he destroyed Beecher, he and his wife would become social outcasts. For three years all three people maintained a complex, well-documented cover-up. The alleged affair remained covered up until Woodhull broke the story two years later.

What happened next is a sad tale with echoes in our own time—but with some significant differences. In contrast to our own jaded response to the Clinton scandal, when the accusations against Beecher broke, the entire country staggered under the impact. This was not a sentimental testament to a lost innocence—the papers of the nineteenth century were filled with lurid sex scandals, including more than a few involving libertine ministers. The difference was Beecher himself.

Beecher made people feel good about themselves. They couldn't get enough of him because they so desperately needed to hear the good things he had to say about them. So when the accusations started to fly, it was not just Beecher, the man of God, who was being assailed; it was this larger-than-life projection of everything Americans wanted to believe about themselves. The anxious question on the tip of everyone's tongues—including my own—was: *Could* a man as lovable and loving as Henry Ward Beecher commit adultery and then lie, allowing others to be destroyed by his lies? If so, what would that say about the millions of people who identified so deeply with him?

Pressured by the newspapers, both Henry and Elizabeth denied the affair. But this was not enough for the preacher's outraged supporters, who set out to discredit not just Woodhull (the accuser) but also Theodore Tilton. (He was accused of having an affair with Woodhull.) Henry's handpicked ecclesiastic investigating committee quickly absolved the minister and ex-communicated Theodore. But Theodore, enraged, then brought Henry to civil trial on the charge of "criminal conversation," providing the court with extensive evidence, including hundreds of private letters.

A spectacular trial was held in Brooklyn, playing out as salaciously and rancorously in Beecher's time as the O. J. Simpson trial did in ours. Although the trial ended with a hung jury, and Beecher lived another ten years as a respected public figure, there is no question that his star was dramatically dimmed by the trial, as were the values he stood for.

Still, his death in 1886 was mourned with all the sentimental extravagance the Gilded Age could offer. The entire city of Brooklyn was officially closed; hundreds of thousands of mourners turned out for his funeral procession; and the most important people in America sent letters of condolence to his widow. Yet by the turn of the century, Henry Ward Beecher had virtually disappeared from the history books and from popular culture. In the twentieth century, those historians who bothered to take note of him dismissed him as a mere humbug, a classic Victorian hypocrite.

Why did someone who was, for most of his life, one of the most influential men in America never find a proper place in history? The more I read, the more I realized that there was a fascinating behind-the-scenes tale that had never been told, a story of intimate secrets and passionate contradictions—a story that would not merely balance the good against the evil, but would reveal the heart-rending human complexities behind a mythic American character. When I finished my research obligations for the exhibit, I went to the library to see what had been published on him, but could find only a slim, dry, academic biography, written almost twenty-five years earlier, and a stack of outdated "fan biographies" written in the 1890s. That day in the library, at the ripe old age of eighteen, I determined that some day I would write this man's real story. After more than ten years and a Ph.D. from Yale, I now feel ready to do so.

My proposed biography, *Breach of Faith,* is, I believe, a book that will restore Henry Ward Beecher to his rightful place in history, not by whitewashing or denouncing the contradictions of his life, but by telling a psychologically complex, and ultimately redemptive personal story. It is also a book that will use Beecher to illuminate his era. His life spanned the heart of the nineteenth century: He helped usher in the end of the culture of Calvinism, the flowering of the American literary Renaissance, the tragic fratricide of the Civil War, and the excesses of the Gilded Age, leaving us on the threshold of the twentieth century. Because Henry was so influential in interpreting public opinion, *Breach of Faith* will also recount the unspoken private history of millions of people who heard their own personal message of redemption in Henry Ward Beecher's gospel.

It is often asked of historians whether the times make the man or the man makes his times. Some men—and women—have the power to grab hold of history and reshape it to conform to their own vision. Others achieve greatness in their own times not by forging ahead of the rest of us but because they *are* us. Their greatness lies in their ability to articulate what we all feel but often vaguely understand, and to lead us where we want history to take us, even when we don't know exactly where that is. This book is a story about the pleasures and perils of that second path.

Breach of Faith takes its title from this central paradox: Henry transformed his life by breaking with his religious forebears and building a new faith on the foundation of self-fulfillment rather than self-denial. The quintessentially human side to this story rests on the sad irony that the road to pleasure can be a slippery slope—when Henry hit bottom, the Gospel of Love turned to heartbreak.

Among the specific questions this book will address are:

- Why did Lyman Beecher's son become the single most important figure, bar none, in ending the Calvinist grip on American culture?

While Henry certainly had personal issues with his father, it is far too easy to suggest that his life was a commonplace generation-gap story, the revolt of a talented and independent spirit against a stern father. For one thing, Lyman Beecher was not a typical father in any way—then or now (see attached chapter for a discussion of Henry's unconventional upbringing). I also hope to show that Lyman and Henry, although very different in their public personas, had much in common in their backstage behaviors and that the push-pull relationship between father and son propelled Henry's career.

- Why did Abraham Lincoln call Henry Ward Beecher the most important voice in America at the end of the Civil War, choosing the minister to lead the raising of the flag over Fort Sumter, an act intended to symbolize not just the end of the war but the reunification of the nation?

Beecher was certainly no Lincoln loyalist, and was, at times, the president's harshest critic (behind the Southern Confederates). Moreover, Beecher waffled on all of the great issues of the day, including the secession of the South, the conduct of the war, the Emancipation Proclamation, and the rebuilding of the South. It was only when public opinion had turned firmly against the South, and his sister's anti-slavery novel, *Uncle Tom's Cabin,* had become a blockbuster, that Henry felt safe enough to come down solidly, even radically, in favor of abolishing slavery. Once he did so, he became an unwavering opponent of racism in both the North and South.

- Why did contemporaries express such mixed feelings about Beecher—including his personality, his accomplishments, and his talent—even as they acknowledged his power?

During the adultery trial, for example, his famous family was split. Some of his siblings supported him unstintingly, especially his sister Harriet Beecher Stowe, while others called for him to confess his guilt, most notably his sister Isabella Beecher Hooker, an ardent ally of Victoria Woodhull; and still others simply distanced themselves from him altogether.

More generally, although Beecher's ideas strongly influenced the leading writers and thinkers of the day, including reformers, politicians, and the classic writers of the American Renaissance such as Henry David Thoreau, Ralph Waldo Emerson, Walt Whitman, and Herman Melville, even those who were fascinated by him were often repelled by his unconventional style and by the content of his message. Melville, in particular, was thinking of him when writing *The Confidence Man*.

- How was it that Beecher was welcomed simultaneously into the New York Bohemian culture of writers and radicals, *and* into the consolidated power circle of the Republican party and the New York Robber Barons? Was Beecher ultimately, as history has judged him, a hypocrite?

Only late in his life, after the shock of the sex scandal, would the contradictions of these relationships come to seem hypocritical. But there is no question about the fact that Henry was involved in a number of postwar scandals, and that his involvement influenced Mark Twain's novel, *The Gilded Age*, which gave a name to this corrupt era. In particular, Twain was fascinated by Beecher's involvement in the McFarland trial, in which Beecher conducted the wedding ceremony of an illegally divorced woman and her fiancé, while the fiancé was dying from bullet wounds inflicted by the woman's jealous husband.

- Why did Beecher's sex scandal seem so earth shattering to so many people—commanding more headlines than the entire Civil War, according to one historian?

Beecher's adultery investigation hit just as the nation was rocked by a wave of postwar traumas—including violent labor strikes, the vicious partisan politics of Reconstruction, the unsettling women's rights agitation, an epidemic of government corruption, a deep financial depression, and the crash of the railroad financiers. Yet because so many people were so emotionally identified with Beecher, his adultery trial was regarded by many as the most significant scandal in an era defined by scandal. Like Watergate in our own century, Beecher's trial seemed to throw the most basic assumptions about human behavior into doubt, encouraging people to become more cynical and socially conservative at a crucial turning point in history.

- Way was Beecher so important to his times?

As one contemporary journalist observed of him: "He is eminently and emphatically of this age and this country, and herein lies the secret of much of his success." This biography will use the relationship between Beecher and his audience to illuminate the emotional transformation of nineteenth-century America, as it haltingly moved from a self-denying view of life to a self-affirming view, one in which excesses were tolerated because they were seen as the price of freedom of personal expression.

THE COMPETITION

There are no recent biographies of Henry Ward Beecher, although, I believe, there are several academic studies in the works.

Regarding the larger Beecher clan, a number of books have been written. In the past two decades, two group biographies of the

Beechers have been published, as well as a popular biography of Catharine Beecher, which remains in print, and a prize-winning biography of Harriet Beecher Stowe (published in 1994).

The Beecher-Tilton scandal has been of increasing interest to historians. It was included in *Scorpion Tongues* by Gail Collins—a history of gossip—and *The Rev. Beecher and Mrs. Tilton*—an academic study on the scandal's relationship to the social and political history of Brooklyn. Most notably, two biographies of Victoria Woodhull, both published in the past six months, feature the scandal in some depth and have been greeted with great enthusiasm in the press. The Woodhull biographies interpret the Beecher-Tilton scandal in the context of the sexual and economic double standard of the nineteenth-century, arguing that the scandal was a product of vicious feuds within the post–Civil War women's movement.

The attention paid to the Woodhull biographies suggests that the time is ripe for a definitive biography of Beecher. As the reviewer in *The New Yorker* observed, Beecher is "the most vital character" in both biographies—"Henry Ward Beecher is the only individual in these books whom we can truly see, smell, and touch" ("Sex, Scandals, and Suffrage," 4/20/98, p. 98).

Several factors will lend a novelistic tone to *Breach of Faith*. First, there is an astounding amount of intimate archival material, including diaries, memoirs, well over a thousand letters—to, from, and about Beecher—and a 3,000-page trial transcript. Unlike with most historical figures, there are no gaps in the record at any point in his life. His personal life and social influence are continuously well documented by both public and private accounts.

The book will encompass a large, fascinating cast of characters that includes corrupt Republican politicians, eccentric Yankees, Western pioneers, soldiers, radical reformers, suffragists, spiritualists, and ex-slaves.

The story will be structured as a true-life psychological mystery, climaxing with the ambiguous, if technically "happy," verdict of the adultery trial—an ending which invites reader participation by placing the contemporary reader in the same breathless position as Beecher's original audience.

As a way to build suspense and engagement, the structure of the biography will mimic some aspects of an epistolary novel; each chapter will begin with a particularly poignant piece of "evidence"—a letter or document that evokes the events and themes of that section. This sequence of letters will depict Henry's rise and fall, cultivating readers' emotional identification with Henry while encouraging them to draw their own conclusions about his character and culpability.

Beecher's story will probably be helped by the fact that we live in a time when sexual impropriety and the role of mass media in jumping upon sexual scandals dominates conversation as never before. In addition to the new popularity of contemporary tell-all memoirs and exposes, there has been an increased interest in historical scandals, from the revelations about Thomas Jefferson and Sally Hemings to the narrative retelling of the murder of the architect Stanford White, or the bacchanals of the Harding administration. As part of the renewed interest in Henry Ward Beecher, *The Trial of the Century*, a documentary film on the scandal aimed at a mainstream television audience, is currently in development. The trial also resurfaced recently in the *New York Times*, in an essay on how Beecher's pioneering efforts to create a market for mass-media intimacy help us understand the uproar over Princess Diana's death ("Our Celebrities, Ourselves," 9/8/97).

Breach of Faith also dovetails well with two other publishing trends. The first is the spiraling market for books on spirituality, especially New Age–style spirituality. Beecher was essentially ground zero for the twentieth-century turn toward a therapeutic and ecumenical style of religion. His life story personifies how this movement began and established itself, and what it now means for Americans.

A second trend is the smaller but significant rise in interest in books on the Civil War period (a trend that often recurs when the country is in an extended period of peace). Beecher was one of the most outrageous and influential pundits of the war, the man everyone either loved or hated, and his life offers a number of fascinating new views of the war. As a newly rediscovered drama of the war years, the book has the potential to tap into the lucrative Civil War buff market.

THE AUTHOR

I have spent twelve years researching and writing about Henry Ward Beecher and am well prepared to complete his biography in a relatively short time. My research has taken me to a wide variety of archives, including the Beecher Family Papers at Yale, various collections in the Schlesinger and Houghton libraries at Harvard, the Beecher-Stow Collection at the Stowe-Day Foundation, several collections at the Library of Congress, including the Robert Todd Lincoln and Andrew Johnson Papers, the Robert Bonner Papers at the New York Public Library, the Henry Whitney Bellows Papers at the Massachusetts Historical Society, the Bowen Family Collection and George B. Cheever Papers at the American Antiquarian Society, the Brooklyn Historical Society and the Brooklyn Public Library.

I am also a historian, professor, and writer specializing in American popular culture, with a wide background in nineteenth-century social and cultural history. I have written for the *New York Times* and for academic publications, including the *Journal of American History, American Literary History,* the *Journal of American Studies* and *Studies in American Fiction.* I have spoken in political and academic arenas, and in 1996, I moderated a national forum, the transcripts of which were published in *Social Text* and *Will Teach for Food* (University of Minnesota Press, 1997).

I was awarded a B.A. summa cum laude in American Studies at Amherst College in 1989, and a Ph.D. in American Studies at Yale University in 1997. Most recently, I taught courses at Yale on American culture in the nineteenth and twentieth centuries. In 1996–97, I was the director of the Yale Graduate School's teacher-training program. I have received numerous academic awards, prizes and fellowships, including a Ford Foundation Research Grant, the Doshisha Prize in American Studies, Amherst Memorial Fellowship, Roswell Dwight Hitchcock Fellowship, Beineke Research Fellowship, Yale University Fellowship, Yale Dissertation Fellowship, and the Sterling Fellowship at Yale University. I have served as a researcher at Old Sturbridge Village, New York University School of Law, the Amherst College Manuscripts and Archives, and the College Board.

Breach of Faith: A Biography of Henry Ward Beecher

In June of 1834, only days from his twenty-first birthday, Henry Ward Beecher boarded a stage coach in western Massachusetts, bound for Albany, New York. His final destination was Cincinnati, Ohio. It was a hard trip, about a week long, with stretches by stage coach, canal boat, and steamer. But it was neither the hardships of the road nor the anticipation of adventure that marked the journey so vividly in Henry's mind. It was the anxiety he felt as he crept closer and closer to the Beecher family fold.

Less than two weeks earlier he had graduated from Amherst. His college years had been good to him, years in which he had come into his own and transformed himself from an awkward boy who lacked confidence into a popular, charming young man. In the days after graduation, he exchanged heartfelt good-byes with his class-mates and paid one last, tearful visit to his fiancé, Eunice Bullard. He would not marry Eunice for seven more years and would see her at most once or twice in all that time; yet she would one day refer to those seven years as the best in their relationship.

Unlike most of his classmates, Henry was not planning to take some time off to relax and think through the good use to which a young man might put a hard-earned Amherst education. After four years of freedom from the daily presence of his famous and powerful father, the Reverend Lyman Beecher, Henry Ward Beecher was returning home to fulfill his father's plans for him, plans that had been laid on the very day of his birth. By this time, he surely had doubts about those plans, but as he later said, rather bluntly, "I had no choice." He was going to Cincinnati to train for the ministry and to do so under his father's tutelage at the Lane Seminary in Ohio, where his father had recently become president. Others would describe Henry's dilemma more bluntly. "Henry Ward Beecher," as one common saying went, "was born in a Puritan penitentiary of which his father was one of the wardens."

Henry's arrival in Cincinnati to fulfill his father's plan for him coincided with the summit of Lyman's own illustrious career. At a time when the Bible was the only book most Americans read, and when ministers were the village aristocrats, the Reverend Lyman Beecher was by then, indisputably, "the most prominent, popular, and powerful preacher in our nation." Henry could personally vouch for his father's influence. As a young boy he had watched his father deliver sermons that moved vast audiences to tears. He had seen great men ride hundreds of miles on horseback just for the opportunity to consult with the eminent Reverend Beecher.

Lyman Beecher was, by all accounts, shrewd, ambitious, and driven all his life by divine orders. ("I was harnessed to the Chariot of Christ," he recalled in old age. "I could not stop.") He was a man on a mission: to save the soul of the new nation. No one who met the Reverend or heard about his successes doubted that had it been solely left to him, even Christ would have relented under the pressure and returned to earth to finish the job He had started.

But the religious movement to which Lyman devoted his life

and was now training Henry and all his other sons for—orthodox Calvinism—was already beginning to lose its appeal. A big part of its decline was directly attributable to the message the Congregationalists delivered.

As orthodox Calvinists, the Congregationalists preached a religion of submission, in which the only hope of salvation was to submit unquestioningly to the will of God and to defer in all earthly matters to the wisdom of His ministers. The Calvinist ministry put special emphasis on the Old Testament, with its graphic tales of plagues and miracles visited on the evil and good alike, of apocalypse and revelations, and with its legalistic commandments and its threats of a divine justice fully exacted for all eternity.

In colonial New England, with its harsh climate, rural isolation, and ancient folk superstitions, this Old Testament vision of God as an all-powerful, wrathful judge, and of society as a tightly controlled hierarchy, had tremendous power. But just around the time Lyman was born, in 1776, revolutions in democracy, science, and free speech were beginning to sweep in a new kind of culture. A more diverse, secular America was emerging, one ready to shake off the heavy hand of Calvinist theology as it had the bonds of European monarchy in the previous century.

It is strange that Lyman, a child of the American Revolution, and in many ways a very progressive father and public leader, should have been one of the last God-fearing Puritans in America. But Lyman never shook off the powerful influence of his boyhood in Connecticut, the last bastion of the old orthodoxy. Nor did he ever forget the words of the ministers who preached to him, especially their warnings of divine justice exacted for an eternity. Quite the contrary, as a very little boy, Lyman took all these tales quite literally. Today, we would say he internalized them; they remained vividly imprinted on his personality until the day he died. He would later tell his own children about the critical moment in his childhood when he saw his future.

When he was a boy, he later recalled, children were not allowed to play on Sunday until three stars became visible in the sky—a centuries-old rule based on a biblical definition of the Sabbath. To the end of his life, Lyman remembered another little boy admonishing him because Lyman had wanted to play before the three stars appeared. God would surely put him in a fire, his friend declared, and burn him "forever and ever." "I understood what fire was, and what forever was," Lyman recalled. "What emotion I had, thinking, No end! No end! It has been a sort of mainspring ever since."

There were other mainsprings to Lyman's life. He was born without wealth or station, the son and grandson of common blacksmiths. Two days after his birth, his mother died of consumption (a then-common disease now diagnosed as tuberculosis), leaving him undernourished and small enough to be held in one hand. His father, David Beecher, perhaps resentful of the baby for having killed his "best-beloved wife," sent him to be raised by his brother-in-law, Lot Benton, a pious, childless farmer in Guilford, Connecticut. Lyman never returned to his father's home, except for a few visits, and his father played almost no role in his life—which may account for Lyman's unusually deep attachment to his own children.

Uncle Lot was a gruff but affectionate Yankee who treated his nephew like a son, with the expectation that he would inherit the farm. But Lyman showed little talent or inclination for farming, preferring to read or fish or daydream. When he was put in charge of Spring plowing, he was often so distracted he let the oxen wander across the field.

According to family lore, when Uncle Lot came into the barn one morning and saw a saddle and bridle just lying in the middle of the yard, he concluded that "Lyman would never be good for anything but to go to college." Lyman jumped at the chance and later liked to say that it was oxen that had sent him to college. It certainly was not his father, who balked at paying school fees for a son he barely knew.

Lyman was admitted to Yale; in his junior year he was introduced to the great Puritan drama of conversion—a complex process of anguish, submission, ecstasy, and rebirth. His mentor would be the newly appointed president of Yale, the Reverend Timothy Dwight, a grandson of the legendary Puritan preacher Jonathan Edwards.

"Old Pope Dwight," as he was nicknamed, taught his students that man was born in sin, damned to hell for his rebellion against God's authority—a criminal tendency first revealed in Adam's fateful decision to eat the serpent's apple. But God was not an irrational tyrant, Dwight insisted, who would create an entire race with a fatal flaw and then make it suffer eternally for that flaw. If a man will strip away his sinful, rebellious impulses, Dwight informed his students, and submit himself utterly to God's will—to the point where he longs to burn in Hell if doing so will add to God's glory—then perhaps he will be shown mercy.

However, Dwight warned, man cannot bribe God with good behavior. It was a mystery how God chooses whom to save and whom to damn, but in his mercy God will give a sign to those he has granted salvation. Those who sincerely repent and submit to God's will might experience a sudden surge of feeling, a glorious cascade of relief and joy, that would "convert" them from sinner to saved and allow them to become full members of the church.

With Lyman's childhood memories of heaven and hell deeply etched in his mind, Dwight's grisly depiction of God's wrath threw Lyman into a deep depression over his own sinfulness. After all, he had certainly not experienced anything like the surge of feeling Dwight described. His despair deepened, until one week in his junior year of college when he went home for the weekend to visit with his aunt and uncle. There his aunt, seeing a drunkard stumble past the house, remarked on the poor man, "He was under conviction once, and thought he had religion; but he's nothing but a poor drunkard now."

As soon as she left the room, Lyman later told his children, he felt a need to pray. "I was not in the habit of prayer. I rose to pray and had not spoken five words before I was under as deep a conviction as I ever was in my life. The sinking of the shaft was instantaneous," he told his children. "The commandment came, sin revived, and I died, quick as a flash of lightning." He knew then that he had been saved. By the end of his senior year he had dedicated his life to making America a Kingdom of Christ.

Years later, when he started his own family, Lyman would be consumed by the possibility that his own children would not be saved from damnation. At a time when many, many children died in early childhood, Lyman's anxiety for their souls mingled with a fear of losing his beloved family to disease. Lyman would father eleven children in all. One part of him, the modern secular part, would devote himself to seeing all his children accomplish great things. Here he would achieve great success, using very modern ideas about parenthood. All seven of his boys would become ministers. His son Edward would also become a noted abolitionist and scholar, his daughter Isabella a suffragist and spiritualist, and his daughter Catharine a pioneering female author and educator. Henry's favorite sister, Harriet (Beecher Stowe), would become an international celebrity as the author of the history-transforming novel, *Uncle Tom's Cabin*. (Upon meeting her, Abraham Lincoln was said to have exclaimed: "So you're the little woman who wrote the book that started this big war!") And Henry would become the most famous Beecher of all.

But the religious soul of Lyman knew that earthly success was not enough to save a person's soul. And over time, Lyman's anxiety for his own children's souls became almost an obsession—with disastrous results. Though all were good children who would become otherwise excellent Christians, none ever reported having experienced that singularly glorious lightning bolt of salvation the way their father had. Lyman's unrelenting pressure on them to repent harder and more often, to give themselves up more fully to God in the hope that the conversion might occur, had the opposite effect: it left the children depressed, ashamed, and hopeless. They were genuinely afraid of God's wrath, yet the fear of disappointing their father made it impossible for them to surrender to the kind of ecstatic release that he had experienced as a young man.

After her father's death, Harriet captured their bewildering childhood dilemma—a dilemma faced by many children of their generation: "Tell a child that he is 'a member of Christ, a child of God, and an inheritor of the kingdom of heaven,' and he feels, to say the least, civilly disposed toward religion," Harriet wrote in her novel, *Oldtown Folks.* "Tell him 'he is under God's wrath and curse, and so made liable to all the miseries of his life, to death itself, and the pains of hell forever,' because somebody ate an apple five thousand years ago, and his religious associations [will not be] so agreeable—especially if he has the answers whipped into him, or has to go to bed without his supper for not learning them."

Eventually all the Beecher children were admitted as members of the church—although Henry, in particular, seems to have fudged his conversion—and all seven of Lyman's boys became ministers. But it is clear from their lives as well as their letters to each other that the years of morbid fear and the self-loathing inculcated in them took a heavy toll. All would suffer extreme mood swings, ranging from debilitating depression and hypochondria to exultant optimism and a reckless religious ecstasy that sometimes seems to have been fueled by erotic impulses.

In the end, Lyman would lose his children in the way that mattered most to him. After their father's death in 1863, both Catharine and Harriet would convert to their mother's more gentle Episcopalian faith. Isabella would become infamous for speaking to the spirit-world, and Henry and his less famous brothers would completely overhaul the harsh traditions of Calvinism. Two of his sons, George and James, would commit suicide.

But as Henry headed back to his family after graduation from Amherst in 1834, all that lay far in the future.

Henry was born in 1813 in Litchfield, Connecticut, when his father was thirty-eight years old. Lyman had accepted a position in Litchfield three years earlier, after a period ministering to the Montauk Indians and taciturn Yankee settlers of East Hampton, Long Island. The Long Island job had been demanding and the salary low, and while Lyman threw himself into the work, eventually he began to search for a position with an income sufficient to allow him to better support his growing family.

The appointment in Connecticut allowed him to buy a rambling white house on an acre and a half of land with an orchard, a wood-shed, two barns, and a workshop, right next to the Congregational Church (both still stand today). The parsonage was "a wide, roomy, windy edifice," as Harriet described it, with a large parlor and kitchen, a well room, three bedrooms downstairs, and four small bedrooms upstairs. Like many old houses, it was wickedly cold in the winter and had a colony of field mice and rats living in the walls. But for the Beecher children it was the setting for many of their happi-est family memories.

As his father's eighth child, Henry came into a household that was literally bursting with life. Besides his older siblings, Catharine, William, Edward, Mary, and George, the household included an orphan cousin, Betsy Burr, two black servants, Rachel and Zillah Crooke, several students from the Litchfield Law School and as many as eleven boarders from the Litchfield Female Academy. Aunt Mary and Uncle Samuel from Guilford visited long and often, and were joined by Grandma Beecher and Aunt Ester, Lyman's stepmother and half-sister, who eventually moved to a house nearby.

Despite their earnest piety (family prayers were held twice daily,

Christmas and birthdays were celebrated with more prayers, and Sundays were spent in silent contemplation—a special torment for a fidgety little boy like Henry), the Beecher house was also boisterous, high-spirited, and affectionate. "There is the strangest and most interesting combination in our family of fun and seriousness," Lyman's youngest daughter, Isabella, observed. The parsonage was filled with lively conversation, practical jokes, books, and music. It was a social center for the cosmopolitan little village, with a constant flow of visitors stopping by and a regular stream of traveling clergymen in need of a bed. The family hosted musical evenings, with the girls on piano and flute, and Lyman himself playing the fiddle with a vengeance.

As a father, Lyman was uncommonly devoted to his children. Deprived of his own natural parents during his growing-up years, he compensated by becoming an exceptionally engaged and affectionate father. "Toward his children I never knew a man to exhibit so much," Isabella said, "—all the tenderness of a mother and the untiring activity and devotedness of a nurse, father and friend." He loved to romp with the children, playing games with them or, when his heavy schedule permitted, taking them fishing or apple picking. As a disciplinarian, he relied, not surprisingly, more on guilt than on punishment. "There was a free and easy way of living," Catharine remembered, "more congenial to liberty and society than to conventional rules."

Still, as a young boy, Henry often felt lost within this large, clamorous family. His childhood was scarred at the age of three by the death of his mother, Lyman's first wife, Roxanna Foote Beecher. As one of the last children born to Roxanna and Lyman, Henry would grow up a classic middle child in what we would now call a "blended" family. Later in life, Henry maintained that despite her early death, his mother was the most important influence on the course of his career.

Unlike her rough-hewn husband, Roxanna Foote came from a well-to-do, educated, Episcopalian family in Guilford. She was shy but gracious, an extremely strong and intelligent woman. By all accounts, she was a model of calm, gentle piety—providing a steady contrast to Lyman's turbulent mood swings. Had they been Catholic, her family would have called her a saint.

Lyman began visiting the Foote family after graduating from Yale, and was smitten with Roxanna almost immediately. "I had sworn inwardly never to marry a weak woman," Lyman later said, and Roxanna seemed to suit him perfectly. For her part, Roxanna once claimed that she would never marry until she met a man like Sir Charles Grandison, the dashing, sentimental hero of Samuel Richardson's bestselling novel of the same name. "I presume she thought she had," Lyman smugly told his children years later. Although he lacked a noble pedigree and sophisticated manners, the young minister radiated a passion and charisma that more than matched that of any fictional hero. Soon the two were deeply in love.

Roxanna easily agreed to join her fiancé's faith, but as the engagement progressed, Lyman began to worry that because Roxanna was not as demonstrative or anguished in her religious devotion as he, perhaps she was not truly saved. He became increasingly upset by this idea, until finally he rode to Guilford, resolved to take the painful step of breaking off the engagement if Roxanna found it impossible to commit herself to his religious principles. "I explained my views," as he told the story, "and laid before her the great plan of redemption. As I went on, her bosom heaved, her heart melted, and mine melted too; and I never told her to her dying day what I came for." Lyman swore that this was as close to a true disagreement as they ever got.

In the Fall of 1799 the two were married. By then, Lyman's only concern was that his great love for Roxanna might overwhelm his love for God. Well it might have, had Roxanna lived. One night in the winter of 1816, when Lyman was immersed in a bitter, losing fight to save Connecticut's state-mandated religion, Roxanna and Lyman were riding home from a parishioner's house. It was a clear cold night, Lyman remembered, when a sudden chill took the air. Roxanna abruptly turned to him and announced, "I do not think I shall be with you long." Six weeks later, when Henry was three years old, Roxanna died of consumption. She knew she was going to die, she explained to Lyman, when she began to have celestial visions.

Her deathbed scene was a remarkable testament to her faith— she expressed no fear or regret, only joyful anticipation of heaven. As for the family, Lyman said, "there was not a dry eye in the house." Before she passed away she gathered her eight sobbing children around the bed, including baby Charles, who had been born only nine months earlier, to say goodbye and to dedicate her sons as missionaries for God. She consoled them by whispering that God would take better care of them than she had. It seemed, as one friend observed with bleak optimism, like "a victory over the grave."

Lyman was shattered by his wife's death. "Both intellectually and morally he regarded her as the better and stronger portion of himself," Harriet later wrote, "and I remember hearing him say that, after her death, his first sensation was a sort of terror like that of a child suddenly shut out alone in the dark." "The whole year after her death was a year of great emptiness," Lyman remembered with fresh sorrow, "as if there was not motive enough in the world to move me. I used to pray earnestly to God either to take me away, or to restore me to that interest in things and susceptibility to motive I had had before."

The older children were overcome by their mother's death and their father's grief. Harriet, five years old at the time, recalled her brother Henry frolicking like a kitten in his golden curls and little black frock, too young to go to the funeral or to understand what had happened. A few days later, the meaning of his mother's death and her burial had begun to sink in, it seems, for Catharine found Henry digging a hole in the dirt under her window. "I'm going to heaven to find Ma," he explained cheerfully.

As he grew older, listenning to stories and reading the letters of the mother he never knew, Henry came to believe that his mother's death was the defining tragedy of his life. "After I came to be about fourteen or fifteen years of age I began to be distinctly conscious that there was a silent, secret, and, if you please to call it so, romantic influence which was affecting me," Henry later said. "It grew and grows, so that in some parts of my nature I think I have more communion with my mother, whom I never saw except as a child three years old, than with any living being. . . . No devout Catholic ever saw so much in the Virgin Mary as I have seen in my mother."

After Roxanna's death, Henry was left to be raised in the competent but cool care of his spinster aunt, Ester, and later a stepmother, Harriet Porter Beecher. As a widower with eight children, a houseful of boarders, and a parish full of obligations, Lyman considered it his duty to remarry quickly, despite his debilitating grief. Like Roxanna, Harriet Porter was an elegant woman from a prestigious New England clan, who possessed a genteel but unshakable piety. She and Lyman had three more children, Isabella, Thomas, and James.

The overwhelming obligations of managing such a large household, combined with her own formidable godliness, made Harriet Porter seem distant and cold to her stepchildren. "I was afraid of her." Henry said. "It would have been easier for me to lay my hand on a block and have it struck off than to open my thoughts to her." No matter what her gifts, it is unlikely that Harriet Porter could ever have approached his idealized memory of Roxanna.

From birth, Henry was considered a special child. He was blessed with a sunny, gregarious nature, along with his father's quick wit. When he was very little, his friends from Litchfield recalled, he would dress up as a minister, wearing huge "blue goggles" he had scavenged for eye-glasses, and pretend the back barn was a church. He would then mount a pile of hay and "begin his sermons to his school-mates; he used no articulate words, but a jargon of word sounds, with rising and falling inflections, wonderfully mimicking those of his father. The rotund phrasing, the sudden fall to solemnity, the sweeping paternal gesture, the upbrushing of the hair, were all imitated perfectly by the son." As a grand finale, Hank, as he was nicknamed, would tumble dramatically down into the hay. (As an adult he turned these performing talents to good use, becoming famous for sermons that seemed more like stand-up comedy than preaching.)

But in front of the other members of the family a different Henry emerged. After his mother's death, he developed a "thickness of speech," a nervous twisting of syllables that made him difficult to understand—an enormous disadvantage in a family where words were the common currency. Like many other gifted children, he was, according to his sister Harriet, "excessively sensitive to praise and blame, extremely diffident. . . ."

Even more noticeable was that he lacked the intellectual aspirations and solemn sense of purpose that were passed down to the other Beecher children. When Henry was only six and Harriet eight, Lyman confessed to his brother-in-law George Foote, "I would give a hundred dollars if she [Harriet] was a boy & Henry a girl—She is as odd as she is intelligent & studious—Henry is Henry."

Henry hated school, which put him further at odds with his bookish family. Instead of studying, he wandered the woods hunting, fishing, and daydreaming. He was shifted from school to school, looking for some mentor who could nourish his natural talents, but the only skill he seemed to cultivate was the ability to read answers from a crib sheet tucked in his hat without getting caught.

Around age ten, he was sent to study under his sister Catharine, who had established a school for girls in Hartford that Harriet attended. It was hoped that perhaps a family member would have more luck. Unfortunately, being surrounded by thirty or forty girls only seemed to bring out Henry's instincts as a class clown. He played practical jokes endlessly and kept a running commentary of wisecracks that Harriet later saw as a sign of his insatiable need for attention and approval.

A body of family stories built up around the subject of Henry's less-than-serious academic commitment. As Catharine liked to describe his classroom attitude, maybe heightening the story's entertainment value, he was pulled aside by a teacher for help with grammar and syntax.

"Now, Henry, *a* is the indefinite article, you see, and must be used only with a singular noun," coaxed the teacher. "You can say, a man but you can't say a men, can you?"

"Yes, I can say amen too," was Henry's reply. "Father says it always at the end of his prayers."

"Come, Henry, now don't be joking! Now decline he. Nominative, he, possessive, his, objective, him. You can see his is possessive. Now, you can say 'his book' but you can't say 'him book'."

"Yes, I do say hymnbook, too," shot back Henry.

"But now, Henry, seriously, just attend to the active and passive voice. Now 'I strike' is active you see because if you strike you do something. But 'I am struck' is passive because if you are struck you don't do anything, do you?"

"Yes, I do—I strike back again!"

Today we would relish such insouciance in our own child and repeat such charming-child stories with a certain pride—and years later, when Henry's future was secure, his own family did. But back then, Henry lasted only six months before Catharine packed him up and sent him back home. When he returned home, his boyish transgressions were mentally transcribed into one more black mark to be recorded in the book of sins by which he had been told he would be judged and for which he would likely spend an eternity in hell.

He would later write: "I remember thinking, 'Well, it is no use for me to try to be a good boy'. My innumerable shortcomings and misdemeanors were to my mind so many pimples that marked my terrible depravity."

The crucial turning point in Henry's life came when he turned fourteen and the family was living in the port city of Boston. He resolved to run away to sea, but the thought of hurting his father kept him from leaving home. Finally he decided to write a note to one of his brothers describing his plan and saying that he wanted his father's permission but would leave without it, if necessary. Whether consciously or not, he then left the note where his father was certain to find it. When Lyman read the note he said nothing, but invited Henry to come saw wood with him—a flattering sign that he wanted to talk to Henry man to man. At the woodpile, Lyman casually turned the subject to his son's future, asking him what he planned to be when he grew up. Henry replied that he wanted to go to sea. "But not merely as a common sailor, I supposed?" Lyman asked slyly.

"No, sir; I want to be a midshipman, and after that a commodore."

"I see," said the doctor. "Well, Henry, in order for that, you know, you must begin a course of mathematics and study navigation and all that."

"Yes, sir: I'm ready." Henry replied with surprise. Within a week, Henry found himself a student at Mt. Pleasant Academy in rural western Massachusetts. Now thoroughly landlocked, his interest in the sea waned, and soon he was well on his way to graduation.

"I shall have the boy in the ministry yet," Lyman predicted.

Acknowledgments

Deepest thanks to our editor, Ed Barber, to whom we pay the highest compliment. He is, by every definition, an editor's editor.

Our agent and friend Gerard McCauley has served us enormously well, especially in placing this project with W. W. Norton, a cherished publishing house.

Very special thanks to Debby Applegate for allowing us to use her proposal as the sample in the back of this book. As brilliant as her proposal is, her book will be even better.

Michael Fortunato, Dick Fortunato, Helena Schwarz, Sarah Schwarz, Eileen Fallon, and Archie Schwartz were our first readers. Their comments and encouragement made the task of writing this book so much easier.

Throughout the years our lives have been enriched and sustained by all our wonderful friends and colleagues at Oxford University Press, St. Martin's Press, Pantheon Books, Basic Books, and HarperCollins. Thanks to all of you. And thanks to our new friends at 240.

We could not have written this book without the expressions of love and support we received from family and friends. We can't begin to count the authors who cheered us on. The entire Schwarz clan has been like family to us in so many ways. Thank you Bruce T., Phyllis H., Errol M., Lillian S., David S., and all the other authors who have become our friends.

This book is dedicated not only to the authors and great books but more personally to our children—Michael, Mimi, Ricky, Alice, Al, Annie, and Evan Matthew.

Index

academic books:
  coded language in, *see* coded
    language
  narrative tension in, 31, 187
  narrow subject matter of, 29,
    30
  stylistic standards in, 29–30
  trade books vs., 29–31, 44, 114
  see also university presses
academic trade books, 29*n,* 137
acknowledgments, 231
acquisition editors, 23, 27, 28
advance orders, computers and,
    35–36
advances, 28, 225
  amount and schedule of, 134
  book sales and, 237
  preemptive offers and, 132
  proposals and, 62–63, 83
African-Americans, books on,
    21–22
agents, *see* literary agents

aggressive advocacy:
  fairness vs., 155–61
  in newspapers, 157, 160, 161
  in television news, 157, 158–59
  in topical books, 155–56, 160
AIDS, 207
Amazon.com, 18
American Lawyer, 41
Anderson, Terry, 92
argument, 141–76
  aggressive advocacy in, *see*
    aggressive advocacy
  command of subject matter
    in, 147–50
  conclusions in, 150–52
  facts vs., 143
  fairness of, *see* argument,
    fairness of
  narrative tension in, 179, 191
  purpose of, 142
  thesis-driven vs. data-driven,
    152–54

argument, fairness of, 32, 160,
161–76
aggressive advocacy vs.,
155–61
alternative interpretations
considered in, 171–72
analogies in, 172–73
attribution of motivation in,
173–74
causation in, 172
dictionaries and, 172
establishing presumptions in,
170–71
lies and near-lies in, 168–69
presentation of other side in,
161–65
respecting self-chosen names
in, 174–75
setting uniform standards in,
165–66
skepticism toward new
discoveries in, 169–70
argument-based books, 160
dramatic elements in, 116
information kept succinct in,
115–16
narrative-based books vs.,
90–91
reason and respect in,
116–17
sample chapters for, 111,
115–17
Arnold, Martin, 182
art books, 40, 45–48
atom bomb, 170
auctions, 134

audience, 22–23, 39–57,
211–14, 238
and argument-based vs. narrative-based books, 116–17
art world, 40, 45–48, 56
for business books, 212
as defined in proposal, 67,
95–96, 211
for explanation-driven books,
118
general-interest, 24–25,
49–50, 53–54, 56
keeping interest of, 103–4
law book, 40–41, 48–49, 213
magazine vs. book, 41–42,
54–55, 56
respect for, 151, 238
technical language and, 118,
213–14
three groupings of, 175–76
true crime, 53
authorlink.com, 124–25
authors:
credentials of, *see* authors,
credentials of
editorial problems of, 228,
229, 230
editors pestered by, 223–24
manuscripts placed by, 122–23
mediagenic, 36, 133–34
most respected by editors,
230
multiple offers entertained by,
134–36
professional reputation of,
142, 143

self-published, 24–25
"tracks" of, 35
in transition from academic to
    trade books, 30–31
writer's block and, *see* writer's
    block, overcoming of
authors, credentials of, 88, 90,
    91–94
blurbs and, 93
editors and, 56–57, 79–80, 83
establishment of, 92–93
platforms vs., 91–92

background chapters, *see*
    context chapters
Barbarians at the Gate
    (Burrough and Helyar),
    178
bar codes, computerized
    inventories and, 34–35
Barnes & Noble, 37, 235
shelving policies of, 15–20,
    21
Basic Books, 15, 50, 130
Bernstein, Richard, 216
best sellers, 16–17, 21, 23, 37,
    155
Bible, 180
Big Bang, 73, 96
Big Five questions for proposals,
    see proposals, Big Five
    questions for
Bill of Rights, 213
biographies:
introductions in, 202–3
narrative tension in, 188–90

sample chapter for, 111–14
of women, 46–47
blurbs, 93, 196
Boltzmann's Atom (Lindley),
    153
*Book Business: Publishing: Past,
    Present, and Future*
    (Epstein), 34
book jackets, 24
blurbs on, 93, 196
design of, 63, 64, 129, 236
flap copy on, 235–36
books:
academic, *see* academic books
backlisted, 17
best sellers, 16–17, 21, 23,
    37, 155
character-driven, 50, 178, 187
course-use potential of, 135
digitization of, 34
influence of computers on
    sales of, 34–36
jackets, *see* book jackets
journalism compared with,
    54–55, 56, 110
self-published vs. traditionally
    published, 23–24
thesis-driven vs. data-driven,
    152–54
titles and subtitles of, 231–32
trade, *see* trade books
Books-A-Million, 16
bookstores, 238
computerized inventories in,
    34–36
independent, 16

bookstores, chain:
  buyers for, 18, 19–20, 21, 35,
      238
  co-op money and, 18, 21,
      237
  double shelving in, 20–21
  independent bookstores vs., 16
  Star Trek section in, 16, 18, 19
  stocking and shelving policies
      of, 15–22
Borders, 16, 37, 235
bound galley, 93
Breach of Faith, 232
  sample proposal for, 241–53
break-narrative chapters, 101,
      103, 106, 107, 109, 178,
      204, 211
  tangential topics in, 206–7
business books, 205
  core audience for, 212
buyers, for chain bookstores, 18,
      19–20, 21, 35, 238

Capablanca, José Raúl, 208
captions, 231
catalog copy, writing of, 234–35
causation, chronology vs., 172
CBS, 158
chains, *see* bookstores, chain
Chang, Iris, 104–5
chapters:
  opening, 203–6
  sample, *see* sample chapters
  types of, 101, 204
character-driven books, 40, 178,
      187

Chauncey, George, 198–200
chess, 162, 208
Children Who Kill, 51
Children Who Kill Children, 54
China, People's Republic of,
      171
chronology, causation vs., 172
Churchill, Winston, 166, 170
Civil Action, A (Harr), 41, 49, 50,
      178
cliffhangers, 185
Clinton, Bill, 69–70, 169–70,
      173
  presidential pardons of, 167
Cluetrain Manifesto, The (Levine
      et al.), 236
coded language, 30, 32, 214–16
  reviewers as critical of,
      215–16
Commentary, 160
communism, 166
computers, changes in publish-
      ing influenced by, 34–37
conclusions, supported by facts
      in text, 150–52
conflict, in nonfiction, 164–65
Constitution, U.S.:
  Sixth Amendment, 106–7
  Fourteenth Amendment, 213
context chapters, 101, 102,
      108–9
  as opening chapters, 204–5
contracts, 32, 136
  extensions on, 150
co-op money, chain bookstores
      and, 18, 21, 237

copyeditors, 234
Counterpoint, 130
covering time, narrative tension
    vs., 184–85, 188–94
credentials of authors, *see*
    authors, credentials of
credibility calculus:
  newspapers and, 157–58
  for serious nonfiction, 160–61
Crossfire, 157
CVs, of authors, 61, 94

dangling participles, 219
Dartmouth v. *New Hampshire,*
    71–72
dedication pages, 231
dictionaries, 172
digitization, of books, 34
dissertations, 29, 31
  revising of, 203
"Does Nonfiction Mean
    Factual?" (Arnold), 182
Donald, Aida, 80
dotcom businesses, 205
drug treatment centers, 193–94
Dutch (Morris), 181–82, 183

editorials, credibility calculus
    for, 157–58
editors, trade:
  acquisition, 23, 27, 28
  author credentials as viewed
    by, 56–57, 79–80, 83
  authors most respected by, 230
  in Big Five questions, 66,
    67–96

busy schedule of, 223–24
  copyeditors, 234
  editorial vs. financial decisions
    of, 17
  freelance, *see* freelance editors
  manuscripts rejected by,
    225–27
  manuscripts solicited by, 122
  manuscript submissions and,
    223–30, 234
  in publishing acquisition
    process, 122–23, 131–33
  in responses to proposals,
    64–65, 122
  as surrogate book buyers, 31
  technical material as handled
    by, 78–80
  university press editors vs., 56
  writing ability as judged by,
    28
editors, university press, 29
  trade editors vs., 56
Einstein, Albert, 190–92
election of 2000, U.S., 161–62
electromagnetism, 192
Eliot, T. S., 195
epigraphs (quotation pages), 231
epilogues, 107, 109, 220
Epstein, Jason, 34
explanation-driven books:
  avoiding "going technical" in,
    118
  definition of, 117–18
  narrative tension in, 190–93
  sample chapters for, 111,
    117–19

fallacies, logical, 172–74
Farrar, Straus & Giroux, 130
fascism, 166
fiction:
  as expressive medium, 142–43
  narrative tension in, 179,
    185–86
  serious nonfiction compared
    with, 164–65, 182–84
first print runs, 64
  changes in, 35–36
Fish, Stanley, 182
flap copy, 235–36
foreign rights, 132
foreshadowing, 185
Foster, Vince, 169–70
Fourteenth Amendment, 213
freelance editors, 225
  fees of, 226
free trade issues, 167
front matter, 231

Gallo, Robert, 207
Gay New York (Chauncey),
  198–200
general-interest audience,
  24–25, 49–50, 53–54, 56
general theory of relativity, 190,
  192
Gideon's Trumpet (Lewis), 106–7
Gladwell, Malcolm, 200–201
Gotti, John, 173
Grisham, John, 19
"guided tour" books, 210

HarperCollins, 15, 130, 135

Harvard University Press, 79
Hawking, Stephen, 15
history books, 189–90
Hitler, Adolf, 173, 175
HIV, test for, 207
Hochschild, Adam, 194n, 198
Holt, 130, 135
Holtsbrinck group, 130
hooks, 185
Houghton Mifflin, 130, 135
human-interest stories, intellec-
  tual ideas discussed in, 106
Hungry Years, The (Watkins), 86
Hyperion, 130
hypothetical projects, *see* proj-
  ects, hypothetical

Ice Bound (Nielsen), 232
Icebound (proposed title), 232
illustrations, book, 231
"Indoctrinology," 163n
In the Heart of the Sea
  (Philbrick), 236
introductions, 32, 107, 109,
  150–51, 196–203
  anecdotes in, 197–98
  in biographies, 202–3
  exposition in, 197
  questions answered by, 197,
    202
  to revised dissertations, 203
  thesis spelled out in, 197,
    198–202
  used in marketing and
    publicity, 201
  writer's block and, 208

inventories:
  computerized tracking of,
    34–36
  "just-in-time," 35–36
investigative journalism, 143
Islam's Black Slaves (Segal), 194
Iwo Jima, 170

jackets, book, *see* book jackets
Japan:
  atom bomb dropped on, 170
  Nanking invaded by, 104–5
journalism:
  book writing compared with,
    54–55, 56, 110
  composite characters used in,
    180, 181
  investigative, 143
  pyramidal story organization
    in, 108
  questionable attributions used
    in, 180–81
Julius Caesar (Shakespeare),
    164
"just" war theory, 166

Kahlo, Frida, 46
Kakutani, Michiko, 181–82
Kazin, Michael, 86
Kennedy, John, Jr., 70
Kennedy, John F., proposed
    biography of, 70, 87–90
King, Stephen, 24
King Leopold's Ghost
    (Hochschild), 197–98
Kipling, Rudyard, 51

Knopf, Alfred A., 17
Kurosawa, Akira, 105

law books, 48–50
  core audience for, 40–41,
    48–49, 213
Levine, Rick, 236
Lewinsky, Monica, 70
Lewis, Anthony, 106
Lindley, David, 153
literary agents, 23, 27, 32,
    124–31, 177–78, 229
  auctions and, 134
  in choosing between multiple
    offers, 134–35
  fees of, 129
  manuscript rejection and,
    226–27
  manuscript submission
    without, 121–23
  projects turned down by,
    127–28
  proposal revisions suggested
    by, 129–30
  purpose of, 124
  selection and contacting of,
    123, 124–27, 129
  submission strategies of,
    130–31
literature reviews, in dissertation
    introductions, 203
Little, Brown, 130
LMP (*Literary Market Place*),
    124
logical fallacies, 172–74
longitudinal studies, 50–51

magazines, book excerpts in,
    233
magazine vs. book audiences,
    41–42, 54–55, 56
manuscripts:
    copyediting of, 234
    editing of, 224–30
    finding provocative questions
        to answer in, 210–11
    for "guided tour" books, 210
    making suggested changes to,
        230, 234
    placing of, with other pub-
        lishers, 225–27, 228
    rejected, 225–27
    submission of, 223–30, 234
    unsolicited, 121–22
    waiting for return of, 223,
        230–33
marketing and publicity, 18, 21,
    36–37, 61, 63–64, 119, 129
    author participation in, 36,
        133–34, 232–33, 237, 238
    introduction as resource for,
        201
    newsworthiness of book
        emphasized in, 233
    in print media, 237, 238
    radio and television in, 36–37,
        133–34, 237
    targeting audience in, 232–33
Marshall, John C., 72
Maxwell, James Clerk, 192
mediagenic authors, 36, 133–34
medicine, politicizing of, 163
memoirs, 20, 21–22, 92

Metropolitan, 130
Miller, JoAnn, 50
mind story, narrative tension
    and, 189, 191–94
Miramax Talk Books, 130
Morris, Edmund, 181–82,
    202–3
Morrison, Toni, 37
motivation:
    attribution of, 173–74
    motive vs., 174
Murphy's Brother's Law,
    147–48

NAFTA, 167
Nanking, Japanese invasion of,
    104–5
narrative-based books:
    biographies, 111–14
    demonstrating command of
        material in, 114
    dramatic endings in, 114–15
    first chapters in, 206
    narrative chapters in, 101,
        102–3, 106, 107, 108–9,
        204, 211
    readers and, 116–17
    sample chapters for, 111–15
narrative nonfiction, 178
narrative tension, 31, 164,
    177–95
    in academic books, 31, 187
    argument and, 179, 191
    in biographies, 188–90
    covering time vs., 184–85,
        188–94

down side of, 186–87
in explanatory books, 190–94
mind story and, 189, 191–94
narrative thread in, 185,
     186–87, 189
reasons for use of, 179, 184–88
writing humanized by, 187–88
narrative thread, 185, 186–87,
     189
National Institutes of Health
     (NIH), 207
Nazis, 175
New Republic, 163
NewsHour, 157
newspapers:
     credibility calculus for,
          157–58, 160, 161
     see also specific newspapers
New Yorker, 54, 180–81
New York Review of Books, 160
New York Times, 53, 106, 160,
     181, 182, 215–16
New York Times Book Review,
     36–37, 86, 194
nicotine, 159
nonfiction, serious:
     fiction vs., 142–43, 164–65,
          179, 183–84, 218
     narrative in, 177–95
     reluctance of authors to use
          narrative techniques in,
          180–83

Okinawa, 170
Onassis, Jacqueline Kennedy, 70
op-eds:

electronic, 158
newspaper, 157, 160, 161
Overworked American, The
     (Schor), 111, 201
Oxford English Dictionary
     (*OED*), 172

Pacific War, 170
paperback rights, selling of,
     135–36
parenthetical mania, 216–17
Penguin Putnam, 130
Perfect Storm, The (Junger), 178
permissions, obtaining of, 231
Perseus Books Group, 130
Philbrick, Nathaniel, 236
photo inserts, 201
physics, 44, 45*n,* 190–92
Physics of Star Trek, The (Krauss),
     15–21, 238
post hoc, ergo propter hoc fallacy,
     172
preemptive offers, 132, 134
press kits, 237
pro-choice movement, 174
projects, hypothetical:
     audience and, 39–57, 211–14
     biological clock (#4), 41–42,
          54–55, 56
     environmental pollution case
          (#2), 40–41, 48–50, 56
     female artist biography (#1),
          40, 45–48, 56
     women who kill (#3), 41,
          50–54, 56
pro-life movement, 174

proposals, 27, 31, 61–96
  advances and, 62–63, 83
  appropriate amount of detail
      in, 70–73
  better books as result of good,
      65–66
  Big Five questions about, *see*
      proposals, Big Five
      questions for
  editorial response to, 64–65
  for hypothetical Kennedy
      biography, 70, 87–90
  and marketing of book,
      63–64
  as narrative, 67–68
  previous treatments discussed
      in, 80
  question vs. thesis in, 76–86
  revisions to, 129–30
  sample, 241–53
  and table of contents, 98–99
  unsuccessful, 39
  "what is talked about" vs.
      "what is said" in, 74–76
proposals, Big Five questions
      for, 66, 67–96
  author's credentials in, 91–94
  book's argument/thesis in,
      73–91
  book's content defined in,
      69–73
  core audience in, 67, 95–96
  timeliness of publication in,
      94–95
Psychology Today, 41, 52
Public Affairs, 130

publicity, *see* marketing and
      publicity
publishers, publishing, 49, 130
  aggressive advocacy and,
      155–56, 160
  auctions held by, 134
  businesslike attitude of, 17
  in competition for proposals,
      64–65, 134
  computer-influenced changes
      in, 34–37
  editorial meetings at, 132–33
  marketing and publicity by, *see*
      marketing and publicity
  "meeting the author" at, 36,
      133–34
  Murphy's Brother's Law in,
      147–48
  placing manuscripts with
      other, 225–27, 228
  preemptive offers of, 132, 134
  rights departments at, 131–32
  seasonal catalogs of, 234
  title meetings at, 231
  traditional vs. alternative,
      23–24
  university presses and, 29–31,
      91, 137
  unsolicited manuscripts and,
      121–22
  see also editors, trade
publisherslunch.com, 125
Publishers Weekly, 125
publishing acquisition process,
      120–37
  agents in, 124–31, 134–35

auctions in, 134

authors approached by editors in, 122

choosing between multiple offers in, 134–36

editorial decisions in, 131–33

editors approached by authors in, 122–23

preemptive offers in, 132, 134

self-represented authors in, 121–23

unsolicited manuscripts in, 121–22

Pulitzer Prize, 36

Puritans, 204–5

pyramidal story organization, 108

qualifier mania, 217

quotation pages (epigraphs), 231

quotations, for book publicity, 233

radio, book publicity on, 133, 237

Random House, 130, 135, 181

Rape of Nanking, The (Chang), 104–5, 235

Rashomon, 105

readers, *see* audience

Reagan, Ronald, 181, 182*n*

reject letters, 131

research:

argument derived from, 144–54

editing of, 148–49

limiting scope of, 147–48

minimizing period of, 149

students and, 148

reviews, reviewers, 61, 194

book sales and, 36–37, 237–38

coded language criticized in, 215–16

credibility and, 162, 163

introductions used in, 201–2

Rise of Theodore Roosevelt, The (Morris), 202–3

Rousseau, Henri, 71

Rousseau, Jean-Jacques, 71

Rule, Anne, 53

St. Martin's Press, 130

sample chapters, 61, 97, 98, 110–19

academic journal article as, 110–11

for argument-based books, 111, 115–17

for biographies, 111–14

for explanation-driven books, 111, 117–19

journalists and, 110

for narrative-based books, 111–15

published work as, 110–11

as showcase, 110

Schor, Juliet, 201

science books, 15–21, 44, 45*n*, 84–85, 238

core audience for, 211–12

covering-material vs. narrative tension in, 190–93

Scotland, 84–85, 205–6
section essays, 206
Segal, Ronald, 194*n*
sentences, wordy, 216–18
Shakespeare, William, 19, 164
Simon & Schuster, 130, 201
Simpson, O. J., books about
    trial of, 154
Sixth Amendment, 106–7
60 Minutes, 54, 158
slush pile, 121
Song of Solomon (Morrison),
    37
special theory of relativity, 190,
    191–92
Stalin, Joseph, 166
Star, 41
Star Trek, 16, 18, 19
submission package, 23, 61–119
    agents and, 126–27, 130–31
    elements of, *see* CVs, of
        authors; proposals; sample
        chapters; table of contents
    focused, 31–32
subtitles, 231
Supreme Court, U.S.:
    Dartmouth v. *New Hampshire*
        and, 71–72
    Gideon's Trumpet case and,
        106–7
    Times v. *Sullivan,* 158*n*
    2000 presidential election
        and, 168–69

table of contents, 61, 97–110, 210
    as blueprint for book, 99

chapter descriptions in,
    99–100
chapter organization in, 101–9
chapter titles in, 100–101
formatting of, 98–99, 107
in manuscript vs. submission
    package, 97–98, 231
proposal and, 98–99
revisions of, 99, 107, 109–10
simplicity in, 101
technical language, 118, 213–14
    see also coded language
television:
    aggressive advocacy in, 157,
        158–59
    book publicity on, 36–37,
        133–34, 237
thesis, 145
    in introduction, 197, 198–202
    protection of, 75–76
    vs. answer in book proposals,
        86
    vs. question in book
        proposals, 76–86
Times v. *Sullivan,* 158*n*
Time Warner publishing group,
    130
Tipping Point, The (Gladwell),
    200–201
Titanic, 185, 198
titles, book, 231–32
tobacco companies, 159
tours, book, 237
trade books:
    academic books vs., 29–31,
        44, 114

audience for, *see* audience
general-interest, 53–54
"guided tour," 210
marketing of, *see* marketing
and publicity
see also specific types of books
Triangle Shirtwaist Factory fire,
102–3
true-crime books, 53
Truman, Harry S., 161
Twain, Mark, 198

"Uncounted Enemy, The: A
Vietnam Deception," 158
United States:
democracy in, 171
in Vietnam War, 165–66
in World War II, 165, 166,
170
university presses, 27–28, 160,
166
commercial publishers vs.,
29–31, 91, 137
editors, *see* editors, university
press
finding literary agents
through, 125
outside vetting process used
in, 79
trade programs at, 29, 121,
131, 137, 215
see also academic books
USA Today, 41, 53

Vietnam War, 165–66
Viking Penguin, 135

Walker, 130
Warner, 130
Web:
finding literary agents on,
124–25
writing books for, 24
Webster, Daniel, 72
Weisman, Steven, 182*n*
Westmoreland, William, 158
women's biographies, 22,
46–47
women's studies, books on, 22
Women Who Kill (hypothetical
project), 41, 50–54, 56
Women Who Kill (Jones), 54*n*
workers' rights issues, 167
World War II, 165, 166, 170
writer's block, overcoming
of, 207–10
brute force method of,
208
introductions and, 208
and meeting daily minimum
standard, 209–10
and not starting at beginning
of book, 208–9
and overcoming fear of
turning in poor work,
210
writing process, 141–220
narrative tension in, 31,
164, 177–95
precision in, 218–19
uses of argument in,
141–76
wordiness in, 216–18

writing samples:
  for *Breach of Faith,* 254–68
  see also sample chapters
writing skills:

of academics, 29–30, 32
  editorial view of, 28
WTO, 167
W. W. Norton, 130, 135